NELSON AT WAR
1914–1918

SUPREMA MULTIS HORA FORSAN TIBI

(It is the last hour for many – perhaps for you)

NELSON AT WAR
1914–1918

A HISTORY OF NELSON BATTALION OF THE ROYAL NAVAL DIVISION

by

ROY SWALES

First published in Great Britain in 2004 by
Pen & Sword SELECT
an imprint of
Pen & Sword Books Ltd
47 Church Street
Barnsley
South Yorkshire
S70 2AS

Copyright © R. C. Swales, 2004

ISBN 1 84468 018 5

Typeset in 10pt Plantin by
Phoenix Typesetting, Auldgirth, Dumfriesshire

Printed and bound in England by
CPI UK

Pen & Sword Books Ltd incorporates the Imprints of Pen & Sword
Aviation, Pen & Sword Maritime, Pen & Sword Military,
Wharncliffe Local History, Pen and Sword Select, Pen and Sword
Military Classics and Leo Cooper.

For a complete list of Pen & Sword titles please contact
PEN & SWORD BOOKS LIMITED
47 Church Street, Barnsley, South Yorkshire, S70 2AS, England
E-mail: enquiries@pen-and-sword.co.uk
Website: www.pen-and-sword.co.uk

This book is dedicated
to my father and
to the other
Officers and Men
who served in
Nelson Battalion of the Royal Naval Division
21st August 1914 – 23rd February 1918

CONTENTS

ACKNOWLEDGEMENTS

The curatorial staff of the Fleet Air Arm Museum at Yeovilton, which now holds a large number of the personnel records of the men who served in the Royal Naval Division, have been especially helpful in allowing me the regular access to those papers without which this history would be devoid of much of the personal narrative. The Royal Marines Museum at Southsea has been very cooperative in allowing me to use documents and photographs concerning the RMLI officers who commanded Nelson Battalion. Dr Rosalind Moad was very kind in helping me to obtain photographic material from the Modern Archive, King's College, Cambridge. The National Archive at Kew has been the source of most of the detailed historical narrative.

I am grateful to the Brotherton Library (Special Collections) at the University of Leeds, who have allowed me to use material from the Liddle Collection, and to the Imperial War Museum (Photographic and Sound Archives) who have kindly permitted the use of interviews and photographs.

I am indebted to authors and publishers for their approval to quote extracts from the following:

The Royal Marines. From Sea Soldiers to a Special Force, by Major General Julian Thompson, published by Sidgwick and Jackson.

Gallipoli, by Sir Robert Rhodes James published by Pimlico. Used by permission of The Random House Group Limited.

Gallipoli by Colonel Michael Hickey published by John Murray (Publishers) Limited.

Command in the Royal Naval Division. A Military Biography of Brigadier General AM Asquith DSO by Captain Christopher Page published by Spellmount Limited.

For God's Sake Shoot Straight! The Story of the Court Martial and Execution of Sub Lt Edwin Dyett by Leonard Sellers published by Leo Cooper.

RND Journal edited and published by Leonard Sellers.

The author and publishers are grateful to the following for permission to reproduce copyright photographs in this book: the Brotherton Library, University of Leeds, 2, 5, 7, 8, 9, 10, 11, 12, 13, 14, 15, 23, 26, 27, 28, 30, 31, 32, 33; the Imperial War Museum, 6, 25, 29, 35, 36; K. Dodgson Esq., 17, 19, 20, 21; the Provost and Scholars, King's College, Cambridge, 3. Nos 16, 18, 22, and 24 come from the collection of the author, who is particularly grateful to the Royal Marines Museum for permission to reproduce Nos 1 and 4.

MAPS

PREFACE

My father, like so many First World War veterans, never spoke very much about his experiences at Gallipoli but he was clearly proud of having served as an able seaman in Nelson Battalion of the Royal Naval Division. He was relatively lucky to be seriously wounded on his third day ashore at Anzac, for nearly one third of his platoon, comprising an officer and fifty men, would die on the peninsula in the course of the Gallipoli campaign. When the men wounded are added to those killed, his platoon's battle casualty rate rises to seventy per cent. None of his chums who avoided death or wounding in combat managed to steer clear of the dreadful fly-borne sicknesses that plagued the summer months on Gallipoli. So my father was very lucky indeed: lucky to be brought down from the heights of Dead Man's Ridge with a horrible compound fracture of the thigh bone; lucky to be put into HS *Gascon*, the only proper hospital ship off Anzac; lucky to survive the transit to Egypt; and lucky to live through his stay in the makeshift 17th General Hospital (formerly Victoria College) in Alexandria, where the smell of gangrene and the cries of the wounded in an age without antibiotics must have lowered morale to the depths. He was lucky to have his shattered femur more or less rebuilt in the RN Hospital at Haslar and he merely had to put up with a left leg three inches shorter than the right for the next forty-seven years of his life.

Inevitably, it was not until nearly forty years after my father's death in 1962 that I decided to research his service in Nelson Battalion. My work was triggered by the discovery that his brief 1914/15 diary contained the names of all the members of his platoon. Tracking down these men through the records in the National Archives at Kew and, latterly, in the Fleet Air Arm Museum at RNAS Yeovilton was a rewarding and humbling experience. The result of my research was a short memoir about the war experience of my father's platoon, written mainly for family purposes.

Clearly, however, there was a much fuller story to be told about the men of

Nelson Battalion and it was with the encouragement of Captain Christopher Page, Head of the Naval Historical Branch, Ministry of Defence, that I set out to write a history of that battalion. I hope it will complement those that have already been written for Hawke Battalion, just after Great War by Douglas Jerrold, and of Hood Battalion, more recently by Leonard Sellers. Captain Page's own efforts to publicize the half-forgotten RND, not least through his excellent military biography of Arthur 'Oc' Asquith, and Len Sellers' tireless production of the *RND Journal* since 1997 have been an inspiration to many 'sons of the RND'.

Much has already been written about the military history of the RND and this work about Nelson Battalion does not attempt to re-tell that story. Rather this is a narrative of what the men of the Nelson lived through. I have tried to illustrate the comings and goings of Commanding Officers and officers and detail the gallantry shown by so many officers and men. This history also provides a record of the names of all the men who gave their lives while serving in the battalion. It traces the day-by-day movements of Nelson Battalion as the war unfolded, drawing on the war diaries in the National Archives. Above all it records the tragedies and the successes of a battalion that lived for three and a half years and carried the illustrious name of Britain's most beloved Admiral into the incongruous arena of the Twentieth Century's most bloody battle-fields. If this account tends to ignore the wider context then that is my decision, for this is above all the story of the officers and men of Nelson Battalion.

1

THE BIRTH AND INFANCY OF NELSON BATTALION:

21 AUGUST – 3 OCTOBER 1914

In 1905 Acting Sub Lieutenant Cyprian Dunstom Charles Bridge was serving at the Royal Naval College, Greenwich, training for a life as a seaman officer in the Fleet. He can have had little idea of the unusual path that his naval career would take less than ten years later on the outbreak of the Great War in the summer of 1914. His academic achievements while under training at Greenwich had included the award of the Ryder Memorial Prize for passing the best examination in French – useful for the war duties in Belgium that were in the future. On completion of his training he joined the Fleet and was promoted to lieutenant with seniority as of 15 November 1905. He served as a junior lieutenant in HMS *Triumph*, joining the ship in July 1906 and remaining with her for about three years. *Triumph* was one of two pre-Dreadnought battleships of the Swiftsure Class. She would have been a new ship when Lieutenant Bridge joined: she was originally laid down for Chile in 1902 but was bought by the British Government and completed in 1904. The service of HMS *Triumph* would end on the bottom of the Aegean off Gallipoli in May 1915, when she was torpedoed by the German submarine *U.21*. Lieutenant Bridge's next appointment in August 1909 was to the gunnery school in HMS *Excellent*, as a student, to qualify for gunnery duties. For reasons that are unrecorded he retired from the Royal Navy later that year after a very short career and the 1910 Navy List shows him as a retired officer. He does not appear to have qualified in gunnery.

On 1 August 1914, three days before the outbreak of war with Germany, Lieutenant (Retired) Cyprian D.C. Bridge RN was recalled from retirement and appointed to HMS President (the accounting base for London-based officers) for Special Service in the Admiralty. Three weeks later, on 21 August, he was appointed in command of Nelson Battalion of the Royal Naval Division (RND) and was promoted to the rank of Acting Commander RN on the following day. It is inconceivable that Commander Bridge's short naval career as a junior officer had prepared him for exercising the battlefield skills of a battalion commander, a post that, in the Army, would have been filled by a lieutenant colonel with long experience of handling soldiers. Nevertheless, such were to be his new military duties. To compound his problems, his 'soldiers' were to be a strange collection of naval ratings pulled together in short order at the instigation of the First Lord of the Admiralty, Winston Churchill, to form the RND.

Churchill had become First Lord three years earlier, in 1911, at the age of thirty-six, having already served in the Liberal government in the previous five years as Colonial Under-secretary, President of the Board of Trade and Home Secretary in succession. As First Lord of the Admiralty, Churchill showed his widely recognized talent for energy, innovation and foresight in preparing the Royal Navy for the war with Germany that he saw as inevitable. It is not known when the idea of creating a force for land-fighting from naval manpower first emerged but the numerous formal minutes which document the formation of the Royal Naval Division are held in the Naval Historical Branch (NHB) of the Ministry of Defence and in the National Archives (NA) at Kew.[1] These show that Churchill's first minute on the subject was sent to the First and Second Sea Lords, the professional heads of the Royal Navy, on Sunday, 16 August 1914. In it he directed the formation of the equivalent of an Army division of three brigades – the formation to be 'completed, so far as resources allow, in the present week'. The manpower for the new force, as yet without a purpose, was to be found from 'surplus naval reservists of different classes', who would be formed into two naval brigades, and from the Royal Marines Light Infantry (RMLI) and Royal Marines reservists, who would form a third brigade.

The demanding deadlines laid down by the First Lord in his following minutes envisaged some four thousand active service, Royal Fleet Reserve (RFR) and Royal Naval Volunteer Reserve (RNVR) seaman ratings arriving at a camp which was to be set up near Deal in Kent, close to the Walmer Depot of the Royal Marines, on the following Friday and Saturday, 21 and 22 August. They would be followed by two thousand RFR stokers and 1,500 Royal Naval Reserve (RNR) ratings to join the camp four days later on Wednesday, 26 August. These 7,500 men forming the naval brigades were to be the subject of an inspection by the Board of Admiralty on the following Monday, 31 August, only fifteen days after Winston's initial minute.

So it was that the newly appointed and promoted Commander Cyprian Bridge RN found himself at Deal on the weekend of 21/22 August 1914 overseeing the formation of Nelson Battalion of the Royal Naval Division. The new naval battalions of the RND were, at Churchill's direction, to be named after renowned Admirals: (1st) Drake, (2nd) Benbow, (3rd) Hawke and (4th) Collingwood Battalions were to form the 1st Naval Brigade; (5th) Nelson, (6th) Howe, (7th) Hood and (8th) Anson would be the 2nd Naval Brigade.

Commander Bridge's Nelson Battalion was under the brigade command of Commodore Oliver Backhouse RN, variously described in the early days of the RND as Brigade Commodore or General Officer Commanding (GOC) of the 2nd Brigade. Commodore Wilfred Henderson RN commanded the 1st Brigade.

Even at the level of GOC the lack of experience was evident in the Naval Brigades. Over the previous ten years Commodore Backhouse, for example, had held appointments as a lieutenant in HMS *Hyacinth*, Flagship of the East Indies Fleet, and in HMS *Excellent*. Promoted to Commander in June 1908, he had then served as Executive Officer (second-in-command) of three ships: in 1908 HMS *Cumberland* (a cruiser which acted as Training Ship for Naval Cadets); in 1911 HMS *Colossus* (a new Dreadnought in the 1st Battle Squadron of the Home Fleet); and, in 1913, HMS Excellent. In June 1914 Oliver Backhouse was promoted to captain and to commodore on appointment as GOC 2nd Brigade on 21 August 1914. Experience of warships' heavy guns and of small-arms drill was really the only military qualification at the higher levels of RND command in these early days.

Nelson Battalion's first RNVR ratings arrived at Deal on 22 August from all over the country, as directed. Typical among them was Petty Officer Euan Fleming, a thirty-year-old Scot from East Glasgow. He had joined No.4 Company of the Clyde Division, RNVR in March 1909 and was employed in civilian life as a draughtsman and engineer. On 2 August 1914 he was drafted to Clyde RNVR HQ but was mobilized on 21 August and joined Nelson Battalion in Kent on the following day. Experienced RNVR senior rates like Fleming, together with petty officers and chief petty officers from the Fleet and RFR were to become the Company and Platoon Senior Rates of the new battalions. Fleming would be the senior NCO in 'A' Company, No.4 Platoon.[2] The missing ingredient was military experience and this was provided to Nelson Battalion in the shape of an officer of the Grenadier Guards, Lieutenant William Raymond Croft Murray, who was appointed to the battalion as Second-in-Command (2i/c) and Adjutant with the rank of Major, RMLI. With such minimal military experience in the command of the naval battalions, but with the benefit of RMLI expertise from the nearby Depot, the work of turning retired and part-time naval ratings into a militarily effective fighting force began in earnest at Deal in late August of 1914, two weeks after the First Lord's directive.

In late August and early September recruiting offices across the country were overwhelmed by patriotic volunteers responding to Kitchener's call, on 25 August 1914, for thirty divisions for his New Army. By the end of the first week of September nearly 175,000 men had been recruited against a target of 200,000 for the first month. RNVR recruiting offices, starting with London and Bristol Divisions on 31 August, were also taking in volunteers for naval service. These men were given 'Z' service numbers (eg LZ/123, BZ/456) to distinguish them from the existing RNVR ratings, whose service numbers were based on their Company number within their Division (eg London 1/789 for the London No.1 Company). The start of London and Bristol recruiting was followed by Sussex and Mersey Divisions on 4 and 5 September respectively and by the Clyde and Tyne Divisions on 7 September. Wales Division opened its 'Z' recruiting much later, on 11 January 1915.

The Army was incapable of handling the huge influx of New Army recruits and, to ease the log-jam, large numbers of men enlisted into regiments in the north of England were transferred in short order to the Navy. In the early days these men came straight from the Army to join the RND at Deal, those joining the 1st Naval Brigade being given 'KW' service numbers, those entering the 2nd Naval Brigade 'KX' numbers. The first man from 'Kitchener's Army' to be drafted into Nelson Battalion was Henry Evans, a coal miner aged twenty-eight from Pelton in Co. Durham, who had joined the Durham Light Infantry as a private on 2 September. By 9 September he had been transformed into an RNVR rating in the RND at Deal. Private Henry Evans was rated Able Seaman Evans with service number KX/31. Many of the earlier 'KX' ratings came from Dundee RNVR and had been transferred into Hood Battalion as members of the battalion band. Others were attached to the headquarters of the 2nd Brigade. For the next three years Henry Evans would serve with Nelson Battalion at Antwerp, Gallipoli and France until late 1917 when he was transferred to sea service.

On 9 September, after barely two weeks under canvas at Walmer, the 2nd Naval Brigade moved to the park on Lord Northbourne's estate at Betteshanger, a couple of miles away. The move would allow training to continue in less cramped conditions and enable brigade and battalion esprit de corps to be built. It was on this day that the first men from Kitchener's Army, including Able Seaman Henry Evans joined the RND.

The earliest of the RNVR 'Z' volunteers to join Nelson Battalion were Oliver Percy Moon, BZ/1, the very first Bristol recruit, and Philip Edwin Allen, LZ/13. They both volunteered, at Bristol and London respectively, on 31 August 1914. The majority of the earlier London recruits had been drafted direct to sea service. Oliver Moon would serve with Nelson Battalion until its disbandment in early 1918. He then transferred to Hawke Battalion in March 1918 and died of wounds received in action just eleven days later. Philip Allen was a twenty year old clerk who lived in Westcliff-on-Sea, Essex and worked in London. He would serve with Nelson Battalion through most of the Gallipoli campaign until invalided sick. Thereafter, he fought with Drake Battalion in France until being taken prisoner in the German attack on the RND front at Welsh Ridge on 30 December 1917.

Unlike the early Kitchener's Army volunteers, who came direct to the RND training camp at Deal, the RNVR 'Z' recruits were sent first for several weeks of naval training to the new Depot which had been set up in the former exhibition buildings at Crystal Palace, south of London, and which opened in mid-September 1914. From there they were sent to sea or to the RND as appropriate. The first 'Z' ratings for the RND did not, therefore, reach their battalions until late October 1914 and they were to miss the RND's first operational experience in the defence of the city of Antwerp.

Meanwhile, the first officers appointed to Nelson Battalion were arriving at the Deal training camp. The Navy List for October 1914 (effective date 18 September 1914) shows the following list of officers:-

Commanding Officer	Cyprian C.D. Bridge *(Lieutenant Commander RN, retired.)*	
Adjutant & 2nd in Command	William R.C. Murray (Grenadier Guards.)	
Lieutenant Commander RN	Henry L. Cheston (Emergency List)	
Lieutenant Commander RNVR	Robert C. Standring	
Lieutenant RNVR	Ralph Leyland	Mungo C. Gibson
	Robert C Primrose	John E. Nicol
Lieutenant RNR	George H. Lloyd	
Sub Lieutenant RNVR	Henry Bremner	Eric Elgood
	Edmund M. Sharer	Charles Micklem
	Thomas McL. Hutchison	Harold T Treves
	James H.M. Clark *(acting)*	Arthur F Austin
	James C.M. Guy(acting)	
Assistant Paymaster RNVR	John E. Macintyre	
Midshipman RNVR	Donald C. Daly	
	Stewart Owler *(Sub Lieutenant 21 August 1914)*	

Of these 21 officers, only Lieutenant Lloyd would not accompany the battalion to Belgium as he was removed from the strength of the RND by the end of September. Two other important officers of the battalion were the Surgeon, Charles H.S. Taylor RN, and the Quartermaster, J. Town (Hon. Lieutenant RM), both of whom would go with the battalion to Antwerp. As with their senior commanders, the military experience among the junior officers was negligible. In addition to the 2i/c, Major Murray, the main store of such expertise for Nelson Battalion resided in a small cadre of seven experienced NCOs from the Royal Marines. These men were recalled pensioners, around fifty years of age, and comprised four Colour Sergeants and two Sergeants of the Plymouth and Portsmouth Divisions of the RMLI and one Sergeant of the Royal Marine Artillery (RMA);[3] almost enough for just two experienced soldiers in each of the four companies of about two hundred men. The in-depth expertise was certainly spread thinly across the battalion and it was fortuitous that additional RMLI experience was available from the RM Depot at Deal. The RND historian notes that training in land warfare for the officers was a particular difficulty:

> The officers with permanent commissions in the RNVR were, of course, as uninstructed in land war as the newest joined civilian, and, as these officers were often of considerable seniority, the difficulty was a real one.[4]

Given their almost exclusively naval experience, already described, such 'difficulties' also applied to the some of highest levels of command. In the 2nd Naval Brigade notable exceptions were the commanders of Hood and Anson Battalions, both Guards officers. Lieutenant Colonel Arnold Quilter of the Hood was noted by Douglas Jerrold, the post-war historian of the RND and of Hawke Battalion, as being 'a tower of strength' in the matter of training for land warfare. In the 1st Naval Brigade only Collingwood Battalion had an Army officer in command.

2

FIRST OPERATIONS – ANTWERP:

4–12 OCTOBER 1914

Winston Churchill's template for the RND had foreseen an RND naval battalion strength of well over nine hundred men, not including officers. The approximate breakdown was to be 424 RNVR, 324 RFR and 187 RNR, for a total of 935 men per battalion. Nelson Battalion would be well below this strength when ordered to embark for operations in Belgium one month later. The Medal Rolls for the award of the 1914 Star to those naval personnel who served in Belgium in October and November 1914[5] give an overview of the size and shape of Nelson Battalion during the Antwerp operations. These show that, not including the twenty-two officers identified in the previous chapter, Nelson Battalion was a little over 830 strong at Antwerp, about 100 short of the First Lord's projection. The great majority of these men were from the existing, pre-war companies of the RNVR Divisions, some 370 in total, representing over 43 per cent of the battalion. Most of these RNVR ratings (just over two hundred) came from Clyde Division, with another large group (some 160 strong) from Mersey Division. RFR stokers, just over three hundred of them, made up some 36 per cent of the battalion. Although less than one month in uniform, the volunteer 'KX' ratings from Kitchener's Army were a substantial minority: nearly 100 of them were to serve at Antwerp, about 11 per cent of Nelson Battalion. The senior NCO expertise comprised just over thirty Fleet/RFR senior ratings (fourteen chief petty officers and eighteen petty officers), a few RNVR senior ratings and the small cadre of RM pensioners already described. Of the total battalion manpower only the 2i/c and the RM NCOs brought experience of land warfare to the Nelson.

The 'rape of Belgium' by the German Army began on 4 August 1914 and the following month of fighting had seen the eventual surrender of the Liege forts on 16 August and the Namur forts on 24 August. By-passing Antwerp, still protected by the Belgian Army, the German armies had struck deep into France, south-west then south towards Paris, and by 4 September the Kaiser was able to boast that his armies were thirty miles from the capital. The Battle of the Marne checked the German advance and forced a retreat. It was not until the end of September that German attention turned again to Antwerp as part of a plan to outflank the Allied armies from the north and to take the Channel ports. The massive siege guns that had reduced Liege and Namur were now, on 28 September, turned on the three lines of defences at Antwerp, effecting a breach on 3 October. It was at this moment that the RND was called forward to help defend the city.

As the RND's only effective fighting force (it, at least, had numbers of experienced marines from the RFR), the 3rd (RM) Brigade had already been called over to Belgium for a few days in late August to defend Ostend against an anticipated German attack. They had returned to England when the attack failed to materialize. In late September the RM Brigade was again sent across the Channel to be based on Dunkirk to protect the Channel Ports and to menace the German lines of communication. As the outer defences of Antwerp fell in early October, the RM Brigade was called to that city to man the defences alongside the collapsing Belgian Army. Shortly thereafter the two Naval Brigades of the RND, despite their lack of training and readiness, were called forward to bolster the defence. They were sent to Belgium at practically no notice, under-trained (many had never fired a rifle) and ill-equipped for military operations.

On Saturday, 3 October Nelson Battalion, under its CO, was on a route march from Betteshanger to Chatham to undertake four days of musketry training on the ranges there. Sub Lieutenant Clark had been left at base in charge of a small rear party of about forty 'sick, lame and lazy' ratings.[6] That night the battalion was in bivouacs at Bekesbourne near Canterbury. Leave had been given from noon and the evening in the camp had been enlivened by the firing of a large bonfire on top of which was an effigy of Kaiser Bill. Most men were very late turning in and their night's sleep was curtailed at 5.00 am by shouting for the CO, turning out of the guard and the rousing of the camp. Commander Bridge briefed his officers that the battalion was to be at Dover by 2.00 pm to embark for an unknown destination. Camp was struck and the battalion set off on the fifteen-mile march to Dover. There they joined up with Sub Lieutenant Clark's rear party. They had spent the morning loading the battalion's gear on wagons before setting off on their three-hour march to Admiralty Pier with the other RND battalions, accompanied by marching bands. The ship allocated to Nelson and Howe Battalions, SS *African Prince*, came alongside at 7.00 pm and loading took the best part of five hours. She sailed for Dunkirk at midnight on Sunday, 4 October, nineteen hours after Commander Bridge had been shaken in his tent alongside Bekesbourne church, a remarkable achievement.

The crossing was calm and uneventful. The *African Prince* lay off Dunkirk for several hours waiting for the tide and finally docked at noon on 5 October, greeted by enthusiastic crowds. Unloading was hampered by a shortage of

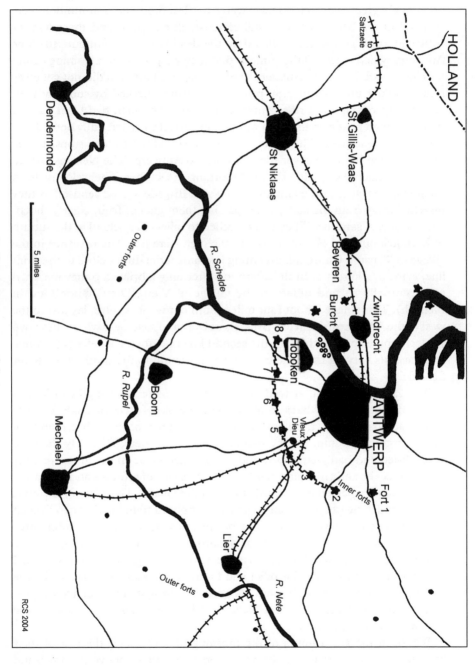

1. Operations around Antwerp.

HOLLAND

to Salzaete

St Gillis-Waas

St Niklaas

Dendermonde

R. Schelde

Outer forts

5 miles

Beveren

Burcht

Zwijndrecht

Hoboken

ANTWERP

8

7

6

5

Vieux Dieu

3

2

Fort 1

Inner forts

R. Rupel

Boom

Mechelen

Lier

R. Nete

Outer forts

RCS 2004

gangways, but Lieutenant Gibson and Sub Lieutenant Clark managed to obtain some chutes which speeded things up considerably. During the afternoon khaki greatcoats, haversacks, water bottles, food and ammunition were issued, but the battalions were still seriously ill-equipped and there was insufficient kit to go round. At this time the destination was announced to be Antwerp, which scotched the rumour that they were all off to a training camp.

The crowded trains to Antwerp carrying Nelson Battalion did not get away from Dunkirk until about 9.30 pm, the departure marked by somebody inadvertently loosing off a rifle round in the train. The men had been warned that a German attack on the train was possible so all travelled 'fully booted and spurred' in readiness. The trains moved slowly with frequent stops, taking more than ten hours to cover the 100 miles to Antwerp. The Nelsons arrived in the beleaguered city early the next morning, 6 October. The welcome from the populace was warm, giving the 2nd Naval Brigade a good send-off as they marched away from the station and passing them gifts of fruit, cigars, chocolate and tins of sardines. They first marched to billets in a school in the suburb of Kiel, just north of Hoboken, where the men were fed. The presence in the village of Winston Churchill, executing his ministerial duties close to the front line, came as a surprise. In the afternoon after only a brief stop they marched on, eventually to find billets in the village of Vieux Dieu (Oude God in Flemish). This village, about four miles south of the city centre, lay just to the west of the Antwerp-Mechelen-Brussels railway and road near where these two strategic routes passed through the second line of Antwerp's defences – a line of great forts curving from the east of the city round to the south at the River Schelde.

The 2nd Brigade had arrived in Antwerp just as orders were being issued for the defenders to fall back to the second line of defences through the forts and it had taken almost the whole of the daylight hours of 6 October, marching over a circuitous route, for the battalions to reach Vieux Dieu. By then the tired, ill-fed and badly-equipped 2nd Brigade had been on the move for sixty hours, since the early morning of 4 October. Streams of refugees and retreating Belgian soldiers passed northwards through the village. The noise of the guns was now much nearer, especially when an armoured train bearing two French naval guns came down the line and began firing in the vicinity. After three hours of waiting at Vieux Dieu for an order to move to the trenches, the Nelsons were directed to find billets in local houses. Lieutenant John Nicol had to break down the door of his billet and found that it had been vacated by the owners in a hurry. At least the Nelsons were in overnight billets for a few hours. The equally tired and ill-fed 1st Naval and RM Brigades were manning the trenches between the forts.

When, in the small hours of the morning of 7 October, the rest of their brigade was called out to man the new defensive positions between Forts 5 and 7 to the west of Vieux Dieu, Nelson Battalion were initially held back in reserve and several working parties were sent off to dig trenches at various places along the line. Sub Lieutenant Clark and a party of fifty ratings of 'A' Company were sent into Antwerp to guard the RND's supply depot situated in a deserted linoleum factory. They worked there for twelve hours, loading buses with food and ammunition. However, German forces, in an out-flanking manoeuvre, crossed the River Schelde about twenty miles south-west of Antwerp at Schoonarde during 7 October, threatening the RND's lines of communication back towards Ostend and Dunkirk. Nelson Battalion was called forward from reserve on the afternoon of that day to extend the RND's defensive line from Fort 7 west towards the River Schelde, taking over trenches from the Belgians. The line of their trenches roughly coincides with the cemetery in today's Antwerp suburb of Schoonselhof (which contains CWGC graves of RND dead). The trenches were useless for defence, having been dug more than a decade earlier. Overgrown with long grass, they were wide enough for horse-wagons to drive along them. The large forts were a mile apart and 'redoubts', manned by Belgian gunners, were spaced a quarter of a mile apart along the trenches between them. The remaining hours of 7 October were marked by continuous firing from the Belgian forts. Occasional alarms initiated heavy machine-gun and rifle fire all along the line from jumpy troops, but no proper targets were identified. After midnight things quietened down a little and some sleep was possible, albeit frequently interrupted by panicky orders to man the trenches. For twenty-eight hours the Nelsons remained in these positions on the right of the line, fortunately suffering minimal casualties as the heavy German artillery barrage passed overhead into central Antwerp.

Thursday, 8 October dawned grey, cold and misty. There was still no sign of a German advance against the Nelson trenches but plenty of artillery over and around them. Fort No.5, some two miles away, received concentrated attention from large German howitzers in the late afternoon. The German gunners had the range to the yard and large shells fell into the fort every five minutes. Behind the Nelson lines the bulk fuel tanks on the east side of the river went up in flames. Meanwhile the interpreter provided to Nelson battalion by the Belgian Army was giving cause for concern. As Sub Lieutenant Clark recorded:

> He seemed desperately anxious to get away on his bicycle – ostensibly to see who had set the petroleum tanks on fire – and he was also found to have on a sort of reversible hat. He was taken to the nearest fort to be examined, and was found to be a German and was shot.

Later that day, as darkness was falling, orders came from the RND GOC, Major General Paris, via GOC 2nd Naval Brigade, Commodore Backhouse, to retire. At 7.30 pm the battalion was fallen in behind the trenches and moved off to the rear on a march which would continue for some twenty-two miles. The nominated route would take them back through the western suburbs of

Antwerp. Through the evening Nelson Battalion pulled back to the north, marching along a line which followed the east bank of the River Schelde through Hoboken, past the burning oil tanks opposite Burcht, described by Sub Lieutenant Clark:

> The place was really a most extraordinary sight, there were about ten acres of fire, six large tanks blazing furiously round the edge of the yard, and in the centre a sort of inferno of small flickering flames. It was pretty hot going past but we got through all right and about half a mile further on we came out on the river.

They crossed the Schelde by a pontoon bridge on which two German saboteurs were arrested as the Nelsons were crossing. They had attempted to light a bomb in one of the pontoons but were apprehended by Marines. One was bayoneted and the other placed in custody. By about 10.30 pm the Nelson Battalion had reached its rendezvous at Zwijndrecht, on the west bank of the Schelde. After a short twenty-minute rest they marched on, heading for St Niklaas. Several false alarms interrupted the march, including a pair of stampeding donkeys being taken, in the dark, for German Uhlan cavalry. One incident, Sub Lieutenant Clark recalled, had provoked a

> great blowing of whistles and a few sound oaths from the road and we all crawled back and formed up again. Then another shot was fired but it was merely some cheerful idiot who had been resting his rifle on his toe and had pulled the trigger.

There followed another nine hours of marching on empty stomachs, with less than an hour's rest in roadside fields in the small hours of the morning. As the battalion approached St Niklaas word was received that the town was in German hands and the RND battalions were diverted to the village of St Gillaes-Waes (St Gillis-Waas), along lanes choked with civilian refugees and retreating Belgian military personnel. There, in the late morning of Friday, 9 October, trains were waiting to take the 2nd and RM Brigades away to the west, north of the advancing Germans, towards Salzaete (Zelzate), Bruges and safety. Nelson Battalion de-trained in Bruges at about 8.00 pm and the men were marched to billets in school buildings in the town.

It was at this stage that it became apparent that, because of poor staff-work, three battalions of the 1st Naval Brigade had been badly delayed in retiring from the Antwerp trenches. Nearly 1,500 men of Benbow, Collingwood, Hawke and the 1st Brigade HQ, led by the GOC 1st Brigade, Commodore Wilfred Henderson, were to end up interned in Holland as they crossed the border to avoid a bloody battle and capture by the German Army. Plymouth Battalion of the RM Brigade was similarly delayed, resulting in nearly one thousand more men being captured by the Germans.

After the first decent night's sleep in days, Nelson Battalion was back at

Bruges Station the following morning. Trains, including a cattle train which travelled at walking pace, took them the fifteen miles to Ostend, where they arrived in the early evening and marched to the quay. They boarded the SS *Lord Tredegar* and slept there for the night. On the following day, Sunday, 11 October, the battalion was transferred to SS *Fremona*, described by James Clark as 'a fairly small and extremely dirty cattle boat', which sailed for England at about 5.00 pm. A thick fog descended during the night and the ship anchored off Dunkirk. After sunrise on 12 October the fog began to lift and the *Fremona* got under way for Dover, where she came alongside the Admiralty Pier at 3.30 pm. The march along the coast got them back to Betteshanger by 8.00 pm, four days after leaving the trenches at Antwerp. Exhausted, like the rest of the RND, the Nelsons had their first proper meal since leaving England a week earlier.

Although no Nelson men had been killed in action, the battalion did leave behind seven men who had somehow got separated from the line of march. Two of these Nelson men became prisoners of the Germans. Able Seaman Roderick Johnstone,[7] remained in the POW camp at Doeberitz for the next four years until he arrived at Leith on being repatriated on 14 December 1918. The record of Junior Reserve Attendant William H. Hall indicates that he too was a prisoner at Doeberitz but also shows that he was discharged 'Shore' from Chatham barracks in August 1915. Other than a statement that he was 'returned to England', details are lacking. He was possibly repatriated as a non-combatant.[8] Hall was one of three ratings of the Royal Naval Auxiliary Sick Berth Reserve (RNASBR)[9] who served with Nelson Battalion at Antwerp. Five other Nelson able seamen were interned in Holland: Alfred Neesham, a Geordie, James Wilson and William Wood, both of 'A' Company, both Scots, and John Love and Arthur Derbyshire, both of 'C' Company, both of Mersey Division RNVR.[10] All remained in internment at Groningen until the end of the war.

The RND returned from Antwerp leaving some 2,500 men behind in internment or in captivity and with four almost entire battalions removed from its line of battle. Although the 2nd Naval Brigade was intact, the losses to the division were very serious. The time needed for the training of replacement battalions would keep the RND well below strength until late-May 1915, when replacement battalions arrived on Gallipoli one month into that campaign. The verdicts on the RND's involvement at Antwerp remain mixed. Douglas Jerrold maintained that the intervention was 'decisive . . . for it saved the Channel ports and the left of the allied army' by postponing the fall of Antwerp from 4 to 10 October, although he also noted that

> the only thing that the British public knew was that the Naval Brigades had their bayonets tied on with string and that this was contrary to Field Service Regulations.[11]

Most historians agree that, despite its lack of training and equipment for combat, the intervention of the RND averted the serious crisis which would have followed upon a quick German capture of Antwerp and with it most of the Belgian Army. The delaying tactics also forestalled a German capture of the Channel coast of Belgium and adjacent France and enabled a defensive line to be formed on the River Yser from Ypres to the English Channel. Little could the men of the RND have known that their Division would be fighting again on that line three years later.

Among the very few men whose services at Antwerp were officially recognized was Petty Officer William Wallace, Dev/211130, of Nelson Battalion who was awarded the Distinguished Service Medal.[12] Petty Officer Wallace would not remain with the RND, however, as he was discharged back to sea service just before the battalion embarked for Gallipoli.

3

RE-SHAPING AND TRAINING THE RND – BETTESHANGER, PORTSMOUTH AND BLANDFORD:

13 OCTOBER 1914 – 28 FEBRUARY 1915

Nelson Battalion returned to Betteshanger camp on arrival in England and within two weeks began to receive newly trained men from the RND Depot at Crystal Palace. These were mostly RNVR 'Z' recruits who had volunteered during late August and the first two weeks of September and had been the 'guinea pigs' for the new system of initial training. Walter Burdon, a Newcastle man, had joined a large number of volunteers in late August at HMS *Calliope*, the RNVR Tyne HQ, having 'tried every place I could think of to join up but I couldn't. They [the army] were all full up.'[13] Having been accepted, he was sent home and then was called back to attest and travel on to Crystal Palace on 11 September. He recalled a batch of about two hundred volunteers travelling south, to most of whom 'it was an adventure. When the call came to do something for my country, I wanted to do it. I wanted to help.' The nineteen-year-old Tyneside patternmaker was impressed by Crystal Palace.

> I thought it was a marvellous place . . . Crystal Palace was great – it was Lyons catering. Good food. I think it got too good because after a while it slackened off and we got very much less.

The syllabus of basic naval training and a fitness regime, which included an early morning run around the Palace grounds and route marches around the local area, was enlivened by friendly, or not-so-friendly, rivalries. Walter Burdon recalled that

> In the Crystal Palace there was a sort of dividing line between the English and the Scots. On a few times there was a right skirmish between them. "To hell with the Scots!" "To hell with the English!" . . . There were fists flying and everything . . . The Scots were a temperamental lot. They

would take umbrage at anything. We had some big fellows amongst our side. They would wade in amongst them and settle them.

Despite this, Walter noted that there was no bullying and he respected his officers and NCOs whom he judged to be fair but firm:

I really had no fault to find with the discipline because if you'd done the right thing you got no bother.

A sizeable number, including Walter Burdon, joined Nelson Battalion from Crystal Palace on 22 October when they were rated ordinary seamen. The author's father[14] was included in this Nelson draft. On completion of their battalion training they were organized into companies and platoons. Walter's Nelson platoon of fifty men was eventually composed entirely of RNVR personnel. His platoon, No.4 Platoon of 'A' Company, would contain newly-volunteered RNVR men from London Division (thirteen), Tyne (twelve), Sussex (two) and Clyde (thirteen). The 'experience' in this platoon was provided by six 'KX' men from Kitchener's Army and three long-serving RNVR men from the Clyde (two petty officers and one leading seaman), all nine of whom had been at Antwerp. The platoon was completed by a 'KP' rating from Benbow and the Platoon Officer[15] also came from that battalion.[16]

Even as newly-trained men were arriving from Crystal Palace, 'old hands' were leaving Nelson Battalion during the autumn of 1914. The senior RNVR officer, Lieutenant Commander Standring, was transferred to the Mobilization Office at Hull, having been found medically unfit, and Lieutenant Leyland was appointed to sea service. All but two of the junior officers were appointed away from the RND, most of them to sea or to gunnery courses in HMS *Excellent*. Sub Lieutenant Micklem left in mid-December to join the Heavy Batteries of the Royal Marine Artillery and Sub Lieutenant Guy transferred to a commission in the RMLI. Experienced men from the RNVR were drafted away from the RND to sea service. Tragically, about sixteen ex-Nelson men from Mersey Division companies, who had been drafted to HMS *Viknor*, were drowned on 13 January 1915, when their ship struck a German mine off Tory Island in the north-west approaches. Formerly the SS *Viking* of the Blue Star Line, HMS *Viknor* had been requisitioned by the Royal Navy as an armed merchant cruiser, part of the 10th Cruiser Squadron. She sank with the loss of all on board: twenty-two officers and 273 ratings.

Both the Commanding Officer and 2i/c of Nelson also left the battalion after Antwerp. Commander Cyprian Bridge was appointed to the Admiralty for 'special duty' in late November. His name had been brought to notice by his Brigade GOC, Commodore Backhouse, 'for exceptionally arduous and meritorious work, in view of the recent creation of the Brigade, at Antwerp'. Major William Murray, the 2i/c, returned to the Army.[17] The new battalion commander for the Nelson was Lieutenant Colonel Edmund George Evelegh, RMLI.

Although he was a professional sea-soldier, Evelegh's recent experience had not been in land warfare. He had been promoted to captain in 1895 and the turn of the century had seen him as Chatham Division's Instructor of Gunnery for a number of years. Afterwards, having been promoted to Major in 1903, he served in HMS *Powerful*, the Flagship, Australia. His subsequent appointment was as a staff officer in HMS *Impregnable*, the training establishment for boy ratings at Devonport. He remained in that post until 1910 when he returned to HQ Chatham Division RMLI as a lieutenant colonel. When the RND was first formed Evelegh was appointed to the 12th (Deal) Battalion of the 3rd (Marine) Brigade as 2i/c. However, the Deal Battalion sent only a relatively small detachment to Antwerp and Lieutenant Colonel Evelegh seems to have served in Chatham Battalion during that operation.[18] Contemporary photographs show Evelegh to have been a rather gaunt, thin officer with a fine moustache, but Douglas Jerrold described him as

> a man of delightful simplicity of character, a fine officer, a staunch Papist, and the only soldier I ever met who would begin a sentence with what I have always regarded as the apocryphal "Damme, Sir . . . ".[19]

Unsurprisingly, his naval ratings had a rather different view of the officer of marines who was now their CO. Walter Burdon remembered the Colonel as

> an old man – or he seemed to us to be an old fellow – but he was very, very abrupt in his manner . . . he used to come and look round. If you moved an eyelid he'd shout, "Still! Keep still!" in that authoritative manner . . . He was very strict.

Born in November 1865, Edmund Evelegh was not quite fifty years old at this time. Was the Colonel popular amongst his men? Walter Burdon's vague opinion was that 'We saw so little of him that we couldn't get an impression of him really.'

The new 2i/c of the Nelson was Lieutenant Commander Henry Lawrence Cheston, RN, who had been with the battalion since it first formed on 22 August. Before the war he had been a lieutenant on the Emergency List, having resigned his active service commission in May 1907. After the October operations GOC 2nd Brigade had also brought Cheston's name to notice for valuable work performed during the defence of Antwerp. However, Cheston would not remain with the Nelsons for long. He would see them through their training during the winter of 1914/15, but he was appointed away just before they embarked for Gallipoli at the end of February 1915. During April and May 1915 he served as 2i/c of the 2nd Reserve Battalion at Blandford, but he was then appointed to the staff of the Inspector of Steel and his nine months in the RND was at an end.

During the last months of 1914, while the personnel arrivals and departures were progressing, Nelson Battalion was on the move. Early November saw the battalion move from camp at Betteshanger to the naval barracks at Portsmouth. They would remain there for about three weeks undergoing musketry training on the ranges at Whale Island (later HMS *Excellent*). Walter Burdon recalled the routine of breakfast in the barracks followed by the march to Whale Island, where they would fire on the ranges starting at 100 yards and working out to 500 yards. As experience was gained they were instructed in rapid fire but not, apparently, in bayonet drill. A midday meal was taken each day on the island: 'bleak, very bleak. Nothing on it, you know, except a bit of hut where we got a bit meal', was what Walter remembered of those cold November days on the ranges.

Having joined the RND in early October, Sub Lieutenant Douglas Jerrold had also joined the Nelson Battalion from Crystal Palace and would spend some three months with what he called 'the friendly battalion' before moving over to the Hawke. He recorded the horrors of a young officer's life at Portsmouth:

> The Naval Barracks was nearly my financial undoing, for I used to eat figs and cream every day for lunch, only to discover that the cream was an extra and that the cost of it depleted my income by exactly 25 per cent – from 4/- to 3/- a day. On top of this I made out my drink chits for whiskies and gins instead of half whiskies and gins (a whisky being what mere civilians call a 'double') and this absorbed far more than the rest of my earnings. The trouble, of course, was that a sub-lieutenant in the Navy is only a sub-lunatic schoolboy (he is not even a Ward Room officer) and is not supposed to have anything but 'pocket money', nor, for that matter, is he allowed to spend more than £2 a month on drinks. Most of our sub-lieutenants on the contrary were nearer thirty than twenty, many of them were over thirty, none of them spent less than £2 a week on drinks and many of them could have spent £2 a day and been none the worse for it.[20]

While Nelson Battalion was at Portsmouth Rupert Brooke also joined for two days, but he was on his way to join what Jerrold called the 'brilliant nucleus' of 'the more distinguished Hood Battalion'. The history of the Hood has been well told in books by Christopher Page[21], Leonard Sellers[22] and Joseph Murray[23].

The completion of musketry training at Portsmouth saw the Nelson as the first battalion to move into the RND's new Depot on the Dorset Downs near Blandford. They arrived there on 27 November 1914. The camp was by no means complete: few accommodation huts had been erected and the roads around the camp had yet to be built. As the first on site, Nelson Battalion had more than their share of hard work in bringing the camp into a workable state. Even some seventy-five years later Walter Burdon recalled clearly the dreadful conditions at the new camp:

Just being built . . . it was in a terrible state. It was in the middle of the Downs. We had to build roads . . . we had ammunition wagons. We used to take the wagon down to the dip and fill it up with pebbles and haul it up to the top. And they had other ones digging the earth up to make a road and we would plant the pebbles in the roads. Of course we got filthy wet. We had our blue uniforms on and it was all chalk down there . . . we had to brush and clean ourselves after every time we were out . . . Oh, mud! That was our enemy . . . We were up to our ankles in mud, no question about it. You were just thrashing about in mud. And you had to appear next morning with clean boots on.

Over the winter months more sub lieutenants were joining from their initial training at Crystal Palace to take up appointments as Platoon Officers. As well as Douglas Jerrold, the Navy Lists show about twenty new junior officers for Nelson Battalion, half of whom would lose their lives at Gallipoli. One of these, a particularly close friend of Douglas Jerrold, was Herbert Clyde Evans,

> a sailor of fortune, who had navigated one of Rozhesturnsky's battleships to the East, and had been on the bridge during the fatal battle of Tsushima, which decided the fate of the Czars and opened the gates of Asia to Japan.[24]

Joining in mid-February 1915 was the former Metropolitan policeman Tom Lewis Price, the first police constable to receive a commission during the war. Evans and he would be promoted rapidly to be the 'D' and 'A' Company Commanders respectively, with the rank of lieutenant commander. Evans would lose his life in June 1915 on Gallipoli in the Third Battle of Krithia. Price would eventually reach the rank of Commander in 1918 as CO of the Regimental Depot at Aldershot.

Walter Burdon recalled one of the new, young Nelson officers, Sub Lieutenant James Bookless, as being:

> Very nice. He was only a little fellow. When we went on a route march we would sing "And A Little Child Shall Lead Them." He says, "Yes, a little child shall lead them but he'll be on horseback!" A canny fellow.

Bookless was lost on Gallipoli during the early defence of Anzac. Sub Lieutenant A.V.W. Cotter, formerly the United States Deputy Consul General at Munich, who had escaped from Germany on a bicycle on the outbreak of war, was transferred, with Jerrold, from Nelson to the new Hawke in early 1915. Jerrold was 'sorry to leave the friendly battalion' and asked himself

> whether the Hawke or the Nelson was intended to be strengthened by this event . . . I imagine that I was regarded as somewhat above the average of incompetence by one officer, who shall be nameless, but who

should have been, had incompetence been the issue, a good enough judge.[25]

Meanwhile, military training continued through the winter months at Blandford. Trench-digging seems to have been a frequent exercise, interspersed with mock battles across the Dorset Downs at platoon, company and battalion level. Able Seaman Joseph Murray of the Hood summed it all up:

> We trudged through the mud looking for an enemy we never found, but kept on looking. When we came to a nice watery patch we would be ordered to lie down . . . We wallowed in the mud all day and cleaned up all night ready for the morrow's mud bath.[26]

On return to camp after training, soaking wet and plastered in mud and chalk, the wooden accommodation huts with no drying facilities were to Able Seaman Burdon less than welcoming:

> There was just a coke stove at one end. You couldn't keep yourself warm and you just had to walk about.

However, for the men from the north of England and Scotland the Dorset winter was probably not too bad. Selected ratings were sent away for specialist training: Walter Burdon had been a signaller in the Boys' Brigade and found himself attending a two-week signallers' course where he was taught morse, by lamp and telephone, and flag signalling. This meant that he would carry extra equipment into action – 'two three-foot flags, one six-foot flag . . . a telescope and . . . a lamp for signalling.'

On 1 January 1915 the Naval Brigades were reorganized. Until the turn of the year the 1st Brigade at Blandford had still consisted of only Drake Battalion, because of the loss of the three other battalions at Antwerp, whereas the 2nd Brigade was at full strength. To balance up the brigades, Nelson Battalion was transferred to the 1st Brigade under the command of Brigadier General David Mercer RMLI, who had replaced the interned Commodore Henderson. Transferred from the 3rd Marine Brigade, Deal Battalion would also come under General Mercer's command, thus balancing the three brigades with three battalions each. At the end of January 1915 some training began at higher formation level with the three under-strength brigades and their supporting formations such as engineers. They would have only four weeks before embarkation. However, despite the increased intensity of training, one expert commentator has strong doubts as to its effectiveness:

> From contemporary accounts and reports, neither the battalions of the RM Brigade . . . nor the rest of the RN Division, did any battalion training to speak of. It is the training of all ranks in a battalion (and a brigade and division), in the articulation of the whole, that turns a crowd of individuals and small groups, however well trained, into a fighting unit. The

majority of the RN Division were not well trained, even as individuals. The sailors and naval officers in the two naval brigades hardly had any basic military training at all. The RM battalions at least had a leavening of experienced NCOs and older men, including regulars, and all the other men had done some military training.[27]

The simple truth was that, in the six months since the formation of the RND, there had been too many short-notice diversions from a coherent pattern of training (operations at Dunkirk and Antwerp, the activation of Blandford, the despatch of the RM Brigade), too many base changes (for Nelson Battalion: Walmer – Betteshanger – Portsmouth – Blandford) and a major reorganization, consequent upon the loss of three-quarters of one brigade and a quarter of another. Post-Antwerp there had also been a major turnover of personnel, which impacted particularly on the officer corps. Full and consistent training would have allowed a battle-worthy division to come together from well-trained units, but this was not to happen. The RND would have to learn its trade in the heat of battle.

The issue of khaki uniforms and pith helmets signified a move overseas, but the rank and file appear to have had little idea where they were going – 'somewhere where it was hot' thought Walter Burdon. February 1915 saw increasing signs of an impending move. The Plymouth and Chatham Battalions of the 3rd RM Brigade sailed for a destination somewhere in the East at the beginning of the month. Winston Churchill arrived at Blandford on 17 February for an inspection. He seems to have looked particularly closely at Nelson Battalion on this visit because the RND historian notes that when Winston returned a week later on 25 February, accompanying King George V, he did not give the Nelson the detailed scrutiny that he gave the other battalions on parade.[28] The RND was now formally under orders, which had arrived on 18 February, to proceed overseas. Six days later Nelson ratings were told to make sure that their allotments of pay, to families or dependants, were up to date. Ammunition and iron rations were issued at this time. Even at this last minute, appointments of officers were still taking place. Lieutenant Commander Robert C. Primrose RNVR took over from Lieutenant Commander Cheston as 2i/c on 25 February. He was the son of the Rev Robert Primrose, a Presbyterian minister, who had been the Hood Battalion chaplain since early October 1914. Two days later the Rev Primrose followed his son into Nelson Battalion.

The Nelson Battalion was now as prepared as it could be for operations. The Hood Battalion left at dusk on 27 February 1915 and just before midnight the Nelsons marched away from Blandford Camp, down from the dark Dorset Downs and into the town of Blandford. Those who were not employed loading limbers onto railway wagons spent the night in the Corn Exchange. In Blandford station and at nearby Shillingstone the trains were waiting to take the RND to the docks at Avonmouth and they departed at intervals through the night and next morning. The Nelsons arrived at Avonmouth early the next morning and embarked in the 18,150 ton former Cunard liner HMT *Franconia*. As well as the RND HQ, the 1st (Naval) Brigade Staff and the other two battalions of the brigade, Drake and Deal, joined the Nelson in the *Franconia*. According to Jerrold's divisional history she also carried the 1st Field Ambulance and a Motor Machine Gun Detachment of the Royal Naval Air Service, but another source places the 1st Field Ambulance in HMT *Royal George* with Howe Battalion, and Deal Battalion in HMT *Alnwick Castle*.[29] According to the same source, the *Franconia* was carrying just over 2100 RND personnel and had 300 spare berths, so she was not over-crowded. The List of Officers published on board *Franconia* on sailing shows clearly that numerous officers of Deal Battalion and the 1st Field Ambulance were embarked, a total of 134 officers. *Franconia* sailed from Avonmouth Docks, escorted by destroyers, at 8.00 pm on Monday, 1 March 1915 as part of the Mediterranean Expeditionary Force (MEF). It was on this day that the RNVR ordinary seamen who had joined from Crystal Palace were rated able seamen. They were probably not informed of this advancement in view of the fact that Charles Swales still thought he was an ordinary seaman when he signed his will six weeks later.

4

THE MEDITERRANEAN EXPEDITIONARY FORCE: LEAD-IN TO THE GALLIPOLI LANDING:

1 MARCH – 28 APRIL 1915

Nelson Battalion at this stage consisted of about thirty officers and between 900 and 1000 other ranks – again sources vary. One record shows the Nelson establishment to be thirty officers and 996 other ranks (ORs).[30] However, the Divisional GOC, Major General Paris, reported the state of the RND on 7 April 1915, showing the present strength of Nelson Battalion to be thirty-one officers and 908 ORs, against an establishment of thirty officers and 1095 ORs. Based on these figures the GOC reported that Nelson Battalion required the addition of 183 ORs.[31] The embarkation record shows the Nelson at thirty-three officers and 996 ORs.[32]

The officer complement of Nelson Battalion in mid-March 1915[33] appears to have been a total of thirty-six, as follows:-

Commanding Officer	Lieutenant Colonel Edmund G. Evelegh, RMLI	
2nd in Command	Lieutenant Commander Robert C. Primrose, RNVR	
Adjutant	Lieutenant Robert J. Carpenter, RMLI	
Chaplain	Rev Robert Primrose	
Lieutenant Commander RNVR	Mungo C. Gibson	John E. Nicol
	Tom L. Price	Herbert C. Evans
Lieutenant RNVR	Edmund M. Sharer	Harold T. Treves
	Percy C. Garnham	Henry G. Andrews
	Alfred Bennett	Herbert J. Starkey

Sub Lieutenant RNVR	Graham M. Paton	James H. Bookless
	Robert E.L. Davies	Frederick W. Sowerby
	Joseph M.F. Dickson	Robert E. Gilbert
	Warren Barclay	Hubert J.I. Whitaker
	John P. Robley	John A.R. McCormick
	John W. Edwards	Hugh D. Lamont-Fisher
	Wilfred V. Gilbert	Roland H. Tepper
	Guy P. Cooke	Eric V. Rice
	Francis H.J. Startin	Tom N. Chambers
Paymaster RNVR	John E. Macintyre	
Quartermaster	J. Town (*Hon Lieutenant RM*)	
Surgeon	Henry B. Parker	Alexander E. Gow

The scale of the turnover of officers since October 1914 can be judged by the fact that only the CO and 2i/c, the Adjutant (who had been brought by the new CO from Deal Battalion), two lieutenant commanders, two lieutenants, the Chaplain, the Paymaster and the Quartermaster had served as officers at Antwerp. Surgeon Taylor had been appointed to a Field Ambulance and would serve with distinction in that role at Gallipoli. Already the RND was selecting suitable ratings to be commissioned as officers, a policy which would serve the division well throughout the war. Of the new sub lieutenants only Cooke and Lamont-Fisher, who had been Benbow ratings, had served at Antwerp.[34] Sub Lieutenant John Edwards was also a former Benbow rating.[35] Sub Lieutenant Eric Rice[36] had originally volunteered as a London Division 'Z' rating. Several officers joined only shortly before embarkation, some on the very day that they marched out of Blandford Camp.

Each lieutenant commander, with a lieutenant as 2i/c and a chief petty officer as the senior NCO, would have commanded one of the four companies (A, B, C and D) each of over two hundred men. Lieutenant Commander Tom Price commanded 'A' Company and Lieutenant Commander Mungo Gibson was CO of 'B' Company. Lieutenant Commander Nicol and Lieutenant Commander Evans were in command of 'C' and 'D' Companies respectively. Each company was subdivided into four platoons, each of about fifty men. The platoons were numbered from 1 to 16, with Nos. 1–4 Platoons in 'A' Company, Nos. 5–8 Platoons in 'B' Company, etc. Each platoon was commanded by a sub lieutenant – Guy Cooke was in command of No.4 Platoon of 'A' Company. Each platoon was sub-divided into four sections each of about eleven to fourteen men with a leading seaman or petty officer as senior rating. The sections were numbered from 1 to 16 within each company – Nos. 1–4 Sections were in No.1 Platoon, Nos. 5–8 Sections in No.2 Platoon, etc.

The passage to the Mediterranean of the MEF transports was generally uneventful. For many men the excitement of going overseas was tempered by the combined effects of inoculations and sea-sickness while crossing the Bay of Biscay, which laid many low. It took nearly two weeks for Walter Burdon to recover from his 'jab'. After three days at sea the *Franconia* passed Gibraltar, where she was stopped and interrogated by patrolling destroyers on the night of 4 March, and passed into the calmer waters and sunny weather of the Mediterranean. Steaming at 17 knots *Franconia* overtook some of the slower transports that had sailed before her. On Sunday, 7 March she anchored off Malta for the night and proceeded into Grand Harbour on the following morning, mooring thirty yards off Valetta with HMT *Royal George* astern. Shore leave was not granted, except for officers. The men on board had to content themselves by trading with the multitude of local boats which came off laden with oranges and figs and souvenirs. While in Malta 'coaling ship' took place. The grimy event was recorded by Private Joseph Clements of the Royal Marine's Deal Battalion. As Clements recalled:

> They opened up the hatches. There were two gangways off the ship. The natives had a little shallow basket filled with coal. They came up this gangway, tipped the coal down the chute, went along and down the other way to go off and get it filled again. There was one continuous stream all day long. Up and down, up and down, coal going in, clouds of dust everywhere.[37]

After little more than twenty-four hours in harbour *Franconia* sailed at 5.00 pm on 9 March, the destination still not disclosed. The routine of the passage was broken by a concert on board that same evening and the following two days were enlivened by a variety of sports events, including single stick fighting and pillow fighting on a spar erected across a canvas water bath, which were captured on film by Lieutenant Commander John Nicol. Passing through the Aegean islands, snow could be seen on the highest peaks. Early in the morning on Friday, 12 March *Franconia* came to her anchor off Lemnos in Mudros Bay, the large natural harbour that had become the main base for the Allied ships that would carry out the assault on Gallipoli.

On the same day Able Seaman Swales noted that he had been presented with Princess Mary's gift. In late 1914 the 'Sailors & Soldiers Christmas Fund' had run an advertisement appealing for contributions. The fund had been started in the name of Princess Mary, the teenaged daughter of King George V and Queen Mary. The fund aimed to give a gift from the Nation to everyone serving in the Army or Navy on Christmas Day 1914. The gift was presented in a brass box carrying an embossed portrait of the princess. Officers and men serving at the front or in ships of the Fleet received a pipe, lighter, one ounce of tobacco and twenty cigarettes in distinctive yellow monogrammed wrappers. Non-smokers and boys received a bullet pencil and a packet of sweets instead.

Two days later, after a fortnight on board, some of the Nelsons went ashore on Lemnos for a route march and again on 18 March they were ashore conducting practice attacks. On the evening of that day all the RND transports, except for *Franconia*, were sailed at short notice, with their troops embarked, to carry out a diversionary manoeuvre to follow up the massive attack by the Fleet on the Dardanelles Narrows. This was to be the great breakthrough. However, as Jerrold described: 'the . . . transports, sailed out of the harbour eastwards [and] arrived off the western shore of the [Gallipoli] Peninsula at 5.30 am on the morning of the 19th.' The flotilla of transports and warships then gathered off the entrance to the Dardanelles, expecting a landing in support of the Fleet's bombardment on the previous day.

> But in fact the movements of the transports, a demonstration planned to divert the attention of the enemy from what should have been the closing and critical stage of a great naval attack, was no longer required. The great naval attack had failed, and within two hours of their first sight of the enemy, the Naval Division received orders to return to Lemnos.[38]

The men of Nelson Battalion witnessed none of this from the *Franconia*, which had presumably stayed at Mudros because the Divisional HQ was on board, and they saw the other transports steam back into harbour on the afternoon of 19 March. Within the week the RND transports had sailed from Lemnos to Egypt where the division would re-group, reorganize and re-load the ships for the amphibious landing which had now become an essential adjunct to the previously naval operation to force the Dardanelles. *Franconia* sailed from Lemnos at 1.30 pm on Wednesday, 24 March and arrived at Port Said in the late afternoon two days later.

On the following day Nelson Battalion disembarked at Port Said and immediately turned-to setting up the RND tented camp in the sands on the outskirts of the town. The heat by day under canvas on the edge of the desert was terrible. A swim in the Sweet Water Canal was about the only way of getting cool. Able Seaman Burdon recalled that:

> We used to go for a bathe – all naked because we had no costumes. We'd just strip off and put our clothes down and we had to put a guard on the clothes. They would pinch our clothes and everything.

Shortened trousers became de rigueur for the well-dressed Nelson sailor:

> Some of the lads they cut their trousers off at the knees. By night time they were looking for them again for to sew them back on again. It was so very cold at night, three or four used to lie together to keep warm, yet you could hardly keep your clothes on during the day.

He also noted that they had 'a plague of dragonflies, all over the tents. Millions of them.' These may actually have been locusts. The dangers of the Port Said fleshpots were the subject of a lecture to the Nelson ratings by the Brigade Major[39], 'about the women and all that . . . It had an impact on most of us.' The local Egyptians made a very poor impression on Walter Burdon, who compared Port Said most unfavourably with his native Newcastle:

> They were Arabs really. What a filthy lot! There was a European Quarter there with all outside tables and lights and everything lit up. They used to clean it. It was like being on Heaton Road – on one side the European Quarter, so nice and clean . . . the other side, a filthy, horrible place, the Arab Quarter on the other side of the road. Some of the lads would go chasing the females and we had to put a guard on the bottom of each street for to stop any of our people going up these streets. Because they were getting clobbered and all sorts of things when they went there.

On 1 April two companies of the Nelson Battalion, as part of an RND detachment, were sent by train to man the Suez Canal defensive trenches at Kantara against the threat of a Turkish attack from the Sinai Desert. The force, under Brigadier General Mercer, was two battalions strong but comprised half-battalions from Drake, Nelson, Howe and Anson. The attack failed to materialize. While they were away the rest of the RND was inspected on the morning of Saturday, 3 April by the Commander-in-Chief of the MEF, General Sir Ian Hamilton, who went on to Kantara to complete his inspection of General Mercer's detachment in the afternoon. The Kantara detachment returned in open trucks to Port Said on the next day, Easter Sunday. The following week saw a continuation of training for the forthcoming landings. Walter Burdon, as a signaller, was taught to use the heliograph, 'a wonderful thing . . . You could see the flash miles away.' Sandstorms made life in camp unpleasant on 5 and 6 April.

During this week, starting on 8 April, after about a fortnight of dockside activity, the re-loaded RND transports began to leave Port Said for Lemnos. Their 'secret' destination was widely rumoured to be Gallipoli. The departures continued through the following five days until, on 13 April, having spent the previous day loading the ship, Nelson Battalion struck their tents and embarked in HMT *Minnetonka*. Formerly on the transatlantic run as part of the Atlantic Transport Line, the 13,500-ton *Minnetonka* had been transferred to government service in early 1915. She sailed at 10.00 am on the following day, the 2nd Field Ambulance and a company of some 160 Army Supply Corps soldiers, sharing the accommodation with the Nelsons. Able Seaman Burdon was no more impressed with the *Minnetonka* compared with the *Franconia* than he had been when he compared Port Said with Newcastle:

> It was a mule-ship. We slung our hammocks up near the top and on top of us were mules. With their stamping all night we got no sleep at all.

His comment is not surprising, since the ninety or so horses and mules which were part of the Nelson establishment had been augmented by about another 100 belonging to the Field Ambulance and 170 belonging to the Army.[40] The constant noise of some 1500 hooves on the deck above the men's hammocks must have been unbearable. Able Seaman Albert Wilson, of 'D' Company, agreed with Burdon:

> Passed the worst night since leaving home. We are sleeping in hammocks and for a start one end of mine slipped the hook. I managed up to midnight and then had to give it up, it was too hot between decks. I slept the rest of the night on the mess table. Tonight I go on deck for a billet.[41]

A two-day passage brought the *Minnetonka* to Trebuki Bay on the island of Skyros on Friday, 16 April, Able Seaman Charles Swales noting that she anchored at 6.00 am. Some of the other RND transports had gone first to Mudros, which was overcrowded with shipping, and they followed into Trebuki Bay later that day. On the same day a sister ship of the *Minnetonka*, HMT *Manitou*, was unsuccessfully attacked with torpedoes by a Turkish gunboat. Survivors of the attack were transferred to the *Minnetonka*. Final preparations for the landings now took place, Nelson Battalion going ashore for training on Saturday, 17 April and, after a Sunday church service on board, on the next day also. Able Seaman Swales briefly noted that they carried out an 'attack uphill' and 'marched through a valley'. Able Seaman Wilson was more specific, observing that the hills of Skyros were 'large enough to pass as mountains – had the job of climbing one of these in full marching order – a very trying job.' Walter Burdon's recollections centred around a great deal of rowing practice – three or four boats would proceed around the harbour with the sailors taking turns at the oars. The battalion was also mustered on board for a briefing on the landings by Lieutenant Colonel Evelegh. Final administrative preparations included the writing of wills for those who had not already done so. Gales and rain on 21 and 22 April delayed the landing by forty-eight hours and prevented training, but the Nelsons' last full day in Trebuki Bay, Friday, 23 April, the day on which the poet Sub Lieutenant Rupert Brooke of the Hood died, included 'hands to bathe' over the ship's side as the weather improved.

On the evening of Saturday, 24 April the RND transports sailed from Skyros. The operation orders required the ships to form up in three divisions. The Nelsons in *Minnetonka* were in the 1st Division, together with the transports *Franconia*, *Alnwick Castle* and *Ayrshire*. Acting as the escort, with General Paris embarked, was the fifteen-year-old pre-Dreadnought battleship HMS *Canopus*.[42] The light cruisers HMS *Doris* and HMS *Dartmouth* escorted the other two divisions and the torpedo boat destroyers HMS *Kennet* and HMS *Jed* also patrolled around the force.

The diversionary operation in the Bay of Saros, which was the task of the RND, began at first light on the following day with the two cruisers opening up a bombardment on the Turkish lines at Bulair at 5.45 am. The bombardment continued all day, drawing the personal attention of General Liman von Sanders, the German commander on the peninsula. From a ridge above Bulair he described the scene below him in the bay:

> About twenty large hostile ships, some war vessels, some transports, could be counted in front of us. Some individual vessels were lying close in under the steep slopes of the coast. Others were farther out in the gulf or were still underway. From the broadsides of the war vessels came an uninterrupted stream of fire and smoke and the entire coast including our ridge was covered with shells and shrapnel. It was an unforgettable picture. Nowhere, however, could we see any debarking of troops from the transports.[43]

The feint landing by the RND would come just before darkness fell. 160 of the Nelsons embarked in *Minnetonka* were detailed off, issued with lifejackets, and were ready to embark in their eight allotted cutters at 6.30 pm, as ordered. At 7.30 pm they left the ship towed by a trawler or steam pinnace towards the designated landing place on the eastern side of the bay. Four other similar tows of cutters were in company as they were towed across the bay, the dusk turning to darkness. Private Joseph Clements of Deal Battalion recalled that they were told by the midshipman in charge of the tow not to worry about making a noise. He estimated that they went, under cover of darkness, to within perhaps 100 yards of the beach but saw no Turks and there was no firing. The tows then circled around and returned to their ships. By 9.00 pm the Nelsons were back at the *Minnetonka* after their ninety-minute trip round the bay.

Some of the transports remained in the Bay of Saros overnight and through the following day. Able Seaman Swales recorded the departure of *Minnetonka* at 8.00 pm on 26 April. Other ships had proceeded earlier down to Cape Helles, where Drake Battalion was landed on 'W' Beach at 8.30 pm on that day. Charles Swales noted the arrival there of *Minnetonka* with the Nelsons: 'Tuesday 27th April – Arrived at Said el Bar [sic] morning 4am. Heavy gunfire on Turk trenches from ships.' The RND transports then remained off Cape Helles ready to disembark the rest of the troops at short notice. The frustration felt by those who watched from the ships while the RND cruised offshore for two days in their transports, when they could have been adding some impetus to the stalled landings, has been well documented.[44] Walter Burdon also remembered this period before Nelson Battalion was landed:

> I had the telescope and I could see figures running back and forward. There was a big battleship there – the *Canopus*, I think. It would fire a

shell and you would see it go backwards with the [recoil] and then you would see the shell burst and see people running all over the place. And I said, "We're going to get amongst that lot!"

His premonition was to prove all too accurate. Within forty-eight hours the sailors of Nelson Battalion would be thrown into 'The Defence of Anzac'.

5

NELSON BATTALION IN THE DEFENCE OF ANZAC:

29 APRIL – 13 MAY 1915

At 9.30 am on 28 April a number of RND transports were sent up to 'Z' Beach at Gaba Tepe. It had become apparent to the command that reinforcement of the ANZAC troops, who had been fighting and digging there unremittingly for more than three days without a chance to rest and reorganize, was becoming essential. Later that day Portsmouth and Chatham Battalions of the 3rd (Marine) Brigade hit the beach at Anzac Cove and were immediately directed to take over the centre of the ANZAC line. The 1st Field Company of the Divisional Engineers (RNDE) went with them to help on the beach. On the following day, 29 April, at 4.30 pm the 1st Naval Brigade (Nelson and Deal Battalions – the Drakes were already ashore at Cape Helles) under Brigadier General Mercer started to land at Anzac as additional reinforcements, together with the 2nd Field Company RNDE. Able Seaman Charles Swales noted that he got ashore with the Nelsons at 8.00 pm and that they came under shrapnel fire immediately. Walter Burdon remembered that they were first transferred from the *Minnetonka*, who lay well off:

> We were taken so far by this ship and then a torpedo boat came. We all got onto a torpedo boat. Then the torpedo boat went inshore as far as it could and towed a whole lot of rowing boats. When he got in as far as he could we had to get into the rowing boats and row ourselves ashore. We weren't bothered much by going ashore but the Australians had to do that and they were slaughtered in hundreds, dozens, scores. Many were fifty in a boat and none would get out alive. But we were fortunate – they got there before us. We lost one or two in the boats – from small arms. As soon as we stepped ashore there were some Australians there and two or three dead ones lying there. I had my flags and that and an Australian says, "You can do away with those. You'll never live to use those. Take

those two" – the crossed flags off an Australian lying there on his pack. "Take those two." So I took the two short ones.

In fact the Nelsons got ashore relatively unscathed, to the extent that nobody was killed in the landing and only six were injured, despite heavy rifle fire (probably many spent bullets) on the approach to the beach. The Deal marines were sent straight up to the front line in the darkness but the sailors of the Nelson were to be held in reserve. Walter Burdon's recollection of that evening at Anzac was:

> We had to get up to the top of the cliffs there and there were ropes hanging down. We had to scramble up the cliffs. Not too difficult because we were young and strong. We didn't mind so much.

The reality was somewhat more terrifying. The inferno of a battle-zone into which they were landed was only about 1,000 metres behind the front-line trenches situated on the high ridges. These were 100 metres or so above the beach and accessible only by climbing cliffs. The conditions must have been daunting, although, in the darkness, the exploding of shrapnel shells could have only given a dim view of the actual conditions.

> The scenes behind the front lines, in the unbelievably restricted area captured by the Anzacs, astounded all new arrivals. They landed at Anzac Cove under a hail of shrapnel-bullets, and splashed ashore to discover a small but active ramshackle town perched on beach and cliff . . . like some extraordinary rookery. At night . . . the Anzac position looked for all the world like a great foundry, working strenuous overtime, sparks flying everywhere, and where shells were bursting great fiery showers flew in all directions like a heavy blow on red-hot metal. This was accompanied by a clanging and cracking that made the likeness complete.[45]

Two Royal Marine Privates of the Chatham and Deal Battalions described the scene at Anzac:

> We . . . landed there in the dark about 9 o'clock at night . . . three days after the big landing. There were no jetties or anything at all, only some stones which the Australians had thrown into the water, which made a very tiny landing place. So we had to get out of the boats and land on the beach like they did, wading through the water. As we landed in the dark we could not see very much, but we could hear a machine gun going "bonk, bonk, bonk", like a motorbike engine. That's just how it sounded with the crackle of rifle fire.[46]
>
> There was very little beach and it was straight up the cliff . . . On the beach you could see a lot of things laying around but we had no idea what it was, cases of this, bundles of something else, quite a shamozzel the whole lot of it seemed to me. It was dark and we went up a gully. I do

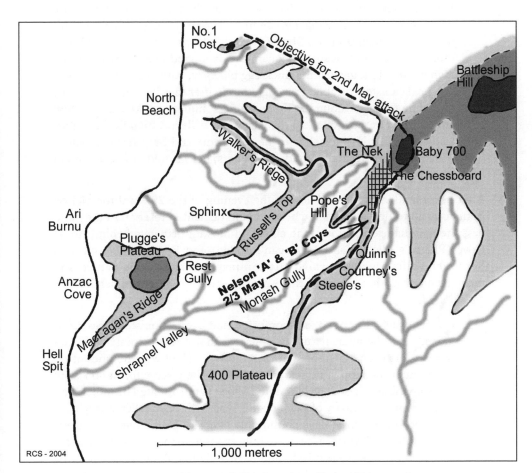

2. Anzac and the Attack on Baby 700.

not know what it was called, I was just looking at the bloke in front and stepping where he was stepping. The one in front of him he got hit with a rifle shot or something. He dropped out and was taken down.[47]

Lieutenant Douglas Hallam RNVR, a Canadian, served in the Royal Naval Armoured Car Division (a unit of the Royal Naval Air Service) and took a machine-gun detachment ashore at Anzac on 29 April.

He had been in uniform just five months and had no military experience whatsoever . . . .Following a guide from a New Zealand unit he and his men carried their guns up Shrapnel Gully. All the time they could hear bullets passing overhead; to Hallam they sounded like the rushing of a high wind. Aloft, against the duck-egg blue sky, could be seen dozens of shrapnel canisters tumbling through the air after they had burst above the front-line trenches along the ridge. Snipers' bullets cracked around him and his men as they toiled up the narrowing valley. A friendly Australian soldier advised him to take off the cap, tunic and Sam Browne belt of which he was extremely proud; the snipers, he was told, made a point of aiming at officers.[48]

After being landed in the darkness of the evening of the 29 April the Nelson Battalion had to find a position where it could be held in reserve. In the darkness the men had to surmount the cliffs and hills immediately behind Anzac Cove (Plugge's Plateau and Maclagan's Ridge) and find a resting-place in Shrapnel Valley, which formed the military administrative centre and main communication route of the Anzac position. The chaos ashore was considerable.

On the beach the crowd and confusion had been astonishing. So great, indeed, was the intermixture of units . . . that it was extremely difficult to assemble even a platoon and march off . . . Here were no lines of re-inforcement or supply, no resting-places for the reserve formations; but every possible piece of level ground had been appropriated by individuals of different units, many of them resting where they had fallen asleep after the exertions of three days continuous fighting. In the darkness it was impossible to tell what places were fully exposed to the view of the enemy. The result to the Nelson Battalion – the only battalion not in the firing line from the start – was that their labours on the construction of dug-outs during the night of the 29th–30th proved in the morning to be fruitless.[49]

Turkish snipers were an ever-present danger in these early days at Anzac, not to mention the possibility of being hit by a spent bullet from the front-line fighting high above the valley floor and the constant barrage of high-bursting shrapnel shells fired from the Turkish guns away behind the ridges. Captain

Eric Wettern of the Royal Naval Division Engineers described the country as 'very good for concealment and it was not surprising that snipers were a beastly nuisance'.[50] As the early days passed and positions were consolidated, the 'safe' (a relative term) routes and billets would become known and marked but for the Nelsons, coming ashore in darkness, there was no such information.

Able Seaman Burdon and his compatriots had to make the best of the conditions. Burdon soon encountered the battle casualties of Anzac:

> I had to step over a dead Australian lying there, his face and neck in a mud pool. The Australians hadn't bothered with him at all. And there was a dead donkey lying there as well. You had to avoid that. And we got to our trenches . . . Well, the first time I didn't get to a trench. There was a big hole in the ground – a big hollow. There were an Australian and a New Zealander in there and I went in beside them. I don't know what time it was but I must have fallen asleep. When I woke up at dawn there was a heck of a skirmish going on. These two were gone – I was left alone.

The arrival of the RND sailors and marines to relieve the Anzacs was essential if the latter were to have any chance to rest and reorganize after the heavy losses of the initial assault but their arrival was not received with universal rejoicing. One historian has written that

> the delight of the exhausted Anzacs was changed to consternation when they beheld the lines of pith-helmeted, pale and bewildered young men.[51]

The ANZAC GOC, General Birdwood, wrote later in his memoirs:

> The Deal and Nelson Battalions of the Royal Naval Division, under Paris, now joined me: nice lads, but very young and untrained.[52]

However, Birdwood wrote very unflatteringly in his diary at the time:

> I have now been given some so-called Marines and Naval battalions who are, so far as I can see, nearly useless. They are the special children of Winston Churchill, immature boys with no proper training . . . children under untrained officers and I feel sorry for them.[53]

They were, indeed, young: the average age of a typical platoon of RNVR ratings was about twenty-one and many lads would have been only eighteen or nineteen when they went into battle. However, the subsequent gallant performance of the RND battalions in the defence of Anzac, including the winning of a Victoria Cross by an RND Marine[54], gave the ANZACs the respite they so desperately needed and soon changed the initial poor impression.

The Nelsons spent the best part of three days in reserve down in Shrapnel Valley, while the RM battalions were holding the line and taking terrible losses on the heights above and Lance Corporal Parker of the Portsmouth Battalion was winning the Victoria Cross. Able Seaman Swales' diary contains brief entries for the first two days. For Friday, 30 April, when a company of the Nelson reserves was ordered forward at 8.30 pm to reinforce in support because of heavy firing on the left flank, it records: 'Dug ourselves in. Called out during night. Heavy battle on.' On Saturday, 1 May: 'Shifted our positions. Battalion splits up in two parts.' On 1 May preparations were being made for a major attack on the Turkish lines, Nelson Battalion moving onto Plugge's Plateau, but the assault was postponed for 24 hours. It was in the first two days of May that the battalion sustained its first fatal casualties of the war.[55] Albert Wilson noted in his diary that although things were 'settling down a little, warships firing overhead and enemy in front rather a trying experience'. At around this time Lieutenant Commander Price, commanding 'A' Company, was hit by Turkish fire and sustained a compound fracture of his right forearm. He was taken by hospital ship to Egypt and did not rejoin the battalion for two months. On 2 May Nelson Battalion was detailed to participate in an attempt to capture the heights which were occupied by the Turks. General Birdwood's plan has been described as

> an excessively ambitious and ill-conceived project to capture the hill Baby 700 by assaults on The Nek and The Chessboard from Russell's Top, Pope's [Hill] and Quinn's [Post], with more troops scaling the almost precipitous cliffs at the head of Monash [Gully].[56]

The Chessboard was the name given to the maze of criss-crossing Turkish trenches on the southern slopes of Baby 700, in front of Pope's Hill. From these commanding positions the Turks had an almost uninterrupted view down Monash Gully and Shrapnel Valley, the main supply route and rest area at Anzac. The Turkish snipers had had a field day picking off scores of men who, initially, had no protection from the fire above.

On 2 May all the RND battalions at Anzac were allotted roles in this ambitious assault on heavily defended Turkish trenches on the high ground, recorded as 'The Attack on Baby 700 – 2nd May' in the Official History of the War[57]. Initially the Nelsons were held in reserve and they were soon called forward to fight. Half of Nelson Battalion, 'A' and 'B' Companies under the command of Lieutenant Commander Primrose, had been allotted as Brigade reserve to Colonel John Monash who was in command of the ANZAC troops assigned to the operation. Charles Swales recorded that they started to reinforce the Anzacs around midnight. They were called forward in the darkness in the small hours of 3 May to climb up the Monash Gully cliffs south of Pope's Hill and support the 13th (NSW) Battalion of the Australian 4 Infantry Brigade. The 13th Battalion had climbed those same cliffs some hours earlier, and had been planned to form the link between the Australian 15th (Queensland & Tasmania) Battalion, who were advancing from the trenches they held on Pope's Hill, and the 16th (S & W Australia) Battalion, who had assaulted the Monash Gully cliffs ahead of them at about 8.00 pm the previous evening. However, in the darkness the timing had gone badly wrong. The New Zealanders of the Otago Battalion, who had to climb the western (left) fork of Monash Gully towards The Nek to form the left of the attacking line, were over ninety minutes late at their rendezvous. Moreover, the 13th Battalion failed to complete the link between themselves, the 15th, on their left, and the 16th, on their right. Utter confusion ensued, organization broke down, the assault faltered and the ANZACs, in the small hours of the morning, were only maintaining a tenuous grip on positions dug on the very edge of the plateau, with a precipitous drop into Monash Gully behind them. The 1st Naval Brigade War Diary[58] noted that

> Firing had practically ceased at 9 pm but at 9.15 pm increased and heavy maxim and rifle fire kept up all night.

It was into this desperate situation that the two Nelson companies climbed in the dark and, after order and counter-order, first to support one battalion and then another,

> They remained . . . till dawn fruitlessly digging in with entrenching tools in rear of the thinly held Australian support line.[59]

Able Seaman Swales wrote that he spent the whole night digging. At dawn on 3 May the exhausted marines of Portsmouth and Chatham Battalions (they had been out of the front-line for less than twenty-four hours) were also being called up the cliffs from reserve waiting positions in the gully below to try and save the deteriorating situation. At the same time

> an ill-fated order was given, in the centre of the battle front, for the Nelson Battalion companies to attempt, by attacking to a flank, to protect the 13th Battalion.[60]

This flanking attack in dawn light, across the flat plateau with no protection, against concealed Turkish machine-gun positions, failed and the Nelsons were ordered to retire. It was probably in this early morning attack that most of the Nelson casualties occurred. The author's father was among those seriously wounded at this time. Among those seen to fall was Sub Lieutenant James Bookless[61], the 'little child' of Able Seaman Burdon's memories.

> Looking around with this heck of a skirmish going on, I saw the officer's servant and another fellow carrying Lieutenant Bookless away. He had been killed. They were carrying him away to the back. [He had been hit] by a machine gun. I seen this fellow and he says, "Booky he had a pistol in his hand and said, 'Get that machine gun! Get it! Get that machine gun!'" and instead that machine gun got him. Practically riddled him.

Many others were killed including Able Seaman John Scrowther of No.16 Section, No.4 Platoon, 'A' Company, whose mortal wounding was also described by his Geordie friend Walter Burdon of No.13 Section:

> Going down the path down the cliff-side, I was with a chap called Jack Scrowther. He were a head bigger than me. [Jack was just over six feet tall, the tallest man in his platoon, Walter was about six inches shorter.] I had my left hand on his right shoulder. I was just saying "Hello, Jack" when 'whooosh' – a bullet whizzed past me and hit him in the neck and the blood spurted out. He staggered and says, "A damned sniper's got us." and he fell down and says, "I'm bleeding at the back." So we always carried an emergency bandage and I was feeling for it in my tunic when I heard a voice say, "Out of the road you bloody fool. That was meant for you." It was a First Aid man just coming up the path. So I scuttled out of the road then. I went down to the rest camp. We were there for a while and then went up again.

Jack Scrowther died of his wounds on Monday, 3 May and is buried in Beach Cemetery at Anzac Cove.[62]

The Official History of the campaign describes the situation as dawn broke over Anzac with stark clarity:

> By this time there was a good deal of confusion in that sector. Streams of wounded were pouring down the valley; the Marine battalions, strung out in an extended line, had lost all cohesion; and though heavy firing could be heard at the top of the scrub-covered heights above them, where the ridge rose like a wall on their right, there was great difficulty in learning the situation. After considerable delay the leading platoons of the Portsmouth Battalion began to climb the steep hill-side, but a moment later a few shells from Australian guns, falling short, dropped on the summit of the ridge. The troops in the neighbourhood came pouring back into the valley, the marines came back with them, and the whole line broke.[63]

After regrouping in Monash Gully, Jerrold records that the Nelsons, under Sub Lieutenant Sowerby, went forward again to the Australian trenches. The Chatham and Portsmouth Battalions, who had been called forward at 2.00 am, arrived at the base of the cliffs at first light and they too fought their way up to the Australian lines. The sailors and marines of the RND held them from 6 a.m. to dusk on 3 May.

> After a fresh delay another effort was made to reinforce a small body of the 16th which still clung to the ridge, but it was too late. By midday all gains in this part of the field had been lost.[64]

In the end, as positions flanking them were given up, the Nelsons and the Marines had to fall back:

> 5.30 the garrison were able to begin an exceedingly cool and well-planned retreat, so well-planned indeed, as to be carried out almost without loss, although it was daylight and the enemy were closing in on all sides.[65]

The timing in Jerrold's account is at variance with the 1st Brigade War Diary. This records that the two Nelson companies which had been with Colonel Monash had collected on the beach at 3.00 pm, were re-organized and joined up with the other two companies of the battalion.

The losses to Nelson Battalion in the attack on Baby 700 were extremely serious: nearly 200 killed and wounded from the two companies engaged – about forty per cent casualties. The Battalion 2i/c, Lieutenant Commander Primrose, took a bullet through his shoulder and was taken to Egypt by hospital ship, later to be invalided home and out of the RND to sea service. The 'B' Company commander, Lieutenant Commander Gibson, was killed and five other officers also lost their lives. 'A' Company had also lost their commander, wounded before the battle was even joined. More than forty ORs of the battalion lost their lives, including the two Company Chief Petty Officers, but only three of these men have graves at Anzac. Most of those killed were un-recoverable. The bodies of the Nelson dead were, perforce, left to decay with those of many Marines and Anzacs in front of the Turkish 'Chessboard' trenches that they had fought so gallantly to take against terrible odds. Their names were all to be commemorated on the Commonwealth Memorial at Cape Helles on the southern tip of the Gallipoli Peninsula. From then onwards this area on the heights above the head of Monash Gully became known as the Bloody Angle and Dead Man's Ridge. Seven Nelson officers and ORs died of their wounds in the hospital ships and were buried at sea. Three ORs died of their wounds in Egypt.

The uncertainty that surrounded the missing was typified by the efforts to ascertain the fate of Able Seaman Charles Poston[66], of No.13 Section, No.4 Platoon, 'A' Company. It was not until four months later that a witness state-ment said he was 'unable to give any definite details as to Poston's death but saw him shot and fall down ridge and never saw or heard anything else about him.' Poston's identity disc somehow made its way back to the RND Record Office in London in late 1915. In May 1916, in response to an RND Missing Circular, a report came in that Poston had been seen 'lying in a gully at Gaba Tepe on May 3rd, shot through chest and shoulder. Dying.' It was not until August 1916 that his death in action was officially accepted.

The attack on Baby 700 had many similarities to the set-piece battles which would take place later in the campaign: a poorly prepared and over-optimistic frontal attack with totally inadequate artillery support, the whole depending on an unachievable, high level of coordination, conducted against well-entrenched troops with good machine-gun defences. The results would become horrifyingly familiar over the ensuing months. The principal feature which sets Baby 700 apart is the fact that the attack took place in darkness on the edge of a precipice rather than across flat ground in daylight.

The survivors of 'A' and 'B' Companies drew breath and counted their luck when they got back with the remainder of the battalion at the 'rest' camp in Shrapnel Valley. Walter Burdon recalled hearing a young officer exclaim in despair after the battle, 'My God, how am I going to account for this lot? I've lost nearly three-quarters of them!' Their rest was short-lived – 4 May was recorded as a 'quiet day' – for at 7.30 am on Wednesday, 5 May General Mercer was ordered to take over the No.4 Section of the Anzac defences from the New Zealand Infantry Brigade. No.4 Section stretched across Russell's Top, where it was confronted by strong Turkish defences south of the Nek and on the summit of Baby 700 beyond. It then ran down Walker's Ridge to the beach, with two small posts, known as Nos.1 and 2 Outposts, thrown forward to the foothills on either side of Sazli Beit Dere.[67] The 1st Brigade arrived on Walker's Ridge an hour after the order to move and three companies each of Nelson and Deal Battalions took over the firing line under Lieutenant Colonel Evelegh. The Turkish trenches were less than 400 yards away and the stench from the rotting, unburied dead was terrible. The two battalions would remain in these positions for the next ten days, with snipers and shrapnel shelling taking a steady toll. The Nelsons lost two ORs killed on each of 4 and 7 May and two more died of wounds in the following days. The warships kept up a steady bombardment on the Turks, Able Seaman Wilson noting that 'at times the shells lifted men clean out of the trenches by the terrific explosion'. On the morning of 6 May General Birdwood visited the 1st Brigade trenches. Occasionally men managed to get back down to the beach, harassed by sniper-fire and bursting shrapnel shells all the way. There they could have a quick bathe. The brigade was relieved on 13 May, orders to embark being received at 8.00 am. As dusk fell, men of Nelson and Deal battalions made their way down to the beach, the rendezvous for embarkation. At 11.45 pm the 1st Brigade embarked in HMT *Alnwick Castle* for Cape Helles, arriving there on the morning of 14 May.

Brigadier General Mercer's report to Major General Paris on the Anzac operations was written as the battalion approached disembarkation at Cape Helles.

From GOC 1st RN Bde to GOC RND   14/5/15

1. I have the honour to submit herewith a short narrative of the events which have occurred during the time a portion of the 1st Brigade was attached to the NZ-A Division.

2. In accordance with your orders the Nelson and Deal battalions were disembarked on the night of 29th April, on the beach to the North of

Kaba Tepe. The battalions were landed from destroyers and on approaching the beach came under heavy rifle fire, 6 men being wounded in the Nelson and 3 in the Deal Battalion.

3. On landing, I received orders to take over the right centre No.2 Section of the defence from Col McKay of the 2nd (Victoria) Inf. Bde. I directed the Deal Battalion to man the trenches and placed Nelson in reserve in the gully in rear of the trenches. There was considerable firing during the night and Deal Battalion sustained a few casualties. On the following night (30th April) several attacks were made on the trenches. Lt Moxham of Deal Battalion was killed and several men of Nelson were wounded by shrapnel fire and spent bullets.

4. On the 1st May I received orders to hand over command of the Deal Battalion to Brig Gen Trotman and to move the Nelson Battalion as a general reserve to Plugge's Plateau overlooking the beach. I was given command of one Battery of 18pdr RFA and 1 Section Mountain Battery. Subsequently 2 companies of Nelson were detached under command of Lt Comdr Primrose to assist Col Monash in an attack which was to be made that night. This attack was subsequently postponed for 24 hours.

5. On 2nd May [should read 3 May], about 150 men of the Nelson joined me. They reported they had taken part in the attack on the previous night, and that Lt Comdr Primrose had been wounded and several officers were killed, and that the two Companies had come under very severe MG fire and had lost heavily. Subsequently, about 150 NCOs and men who had got lost had rejoined. The total losses being about 100 [an under-estimate].

6. On the 3rd May, I was directed to move to the left flank and take over the fourth section of the Defence, from the NZ Inf. Bde. I placed 3 Coys of Nelson and 3 of Deal Battalions in the fire trenches under the command of Col Evelegh RMLI, the remainder manning the Northern Spur, under command of Maj Tupman. We remained in these trenches until relieved on 13th May. We enlarged and improved the trenches, the men being employed most of the day in digging. We suffered a great deal from sniping and were at times heavily shelled. Several men were killed by snipers and others by unaimed infantry fire.

7. I regret to report that Lt Col Bendyshe was killed on the night 2nd/3rd May, under circumstances which have already been reported. I directed Major Tupman to assume command of the [Deal] battalion and, as only two senior Company Officers were left, I organised the Battalion into two wings under Capt Lawrie and Capt Bush.

8. I have much pleasure in stating that the conduct of Officers, NCOs and men has been excellent. The men have especially benefited by their experience in the trenches. At first I do not think they quite

realised their responsibilities but after the first 48 hours quickly settled down. The Bde was re-embarked in *Alnwick Castle* on the night of the 13th inst., two men being seriously wounded while being transferred. We disembark at Cape Helles this morning.

9. I attach a copy of a letter I addressed to GOC NZ-A Division, which I understand he will forward to you in due course. Before leaving, both the Army Corps Commander [General Sir William Birdwood] and Sir H. Godley [GOC NZ-A Division] expressed their thanks for the help we had been able to give. General Godley was particularly complimentary and came down to see us off, and asked me to express this thanks to the officers and men of the two battalions.

David Mercer Brig. Gen.

General Mercer attached to his report a copy of a letter of commendation, addressed to the GOC NZ-A Division, in which he cited the Nelson Battalion Commander, Lieutenant Colonel Evelegh, as being:

worthy of special mention . . . This officer has worked with untiring zeal and ability and has given me his whole-hearted support. He is the most excellent Bn Cdr, and although very much handicapped by a shortage of both Officers and NCOs he has brought the Bn on in a most remarkable manner. The men are mostly young and inexperienced, and his task has been rendered the more difficult on this account.

The Nelson Battalion's two weeks at the defence of Anzac had cost the lives of six officers and forty-nine ORs and nearly 150 had been wounded – about twenty per cent of the battalion. The battalion 2i/c and two company commanders were among the casualties. No.4 Platoon of 'A' Company was probably typical – they may even have fared better than other platoons. This platoon landed at Anzac Cove with one officer and fifty ORs. In the attack on Baby 700 it lost its commander, Sub Lieutenant Cooke, and eight ORs, including the Platoon Petty Officer, Euan Fleming, who had been one of the first to join on 22 August 1914. Of these nine dead, one is buried in Beach Cemetery[68] and one was buried at sea[69]. The remainder have no known grave and their names are on the Helles Memorial. A further seven ORs of this platoon were wounded in the defence of Anzac and evacuated to Egypt. Of these, four later had to be repatriated (the author's father, Charles Swales, was among these 'lucky' men). No.4 platoon had 31.4 per cent casualties – 17.7 per cent killed and 13.7 per cent wounded.[70]

The last of the Nelson casualties at Anzac to die of the wounds he received there was Stoker Michael Mulroy[71] of 'D' Company. His death occurred on 20 May in the hospital on Lemnos and was caused by a gunshot wound in the thigh which had turned gangrenous. His days of suffering, in an era without antibiotics, do not bear thinking about.

NELSONS KILLED OR MORTALLY WOUNDED
IN THE DEFENCE OF ANZAC, 29 APRIL – 13 MAY 1915

RANK/RATING NUMBER	NAME DATE	CAUSE	BURIAL / MEMORIAL	1914*
AB TZ/1440	HUMPHREY, W 02/05/15	KIA	HELLES MEMORIAL	
AB MZ/50	LANCASTER, C 02/05/15	KIA	HELLES MEMORIAL	
AB LZ/282	ANDREWS, CW 03/05/15	KIA	HELLES MEMORIAL	
AB TZ/1357	ARNOLD, J 03/05/15	KIA	HELLES MEMORIAL	
AB CZ/30	AULD, GL 03/05/15	KIA	HELLES MEMORIAL	
AB TZ/35	BROWN, A 03/05/15	KIA	HELLES MEMORIAL	
AB CZ/32	BUCHANAN, J 03/05/15	KIA	HELLES MEMORIAL	
AB LZ/294	COLE, AP 03/05/15	KIA	HELLES MEMORIAL	
SUB LT	COOKE, GP 03/05/15	KIA	HELLES MEMORIAL	1914*
AB LZ/227	DE LA MARE, WE 03/05/15	KIA	HELLES MEMORIAL	
AB MZ/84	EYES, JS 03/05/15	KIA	HELLES MEMORIAL	
PO C4/1545	FLEMING, E 03/05/15	KIA	HELLES MEMORIAL	1914*
LT	GARNHAM, PC 03/05/15	KIA	HELLES MEMORIAL	
AB KW/171	GAVIN, T 03/05/15	KIA	HELLES MEMORIAL	
LT CDR	GIBSON, MC 03/05/15	KIA	HELLES MEMORIAL	1914*
AB CZ/64	GREEN, J 03/05/15	KIA	HELLES MEMORIAL	
AB LZ/288	GREENING, WB 03/05/15	KIA	HELLES MEMORIAL	
LS DEV/281626	GREEP, FT 03/05/15	KIA	HELLES MEMORIAL	1914*
AB LZ/346	HALL, AO 03/05/15	DOW	CHATHAM NAVAL MEMORIAL	
STOKER1 DEV/291735	HARRINGTON, J 03/05/15	KIA	HELLES MEMORIAL	1914*
AB KW/260	LEATHER, GH 03/05/15	KIA	HELLES MEMORIAL	

43

RANK/RATING	NAME				
NUMBER	DATE	CAUSE	BURIAL / MEMORIAL		1914*
STOKER1 SS108431	LONNON, J 03/05/15	KIA	HELLES MEMORIAL		1914*
AB CZ/78	MARTIN, J 03/05/15	KIA	HELLES MEMORIAL		
AB CZ/65	McVICAR, R 03/05/15	KIA	HELLES MEMORIAL		1914*
LS C4/1822	MILLER, J 03/05/15	KIA	HELLES MEMORIAL		1914*
CPO DEV/139490	NORTHMORE, J 03/05/15	KIA	HELLES MEMORIAL		1914*
STOKER1 DEV/282111	O'LEARY, J 03/05/15	KIA	HELLES MEMORIAL		1914*
AB T4/207	PARKIN, JH 03/05/15	KIA	HELLES MEMORIAL		
AB LZ/134	POSTON, CH 03/05/15	KIA	HELLES MEMORIAL		
AB LZ/95	RICHARDS, KJ 03/05/15	KIA	SHRAPNEL VALLEY CEMETERY, ANZAC		
AB KX/88	SCROWTHER, JG 03/05/15	DOW	BEACH CEMETERY, ANZAC		1914*
AB KX/94	SIMMONS, J 03/05/15	KIA	HELLES MEMORIAL		1914*
CPO C3/255	SKELTON, W 03/05/15	KIA	HELLES MEMORIAL		1914*
AB LZ/37	VIDLER, KA 03/05/15	KIA	HELLES MEMORIAL		
LS CZ/73	WARE, LO 03/05/15	KIA	HELLES MEMORIAL		
SUB LT	WHITAKER, HJ 03/05/15	KIA	HELLES MEMORIAL		
LS DEV/297237	WILKINS, A 03/05/15	KIA	HELLES MEMORIAL		1914*
AB L10/3446	ARMSTRONG, EA 04/05/15	DOW	BEACH CEMETERY, ANZAC		
SUB LT	BOOKLESS, JH 04/05/15	DOW	HELLES MEMORIAL		
STOKER1 SS108146	DUNPHY, M 04/05/15	DOW	PLYMOUTH NAVAL MEMORIAL		1914*
STOKER1 DEV/296630	HARLING, F 04/05/15	DOW	PLYMOUTH NAVAL MEMORIAL		1914*
AB CZ/6	KNOX, RG 04/05/15	DOW	PORTSMOUTH NAVAL MEMORIAL		
AB M3/180	MASSEY, GA 04/05/15	KIA	HELLES MEMORIAL		1914*

RANK/RATING	NAME				
NUMBER	DATE	CAUSE	BURIAL / MEMORIAL		1914*
SUB LT	PATON, GM				
	04/05/15	DOW	PORTSMOUTH NAVAL MEMORIAL		
AB	PATRICK, J				
KW/136	04/05/15	KIA	HELLES MEMORIAL		
AB	UPTON, B				
SZ/14	05/05/15	DOW	PORTSMOUTH NAVAL MEMORIAL		
AB	COMPTON, H				
KW242	07/05/15	KIA	HELLES MEMORIAL		
STOKER1	FOSS, R				
SS101103	07/05/15	KIA	HELLES MEMORIAL		1914*
LS	STEALEY, RD				
LZ/191	07/05/15	DOW	CHATBY WAR MEMORIAL		
			CEMETERY, EGYPT		
AB	HOWES, WG				
LZ/299	08/05/15	DOW	CHATBY WAR MEMORIAL		
			CEMETERY, EGYPT		
AB	BAIN, D				
CZ/63	10/05/15	DOW	CHATBY WAR MEMORIAL		
			CEMETERY, EGYPT		
AB	DONKIN, H				
TZ/1475	11/05/15	DOW	CHATBY WAR MEMORIAL		
			CEMETERY, EGYPT		
STOKER1	MILES, H				
SS104159	14/05/15	DOW	PLYMOUTH NAVAL MEMORIAL		1914*
STOKER1	FERGUSON, WJ				
DEV/308717	17/05/15	DOW	CHATBY WAR MEMORIAL		1914*
			CEMETERY, EGYPT		
STOKER1	MULROY, M				
SS103567	20/05/15	DOW	EAST MUDROS MILITARY		1914*
			CEMETERY, LEMNOS		

6

NELSON BATTALION AT CAPE HELLES:

14 MAY – 7 JUNE 1915

At 10.00 am on 14 May 1915 Nelson and Deal Battalions, together with the 1st Naval Brigade HQ, disembarked from the *Alnwick Castle* at 'V' Beach. The Nelsons proceeded to their bivouac area, joining up with Drake Battalion, where they would have three days to sort themselves out after the Anzac operations. Digging holes for shelter was a priority in a 'rest area' that was swept with shell fire, both shrapnel and high-explosive, and regularly bombed by German aircraft, which seemed to overfly them with impunity. Efforts to do so were frequently frustrated by either bedrock or water at quite shallow levels. Reunited with their sister RND battalions (for the first time since sailing from England all nine RND battalions were together), the Nelsons would find that both the Hood and the Anson had lost a similar number of their people since landing, especially on 6 May during the Second Battle of Krithia. Within a week of landing at Helles the Nelsons had their first casualty on the new front when Stoker R McLaughlin[72] died of his wounds on 20 May.

A German Taube aircraft dropped leaflets on 16 May announcing that Calais and Warsaw had both been captured and inviting the British to surrender. On the night of 17/18 May the 2nd Naval Brigade and Nelson Battalion took over the RND defensive trenches. These ran south-east of the Achi Baba Nullah (Kanli Dere) to the old telegraph line to Sedd el Bahr which ran parallel to the nullah, a frontage of about six hundred yards. The RND left flank was held by 42nd (East Lancs) Division and the right flank by the French Corps. The Turkish trenches were about half a mile in front. Nelson Battalion moved into the support trenches on 17 May and into the firing line on 22 May, a day of heavy rain which turned the trenches into a quagmire. The last days of May were taken up by efforts to move the firing line forward, aiming to reduce the gap between the opposing front lines to an 'assaulting distance' of about two hundred yards in readiness for the next major attack on the Turkish trenches. The forward ground was 'so far as possible, to be stolen from the enemy by night advances.'[73] The 2nd Brigade moved forward 120 yards during the night 18/19 May and Nelson Battalion was part of a similar advance on the night of 24/25. These night moves forward were not casualty-free and Nelson Battalion had lost an officer and six ORs by the end of May. On 25 May, a day when the skies delivered exceptionally heavy rains and flooded the trenches, the Marine Brigade came forward to start relieving the 1st Naval Brigade. The Achi Baba Nullah, which served as a communication trench to the front line, was fulfilling its function as a storm water drain and, once out of the line, working parties of Nelsons were sent forward to deal with the flood by banking up the earth and rocks.

The loss of Lieutenant Harold Treves at this time illustrates again the confusion over casualties at this early stage of the campaign. Treves apparently received a very severe gunshot wound in the head on 22 May[74], was admitted to 3rd Field Ambulance and then transferred to No.11 Casualty Clearing Station. On the following day he seems to have been embarked in an unidentified hospital ship for transfer to Lemnos 'since which date no trace can be found of him in spite of repeated enquiries which are still being conducted. Possibly succumbed wounds, which were dangerous, and was buried not identified.'[75] He was probably buried at sea and his name is on the Portsmouth Naval Memorial.

On 28 and 29 May the newly re-formed Hawke, Benbow and Collingwood Battalions disembarked on Gallipoli and the RND was back to twelve battalions again for the first time since Antwerp. Hawke and Benbow joined Nelson in the 1st Brigade and Deal returned to the 3rd RM Brigade on 30 May. As May turned into June, preparations for what would be the fatal Third Battle of Krithia were being finalized. Shelling of the rest camps and heavy sniping on the trenches took their toll, the Nelsons having returned to the firing line on 2 June. Sub Lieutenant Wilfred Gilbert[76] and Chief Petty Officer M.D. Williams[77] died of wounds before the Nelsons went into a full-scale battle for the second time on 5 June, the day after the decimation of Collingwood Battalion.

In the small hours of 4 June, as the attacking battalions of the 2nd Brigade came forward to relieve the 1st Brigade, Nelson Battalion came out of the firing line. They went back to the rest camp as part of the Corps reserve under Brigadier General Marshall, whose 87 Brigade of 29th Division formed the other part of that reserve force. The Nelsons remained in their bivouac area at short notice to move. The disposition of the RND for the forthcoming battle was as follows:

First wave of assaulting force: 2nd Naval Brigade – Anson, Hood and Howe Battalions

Second wave of assaulting force: 2nd Naval Brigade – Collingwood Battalion

Divisional Reserve :   1st Naval Brigade – Drake Battalion

Corps Reserve: 1st Naval Brigade – Nelson, Hawke
and Benbow Battalions, and
3rd Marine Brigade – Chatham,
Portsmouth, Plymouth and Deal Battalions

This battle would, sadly, follow the pattern of the previous failed advances conjured up in the under-imaginative mind of the commander at Helles, Major General Sir Aylmer Hunter-Weston, known to some as 'The Butcher of

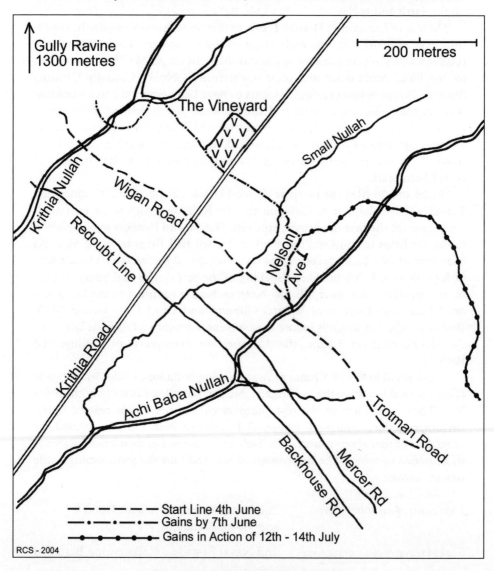

RCS - 2004

- – – – – – Start Line 4th June
- – ·— · — · — Gains by 7th June
- ●——●——●——● Gains in Action of 12th - 14th July

3. The June and July Battles at Helles.

Helles'. His fatal orders for yet another frontal assault in daylight against massed Turkish rifles and machine guns, over ground which was covered by a withering shrapnel barrage accurately directed from the heights of Achi Baba, would achieve the inevitable ghastly result. But then, as Hunter-Weston himself said to General Paris, 'Casualties? What do I care for casualties?'

The attack began along the whole of the Helles front at twelve noon. Within the hour the damage had been done. The first wave of RND battalions had gone forward, with terrible casualties, and had taken the second line of Turkish trenches. There they were enfiladed by Turkish machine-gun and rifle fire from their right where the French Corps had failed to take their objectives on the high ground of the Kereves Dere Ridge. The Collingwoods, comprising the second wave, had met the same hurricane of Turkish fire as they moved forward fifteen minutes later. The results for them were even more devastating. The sensible decision had then been made that the RND assaulting force should withdraw from their untenable forward position. They had pulled back to their start line, leaving behind as casualties about ninety per cent of their officers and half of the ORs. Recognizing the danger of a Turkish counter-attack, General Paris called forward his one reserve battalion, the Drake, and the Corps Commander released Benbow Battalion from his reserve to replace them.

On the RND right the French were also still on their start line, but on the RND left the 127 (Manchester) Brigade of the 42nd Division had successfully advanced their line more than 300 yards, taking three lines of enemy trenches on the other side of Achi Baba Nullah. The RND, in the act of falling back to their start line, now left the Manchesters open to enfilade fire from the right. Because of this, the troops on this flank of their advance also had to fall back. As dusk fell, only the first line of Turkish trenches was held by the Manchesters.

By 4.00 pm on 4 June the remainder of 1st Naval Brigade (Nelson followed by Hawke) had been moved forward to the vicinity of Backhouse Post. Walter Burdon remembered the message coming back: 'Will the Nelson get back to the front line? The Collingwood's been wiped out. Take your machine guns with you.' As the sun was setting, it eventually fell to Nelson Battalion to secure the dangerously uncomfortable 300-yard offset that now existed between the forward troops on the Manchester's right, on the west of Achi Baba Nullah, and those on the RND's left, which was still on its start line on the east of the nullah. The initial Hunter-Weston-style plan was for Nelson Battalion and two companies of Benbow to carry out yet another full-frontal dusk assault on the right flank of the Turkish trenches adjoining the Manchesters to the east of the nullah. The aim, as stated in the Divisional War Diary[78], was that they should 'establish contact with Manchester Brigade and throw back their right to the RND centre and secure the line.' At this point CO Nelson Battalion appears to have put forward a plan less likely to result in yet another RND bloodbath. As the RND historian described it:

> Colonel Eveleigh [sic], after discussing the position with the Brigadier on the spot, hit on a wiser, though still hazardous plan, the execution of which was entrusted to 'D' Company of his Battalion (Lt. Commander H.C. Evans, RNVR). This plan was to construct a number of separate entrenchments covering the gap between the two [British] front lines, and so sited as to afford the maximum protection for the exposed [Manchester Brigade] flank. Protected by covering parties, these posts could be completed before dawn, and could then be joined up during the day into a continuous line.[79]

Such became the Nelson's daunting task on the night of 4/5 June and Colonel Evelegh's plan seems to have been a notable success in that the aim of closing the offset was achieved. The Divisional War Diary notes briefly for 5 June:

> Nelson Bn effected junction with Manchester Bde right 150 yards west of Nullah in Trench F.11 and dug in under heavy fire to RND left and secured the line.

The 1st Brigade War Diary is more detailed:

> Lt Col Evelegh left about 8pm and arrived at Manchester HQ about 9.30 pm. Sent a report to BHQ received at 11pm. On receipt of this GOC 1st Bde saw GOC RND and Nelson were ordered to dig in and connect right flank of Manchesters with RND firing line asap [as soon as possible]. This was done during night 4/5. The Manchester right, about 150 yards west of where F11 crosses nullah, and the right of Manchester old firing line was connected by a trench. To accomplish this the Nelsons had to attack the Turks in F11 near nullah. This Bn was also under close fire from the Turks during the time they were digging in, which they did successfully by daylight.

These few words do not do justice to the difficulty and danger involved, which are more eloquently described by Jerrold.

> Throughout the night the Turkish fire was continuous, and casualties were heavy, but the plan was so far successful that digging was able to continue, which would almost certainly not have been possible had the Turks been led to realize our intentions by a formal attack on their flank. When dawn broke, the fire, aimed from close range by the enemy in the front line to the right of the Manchesters, became intense, but enough cover had been won during the night to enable the posts to be not only held but steadily strengthened and extended throughout the day. By four o'clock (when 'C' Company of the Hawke Battalion relieved the Nelson Company to carry on the work of consolidation), the trench, though

shallow, was almost continuous.

Jerrold had a good knowledge of this new trench because it was his company of the Hawke who relieved the Nelsons. He noted that the Turks had

> merely shot up a company of the Nelson Battalion while they were digging it and proceeded to shoot at us while we completed the work. They shot very few of us because the Nelson had done their work well. On the morning of the 5th, before we relieved the Nelson, the Turks had started throwing bombs at Evans's fleet reserve stokers as they were eating their breakfast. The stokers had retired to finish their breakfast in peace. Then they were ready to resume and without a word from any one they went back with the bayonet. 'Come on, Bill, let's have a prick at the b . . . s' was the nearest to a word of command that anyone had over-heard.[80]

The 1st Brigade War Diary summed up the achievement of the Third Battle of Krithia thus:

> The result of the general attack was the RND section remained on the same line as before, on its old front, while the Nelson Bn connected its left by a manned trench with the right of the Manchester Bde, and also held about 150 yards of the trench on left of RND section as a support to the new trench which had been made during the night.

The gallant efforts of Lieutenant Commander Evans' 'D' Company in consolidating the line merit not even a mention in the Official History of the War.

Nelson Battalion remained holding the left of the RND line, including their new trench running forward half-left to the right flank of 42nd Division. The resulting diagonal fire trench, bridging the dangerous gap between the 42nd and RN Divisions, became known as Nelson Avenue. Turkish counter-attacks continued through 5 June as the dangerous work of consolidating continued. On the following day at least two major attacks on the new line were made by Turkish reinforcements who had been hurried forward in response to the Allied attack. Nelson Battalion continued to take casualties throughout.

With darkness on 6 June the Third Battle of Krithia came to an end as both sides settled into their new front lines. Nelson Battalion's second major operation had again cost them dearly. Yet another company commander was dead. Lieutenant Commander Clyde Evans, Jerrold's friend and veteran of the Battle of Tsushima, was killed in action on 5 June leading his men of 'D' Company on their perilous task to secure the main battle line. His body was taken back to Backhouse Post, where he was buried by Chaplain B.J. Failes, Chaplain to the 1st Brigade. Clyde Evans' courage was to be recognized by his being mentioned in the Despatches of GOC-in-C MEF.[81] Three other Nelson officers, Lieutenant J.A.R. McCormick, Sub Lieutenants J.P. Robley and J.W.

Edwards were killed or died of wounds on 5 June. John Robley's records show that he was 'killed early morning 5th June when Company entrenching under heavy fire. Shot through head died immediately. Buried with two other Nelson officers.' Like his company commander, he was buried at Backhouse Post by Chaplain Failes. All four officers are now buried or have a Special Memorial in Skew Bridge Cemetery, Helles.

The Nelson ORs also took heavy casualties in the Third Battle of Krithia, thirty-four being killed in action on 5 June and in the Turkish counter-attacks on 6 June or dying of their wounds. Nearly half of those killed were veterans of Antwerp. Only six of the dead ratings have graves on Gallipoli and one of those who died of his wounds is buried on Lemnos. Over seventy ORs were wounded. Included in the wounded was Able Seaman Walter Burdon, who had been among the digging party during the night of 4/5 June. He recorded that:

> We were told to go forward at night and dig in . . . we were down to about waist deep, when there was a heck of a yell from the right. The officer shouts, "'Enemy right! Enemy right!" I'd just turned round and was just going to fire, when . . . something hit me in the side of the head . . . I think that the bullet had hit my rifle and splintered it. Blew my rifle all to bits and I got the impact.

That Turkish bullet ended Burdon's fighting career. He was evacuated to Egypt, invalided home and discharged medically unfit in January 1916.

As Jerrold comments,

> the work of the Nelson Battalion on the next night [4/5] had at least prevented the enemy from exploiting his earlier success [in fighting off the RND and French assaults] and had preserved for us some substantial gains. The price paid by the Naval Division for this very negative success was, unfortunately, out of all reckoning.[82]

Nelson Battalion eventually came out of the firing line on the evening of 7 June. They withdrew to the rest camp to sleep in their unprotected holes in the ground under a hail of Turkish shrapnel.

NELSONS KILLED OR MORTALLY WOUNDED ON THE HELLES FRONT. 14 MAY–7 JUNE 1915, INCLUDING THIRD BATTLE OF KRITHIA

RANK/RATING NUMBER	NAME DATE	CAUSE	BURIAL / MEMORIAL	1914*
STOKER1 SS107526	McLAUGHLIN, R 20/05/15	DOW	HELLES MEMORIAL	1914*
STOKER1 DEV/354287	DONOVAN, EM 23/05/15	KIA	HELLES MEMORIAL	1914*
AB KW/225	CROFT, HA 25/05/15	KIA	HELLES MEMORIAL	
AB CZ/454	INNES, JC 25/05/15	KIA	REDOUBT CEMETERY	
PO CH/193730	SEARLE, C 25/05/15	KIA	HELLES MEMORIAL	1914*
LT	TREVES, HT 25/05/15	DOW	PORTSMOUTH NAVAL MEMORIAL	1914*
AB C1/1948	HAY, A 28/05/15	DOW	LANCASHIRE LANDING CEMETERY	1914*
SUB LT	GILBERT, WV 03/06/15	KIA	SKEW BRIDGE CEMETERY	
CPO DEV/165528	WILLIAMS, MD 04/06/15	DOW	LANCASHIRE LANDING CEMETERY	1914*
SUB LT	EDWARDS, JW 05/06/15	DOW	SKEW BRIDGE CEMETERY	
LT CDR	EVANS, HC 05/06/15	KIA	SKEW BRIDGE CEMETERY	
LT	McCORMICK, JAR 05/06/15	KIA	SKEW BRIDGE CEMETERY	
AB CZ/278	MCINTOSH, A 05/06/15	KIA	HELLES MEMORIAL	
AB C5/2524	MENZIES, J 05/06/15	DOW	LANCASHIRE LANDING CEMETERY	1914*
AB KW/237	PAGDEN, C 05/06/15	DOW	LANCASHIRE LANDING CEMETERY	
SUB LT 05/06/15	ROBLEY, JP KIA		SKEW BRIDGE CEMETERY	
STOKER1 DEV/109988	WILLIAMS, RW 05/06/15	DOW	SKEW BRIDGE CEMETERY	1914*
AB KW/145	BULLOCK, H 06/06/15	KIA	HELLES MEMORIAL	
AB KX/117	BURNIP, W 06/06/15	KIA	HELLES MEMORIAL	1914*
AB KW/183	CONNICK, W 06/06/15	KIA	HELLES MEMORIAL	

RANK/RATING	NAME			
NUMBER	DATE	CAUSE	BURIAL / MEMORIAL	1914*

RANK/RATING NUMBER	NAME DATE	CAUSE	BURIAL / MEMORIAL	1914*
AB LZ/479	COX, H 06/06/15	KIA	HELLES MEMORIAL	
AB CZ/417	DAVIDSON, WR 06/06/15	KIA	HELLES MEMORIAL	
STOKER1 SS105269	DAVIES, JL 06/06/15	KIA	HELLES MEMORIAL	
PO CH/188465	EVANS, J 06/06/15	KIA	HELLES MEMORIAL	1914*
AB C4/2209	GIBSON, C 06/06/15	KIA	HELLES MEMORIAL	1914*
AB CZ/329	GOURLAY, A 06/06/15	KIA	HELLES MEMORIAL	
AB S5/258	HIPGRAVE, AE 06/06/15	KIA	HELLES MEMORIAL	
AB TZ/30	HOLLAND, P 06/06/15	KIA	HELLES MEMORIAL	
AB KW/206	HOWARD, A 06/06/15	KIA	HELLES MEMORIAL	
AB LZ/259	HULME, H 06/06/15	KIA	HELLES MEMORIAL	
AB M3/225	JOHNSTONE, G 06/06/15	KIA	HELLES MEMORIAL	1914*
STOKER1 SS108268	JONES, FC 06/06/15	KIA	HELLES MEMORIAL	1914*
STOKER1 SS105392	KERR, WJ 06/06/15	KIA	HELLES MEMORIAL	1914*
AB TZ/1434	LEWIS, JG 06/06/15	KIA	HELLES MEMORIAL	
AB LZ/492	MEREDITH, WT 06/06/15	KIA	HELLES MEMORIAL	
STOKER1 SS108239	OSMOND, D 06/06/15	KIA	HELLES MEMORIAL	1914*
LS C5/2348	O'SULLIVAN, CP 06/06/15	KIA	HELLES MEMORIAL	1914*
AB KX/111	PRIESTLEY, V 06/06/15	DOW	SKEW BRIDGE CEMETERY	1914*
AB LZ/353	PRITCHETT, PA 06/06/15	KIA	HELLES MEMORIAL	
STOKER1 SS107028	RANCE, T 06/06/15	KIA	LANCASHIRE LANDING CEMETERY	1914*
AB TZ/2000	READMAN, H 06/06/15	KIA	HELLES MEMORIAL	
AB TZ/1849	SEWELL, J 06/06/15	KIA	HELLES MEMORIAL	

RANK/RATING	NAME			
NUMBER	DATE	CAUSE	BURIAL / MEMORIAL	1914*
STOKER1	SHEARER, T			
SS104495	06/06/15	KIA	HELLES MEMORIAL	1914*
AB	SPENCER, D			
KW/218	06/06/15	DOW	EAST MUDROS MILITARY	
			CEMETERY, LEMNOS	
STOKER1	TANNER, G			
SS105734	06/06/15	KIA	HELLES MEMORIAL	1914*
AB	THOMPSON, PG			
M7/255	06/06/15	DOW	SKEW BRIDGE CEMETERY	1914*
STOKER1	SEARLE, H			
DEV/K/17715	10/06/15	DOW	CHATBY WAR MEMORIAL	1914*
			CEMETERY, EGYPT	
AB	GUNN, J			
CZ/239	07/06/15	DOW	PORTSMOUTH NAVAL MEMORIAL	
AB	WILLIAMS, W			
M3/223	19/06/15	DOW	CHATBY WAR MEMORIAL	1914*
			CEMETERY, EGYPT	
AB	BARRON, NC			
CZ/40	14/07/15	DOW	GLASGOW WESTERN NECROPOLIS	

7

RECOVERING FROM THE LAST SLAUGHTER, PREPARING FOR THE NEXT:

8 JUNE – 11 JULY 1915

As the Turkish counter-attacks died down with nightfall on 6 June, consolidation of the RND's hard-won gains in the firing line continued round the clock. Nelson working parties were concentrated on digging a second firing line along Nelson Avenue, as well as improving access along the communication trenches towards the rear. Meanwhile General Paris pondered the changes that would be required to compensate for the terrible losses that had been sustained by his Division. The Divisional War Diary recorded these losses as sixty-four Officers and 1,106 ORs. Jerrold puts the casualties at more than sixty officers and 1,300 men of which nearly half were killed. The outcome was to be the disbanding, on 9 June, of the relatively unscathed Benbow Battalion, together with the survivors of the Collingwood Battalion. Their manpower was absorbed in the other six naval battalions. After only ten days at full strength, the naval brigades were back to three battalions each. On the following day, the Divisional War Diary records the strength of Nelson Battalion, after augmentation, as nineteen officers and 723 ORs, the weakest of the three battalions in the 1st Naval Brigade (Nelson, Drake and Hawke).

14 June saw Nelson Battalion move back into the firing line and over the next four weeks they moved in and out of the front and support lines as dictated by the rotation of the brigades. The Divisional War Diary records many of these days as 'quiet days' but this description is purely relative, because sniping and shelling of the camps and bivouac areas continued and all was far from quiet in the RND firing line. On 19 June, at 2.30 am, a further attempt was made to capture Turkish trenches on the RND left. Nelson Battalion gave covering fire from Nelson Avenue and fought off Turkish counter-attacks as 'A' Company of the Hawke moved forward. However, by first light the Hawke gains were untenable because of enfilading machine-gun and shrapnel fire and those trenches that had been won were abandoned with heavy losses. This was not

to be the last attempt on these enemy trenches. The Portsmouth marines were to try again three days later with a similar lack of success and similar losses. These bloody attempts serve to illustrate the wisdom of Lieutenant Colonel Evelegh, when he argued against comparable frontal assaults by the Nelsons on the same trenches on the night of 4/5 June.

As June turned into July the weather got ever hotter and the dust-storms and flies made life sheer hell. The Nelsons were again holding the line from Nelson Trench. Their future CO, Major Norman Burge, was temporarily commanding Howe Battalion at the time and he came forward to inspect the position prior to relieving the Nelsons. He described the situation on 1 July in his diary:

> The Nelson Battn. under Evelegh are in the bit we relieve – the L[eft] of the Naval Division sector, which is the nullah piece, thank you. A most forbidding looking bit about 350 yards long as regards the fire trench, with support trenches at any angle and Turks' trenches only 30 yards off in places. A beastly nullah cuts through it and it's a regular medley of a place including a fatuous redoubt with no field of fire. I can see there's lots of work to be done – but one can't do much or anything at all hardly by day. One place there is a sap thrown out to the Turkish trench, which suddenly ran into one from them to <u>us</u>, to the great embarrassment of both sides – so somehow it got blocked in the middle. I gather there is a certain amount of bombing going on.[83]

A Turkish assault on the RND and French lines on 5 July was beaten off with heavy Turkish casualties. Able Seaman Wilson noted in his diary:

> Turks attacked en masse but were driven off with heavy losses – a sight to see. Wish they would do it every morning. It happened in broad daylight – they were very plucky but had no chance, we just mowed them down.

On the same day orders were received that 52nd (Lowland) Division would take over the RND trenches and on the following day the relief was successfully executed. The RND moved back into reserve south of Backhouse Post but, despite the urgent need for rest and recuperation, Nelson Battalion would only be allowed one week out of the firing line. The toll of RND casualties had continued through the previous four weeks of 'normal' trench routine and working parties, and shelling of the bivouac areas continued when battalions were 'resting'. During this period Nelson Battalion had lost one officer, Sub Lieutenant Alan C. Iliff,[84] who was shot through the head and died of his wounds on 20 June. In addition, twenty-one ORs lost their lives, among whom were the first three Nelsons[85] to die of the diseases which were wreaking havoc in the ranks of all on the peninsula as the summer plague of flies multiplied and the numbers of unburied dead increased. The field ambulances on

Gallipoli transferred the worst cases to Lemnos, where a desperate period of up to two weeks might pass before patients died of dysentery, typhoid or paratyphoid. The surviving worst cases were invalided home to recover, but some succumbed to the disease even there.[86] Many others stayed with the MEF, made a recovery, of sorts, and returned to the fray.

The contemporary Navy List for July 1915 gives a very inaccurate picture of the Nelson Battalion's officers as it includes those who had recently been killed or who had been injured and evacuated. Moreover, it shows officers who had been appointed but had not yet joined from England. Nor does it reflect the disbanding of Benbow and Collingwood in early June. The following is a more complete picture of the parlous state of the Nelson Battalion officers present on Gallipoli in the early days of July 1915, just before their next major battle.

Commanding Officer	Lieutenant Colonel Edmund G Evelegh, RMLI
2nd in Command	*[Lieutenant Commander Robert C Primrose, RNVR had been wounded 3 May, invalided home and was in RNH Haslar, prior to discharge from the RND.]*
Adjutant	Lieutenant Robert J. Carpenter, RMLI
Lieutenant Commander RNVR	John E. Nicol *[wounded 5 June, rejoined from hospital in Egypt on 11 July.]* Tom L. Price *[wounded 1 May, rejoined from hospital in Egypt on 11 July.]* Henry G. Andrews *[promoted Lieutenant Commander 1 July.]*
Lieutenant RNVR	Edmund M. Sharer Alfred Bennett *[wounded 6 May, rejoined from hospital in Egypt on 4 July.]* Herbert J. Starkey Hubert R. Daldwin *[ex-Benbow. Dysentery 15 June, rejoined from hospital in Egypt on 11 July.]* Frederick W. Sowerby

Sub Lieutenant RNVR		
Francis H.J. Startin	Robert E.L. Davies
Joseph M.F. Dickson	William H. Edwards
Hugh D. Lamont-Fisher	Eric V. Rice
Arthur Hobbs	Basil W. Smyth
William Lintott *[ex-Benbow]*	

Paymaster RNVR	John E. Macintyre	
Quartermaster	J. Town *(Hon Lieutenant RM)*	
Surgeon	Henry B. Parker	Alexander E. Gow

It is instructive, but depressing, to compare the list above with that of mid-March 1915, which indicates the strength of the battalion officers on first landing at Anzac on 29 April. In a little over two months Nelson Battalion had participated in two major battles, the Anzac action on Baby 700 involving two companies ('A' and 'B') and the Third Battle of Krithia involving one company ('D'). The losses had been dreadful, including two of the battalion's four lieutenant commanders and two of its six lieutenants killed. Twelve of the eighteen sub lieutenants on the March 1915 list of officers had been lost to the battalion – eight of them dead, two wounded and two sick. Several other officers had only just rejoined after treatment for their wounds.

The list also shows the continuing policy of ratings being commissioned. Sub Lieutenant William Edwards had served as a chief petty officer with Nelson Battalion since its formation and had been with the battalion at Antwerp.[87] He was commissioned as a sub lieutenant in the field at Gallipoli on 5 June 1915, a day when five of the battalion's officers had been killed. Sub Lieutenant Arthur Hobbs had, similarly, been promoted from chief petty officer in the field at the end of the costly defence of Anzac.[88] Serving as an able seaman in Drake Battalion, Sub Lieutenant Basil Smyth was also commissioned in the field and transferred to Nelson on 8 July.[89]

During this period the Nelsons had suffered two unfortunate casualties. Able Seamen J.L. Price[90] and J. Ross[91] had both died of bullet wounds inflicted by other Nelson ratings. In both cases the ratings responsible were charged with carelessly firing their rifles in the trench and mortally wounding the other two men. Both were sentenced to twenty-eight days' detention, the punishment suspended. Price was hit in the legs and died in HS *Neuralia*. He was buried at sea. Ross was shot in the abdomen and was buried on Gallipoli.

As the day of the next big battle approached the fighting strength of Nelson Battalion stood at seventeen officers and 674 ORs, according to the Field State Report (Army Form B.231) raised on 11 July, against a war establishment of thirty officers and 977 ORs.[92]

NELSON KILLED OR MORTALLY WOUNDED ON THE HELLES FRONT OR DIED OF DISEASE, 8 JUNE–11 JULY 1915

RANK/RATING NUMBER	NAME DATE	CAUSE	BURIAL / MEMORIAL	1914*
AB KX/118	CORNER, SH 15/06/15	DOW	PINK FARM CEMETERY	1914*
AB CZ/1595	FORBES, N 15/06/15	DOW	SKEW BRIDGE CEMETERY	
AB M5/152	BATTY, GT 16/06/15	KIA	HELLES MEMORIAL	1914*
AB CZ/20	WRIGHT, D 16/06/15	KIA	HELLES MEMORIAL	
PO LZ/78	BURWELL, J 17/06/15	DOW	LANCASHIRE LANDING CEMETERY	
PO C1/2280	NICOL, J 17/06/15	KIA	HELLES MEMORIAL	1914*
STOKER1 DEV/295083	HOWSE, DE 19/06/15	KIA	HELLES MEMORIAL	1914*
AB CZ/1239	STEPHEN, C 19/06/15	KIA	HELLES MEMORIAL	
SUB LT	ILIFF, AC 20/06/15	DOW	SKEW BRIDGE CEMETERY	
AB TZ/3083	CURSON, RW 21/06/15	KIA	HELLES MEMORIAL	
AB CZ/1611	HENDERSON, J 21/06/15	KIA	TWELVE TREE COPSE CEMETERY	
LS KW/254	HERRINGTON, JO 21/06/15	KIA	TWELVE TREE COPSE CEMETERY	
AB CZ/35	LAYFIELD, HJ 21/06/15	KIA	TWELVE TREE COPSE CEMETERY	
AB KW/108	SAYES, S 27/06/15	SICK	EAST MUDROS MILITARY CEMETERY, LEMNOS	
AB LZ/265	BAILEY, WV 30/06/15	SICK	EAST MUDROS MILITARY CEMETERY, LEMNOS	
AB KW/150	BOLLAND, JE 30/06/15	KIA	HELLES MEMORIAL	
LS DEV/208191	McCANN, P 30/06/15	KIA	HELLES MEMORIAL	1914*
AB CZ/2686	ROSS, J 30/06/15	DOW	LANCASHIRE LANDING CEMETERY	
LS M3/204	RICHARDS, GEW 03/07/15	DOW	LANCASHIRE LANDING CEMETERY	1914*

RANK/RATING	NAME			
NUMBER	DATE	CAUSE	BURIAL / MEMORIAL	1914*
AB	PRICE, EJL			
LZ/236	05/07/15	DOW	CHATHAM NAVAL MEMORIAL	
AB	PEARCE, C			
TZ/396	07/07/15	KIA	HELLES MEMORIAL	
AB	WAREING, J			
M5/162	09/07/15	SICK	EAST MUDROS MILITARY CEMETERY, LEMNOS	
AB	HUTCHINSON, W			
TZ/3394	16/09/16	DOW	NOT KNOWN[93]	

8

THE ACTION OF ACHI BABA NULLAH:

12 – 14 JULY 1915

As preparations for the August landings at Suvla Bay were proceeding apace, the command had decided that the attention of the Turks should be kept on the Helles Front in the south by yet another frontal attack by allied forces. This was scheduled for 12 July. The objectives would be those same Turkish trenches that the RND had taken and given up at enormous cost on 4 June in the Third Battle of Krithia. The 52nd Division would provide the assaulting force, from the old RND trenches, with the French attacking on their right. The difference on this occasion would be that the danger of enfilade fire from Kereves Ridge was diminished because of earlier French gains in that area on 21 June. From 6.00 am on 12 July, less than six days after the RND had been relieved by 52nd Division, Nelson Battalion found itself again nominated as part of the Corps reserve, comprising the 1st and RM Brigades (less Deal).

The uncertainty surrounding the outcome of the main, initial attack by 52nd Division on 12 July was to provide the necessity for the engagement of the RND battalions from the Corps reserve on the following day. At 3.00 am on 13 July Nelson Battalion was ordered to move forward to bivouac in rear of Backhouse Post. In the 52nd Division assault the GOC had not only used up his divisional reserve brigade in its entirety but had also been forced to call upon several battalions of the RND to take over as his reserve. Through the night 12/13 July, if nothing else was clear, it became very certain that any gains that had been made by 52nd Division were, to say the least, precarious, despite the pouring in of reserves, and nobody knew what or where those gains were. The RND, under their acting GOC, Brigadier General Trotman RMLI (General Paris was in Mudros), were invited to sort out the mess by consolidating the existing gains and taking the original objectives, especially those in the most distant Turkish trenches, some of which had turned out to be mere scrapes in the ground.

The RND assault on the afternoon of 13 July would comprise three battalions, with the Nelson again on familiar ground on the left of the line and to the east of Achi Baba Nullah. On the Nelson right would be two RM battalions, first Portsmouth, in the centre of the RND line, and on their right Chatham Battalion. Everything would hang on the success of the RND attack for, if it failed, a withdrawal back to the original 52nd Division starting line seemed the most likely outcome. And yet this difficult task was being given to RND battalions which the Corps Commander, General Hunter-Weston, being realistic for a change, had only recently described as being unfit for offensive operations because of the pounding they had taken since May and widespread sickness. It has been shown that Nelson battalion, on the eve of the battle, had less than twenty officers (about two-thirds strength), with three of the most senior officers just returned from treatment in hospital. The complexity and difficulty of the task was compounded by the fact that RND commanders were neither informed of changes that had been made to the objectives forty-eight hours earlier, nor were they issued with the most up-to-date trench maps. To make matters worse, insufficient time was allowed for orders to be distributed and for the troops to be deployed for the attack: the order to take the trenches was only passed to the attacking battalions at about 4.15 pm, fifteen minutes before the assault was due.

In consequence, at 4.30 pm the artillery barrage lifted but it would not be until nearly 5.00 pm that the Nelson and Portsmouth Battalions alone were ready to execute the 'over the top' attack (in this case literally over the top of the battalions of 52nd Division dug-in in front of them) against forewarned and fully prepared Turkish defences. Chatham Battalion never did complete preparations in time and, wisely, remained in their trenches. The Nelsons' brave attack was launched late and almost blind, given their lack of information and preparation. Able Seaman Wilson recorded that their orders were 'to charge, jump three trenches and occupy the fourth'. They advanced swiftly through a very heavy Turkish shrapnel curtain accurately aimed by the German spotters on Achi Baba.

> Many eye-witnesses speak of the inspiring sight of Lieutenant Colonel Evelegh, RMLI, standing cap in hand, on a trench parapet, cheering his men forward like hounds into cover, and then dashing on himself. He was never seen alive again.[94]

The battalion took a terrible toll of casualties as it pressed forward over open, bullet-swept ground to reach and take its final objectives – former Turkish trenches which were found to be already full of men of 52nd Division. As the Official History succinctly states the situation:

> This very gallant advance by the Portsmouth and Nelson Battalions had therefore been of little or no avail . . . and all that could be claimed for it was that it had provided a small stiffening of very battered reinforcements.[95]

The Nelsons pushed even further forward but the ground could not be held and they fell back. Their forward trench gains, which had to be held through the night, were in a condition which beggars description:

> where many hundreds of men lay dead or dying, where a burning sun had turned the bodies of the slain to a premature corruption, where there was no resting-place free from physical contamination, where the air, the surface of the ground, and the soil beneath the surface were alike poisonous, fetid, corrupt.[96]

The stench from the piles of rotting bodies caused the living garrison of the trenches to vomit even when they were wearing respirators in a futile attempt to stifle it. Able Seaman Albert Wilson noted that the Turkish dead were lying in heaps up to five or six men deep.

Because there were no communications to the rear of the Nelson Battalion and laterally to the Portsmouth Battalion (who were in, if possible, even worse conditions on their right) the command still had no clear view of what had been achieved by the RND. The Divisional War Diary records successive reports back to HQ VIII Corps which clearly demonstrate the 'fog of war' which surrounded this action:

1635	Can see nothing for dust from bombardment.
1650	Continuous stream of Naval Division charging . . .
1655	Men are charging.
1710	Men are charging over crest line . . . Charge successful, nobody appears to go back.
1714	Men appear to be moving . . .
1718	About 30 men running . . . halfway between E.12 and trench beyond.

The situation thereafter remained 'very confused. 52 Divn. and RN Divn. much mixed up.' Not until 10.00 pm could GOC RND report,

> Position as far as known at present as follows: Nelson Bn on line ordered on the left. Ports Bn reported digging in slightly in advance of E.12.

General Paris returned from Mudros and resumed command of the RND at 11.00 pm but still his staff were

> endeavouring to clear up situation 'til 3am but quite impossible owing to hopeless congestion of communication trenches. Very difficult to obtain any coherent idea of what had happened.

Even on the following day, the War Diary records,

> Situation not yet clear but every endeavour being made to get to the bottom of it.

Meanwhile, overnight 13/14 July the Drake came forward to relieve the shattered Portsmouth marines, who were 'withdrawn from trenches which were indescribable – dead and wounded being impossible to clear away.' The remains of Nelson Battalion were still holding on to the most advanced trenches, in front of Drake Battalion, and the morning of 14 July saw the Nelsons in firm touch with 5/Highland Light Infantry on their left, across the nullah. With Drake behind them and on their right and they, in turn, in touch with the Chatham marines on their right, the RND line was complete. The RND War Diary could at last record 'Situation at last clear.' The 52nd Division troops were withdrawn, leaving the RND battalions for the next ten days to the unenviable task of re-building trenches and attending to the scores of dead along the new firing line and establishing communication trenches. The remnants of Nelson Battalion did not come out of the line until 16 July, when 2nd Naval Brigade and Deal Battalion came forward.

The losses in Nelson Battalion in the Action of Achi Baba Nullah were, as Jerrold says, disastrous. The Nelsons had lost their CO, Lieutenant Colonel Evelegh, and seven other officers killed. Again the sub lieutenant Platoon Commanders took terrible punishment – of the nine who were present before the action, five were killed in battle. Sub Lieutenant Francis Startin died six days later in a hospital ship and would be later mentioned in the CinC's despatches. After the wounded officers had been evacuated Nelson Battalion was left, in the immediate aftermath of the action, with only one lieutenant commander, two lieutenants and three sub lieutenants on the fighting strength: Lieutenant Commander J.E. Nicol; Lieutenants A. Bennett and H.J. Starkey; Sub Lieutenants R.E.L. Davies, H.D. Lamont-Fisher and A. Hobbs. The 1st Brigade War Diary records fourteen officers and 273 ORs as casualties (killed and wounded) in Nelson Battalion. Today's records show that ninety-nine ORs were killed in action or died later of the wounds they received in this battle. The day Nelson Battalion went, literally, over the top of the men of the 52nd Division, 13 July 1915, was the battalion's worst day on Gallipoli. On that day alone, from five o'clock in the late afternoon, 92 officers and men of the Nelson are recorded as having lost their lives and none of these men have known graves.

Lieutenant Colonel Burge, whose time to command Nelson Battalion had now come, as a result of Lieutenant Colonel Evelegh's courageous death, recorded in his diary at the time:

> The Nelsons made a most dashing charge but lost poor Evelegh and 16 officers and a lot of men . . . Our casualties were very heavy indeed and it was a victory at great expense.

NELSONS KILLED OR MORTALLY WOUNDED
IN THE ACTION OF ACHI BABA NULLAH 12 – 14 JULY 1915

RANK/RATING	NAME			
NUMBER	DATE	CAUSE	BURIAL / MEMORIAL	1914*
AB	AITKEN, W			
C2/1970	13/07/15	KIA	HELLES MEMORIAL	1914*
AB	ALEXANDER, JG			
CZ/2267	13/07/15	KIA	HELLES MEMORIAL	
AB	ANDREW, WN			
KX/66	13/07/15	KIA	HELLES MEMORIAL	1914*
LT	BALDWIN, HR			
	13/07/15	KIA	HELLES MEMORIAL	
AB	BATTY, PG			
TZ/3093	13/07/15	KIA	HELLES MEMORIAL	
AB	BELL, J			
CZ/2236	13/07/15	KIA	HELLES MEMORIAL	
AB	BELL, JF			
CZ/1575	13/07/15	KIA	HELLES MEMORIAL	
AB	BERG, AH			
LZ/200	13/07/15	KIA	HELLES MEMORIAL	
AB	BROWN, J			
TZ/70	13/07/15	KIA	HELLES MEMORIAL	
AB	BURROWS, J			
M3/230	13/07/15	KIA	HELLES MEMORIAL	1914*
AB	CAMPBELL, J			
CZ/1020	13/07/15	KIA	HELLES MEMORIAL	
AB	CARD, J			
S2/293	13/07/15	KIA	HELLES MEMORIAL	
AB	CARSON, AG			
LZ/1049	13/07/15	KIA	HELLES MEMORIAL	
STOKER1	CARTON, M			
SS103072	13/07/15	KIA	HELLES MEMORIAL	1914*
AB	CARTWRIGHT, G			
KX/123	13/07/15	KIA	HELLES MEMORIAL	1914*
AB	CLARKE, HA			
KW/282	13/07/15	KIA	HELLES MEMORIAL	
AB	CLELLAND, JW			
CZ/2996	13/07/15	KIA	HELLES MEMORIAL	
STOKER1	COLLINS, J			
SS107470	13/07/15	KIA	HELLES MEMORIAL	1914*
AB	COOMBS, V			
BZ/325	13/07/15	KIA	HELLES MEMORIAL	
AB	COULL, GI			
CZ/2227	13/07/15	KIA	HELLES MEMORIAL	
AB	COWIE, JW			
C3/2577	13/07/15	KIA	HELLES MEMORIAL	1914*

RANK/RATING	NAME				
NUMBER	DATE	CAUSE	BURIAL / MEMORIAL		1914*
AB KW/73	CUTTS, H 13/07/15	KIA	HELLES MEMORIAL		
PO LZ/1268	DAVY, BJ 13/07/15	KIA	HELLES MEMORIAL		
SUB LT	DICKSON, JMF 13/07/15	KIA	HELLES MEMORIAL		
STOKER1 DEV/299827	DOCHERTY, M 13/07/15	KIA	HELLES MEMORIAL		1914*
STOKER1 DEV/300914	DOHERTY, W 13/07/15	KIA	HELLES MEMORIAL		1914*
AB TZ/384	DOUGLASS, J 13/07/15	KIA	HELLES MEMORIAL		
AB CZ/2286	DOWNIE, RW 13/07/15	KIA	HELLES MEMORIAL		
AB KX/317	DOYLE, W 13/07/15	KIA	HELLES MEMORIAL		
AB CZ/2070	DRUMMOND, T 13/07/15	KIA	HELLES MEMORIAL		
AB CZ/7764	DUNCAN, C 13/07/15	KIA	HELLES MEMORIAL		
AB CZ/2268	EASSON, W 13/07/15	KIA	HELLES MEMORIAL		
AB TZ/3409	EASTHAM, J 13/07/15	KIA	HELLES MEMORIAL		
STOKER1 SS108020	EDWARDS, HE 13/07/15	KIA	HELLES MEMORIAL		1914*
SUB LT 13/07/15	EDWARDS, WH KIA		HELLES MEMORIAL		1914*
AB TZ/3685	ELLISON, L 13/07/15	KIA	HELLES MEMORIAL		
STOKER1 SS108779	GILLEN, MJ 13/07/15	KIA	HELLES MEMORIAL		1914*
AB KX/124	GOODWIN, L 13/07/15	KIA	HELLES MEMORIAL		1914*
AB CZ/2272	GORDON, A 13/07/15	KIA	HELLES MEMORIAL		
AB TZ/3711	GOWERS, AD 13/07/15	KIA	HELLES MEMORIAL		
AB CZ/2183	HAIR, HG 13/07/15	KIA	HELLES MEMORIAL		
STOKER1 SS107523	HARRIS, RC 13/07/15	KIA	HELLES MEMORIAL		1914*
AB CZ/103	HARRISON, J 13/07/15	KIA	HELLES MEMORIAL		

RANK/RATING	NAME				
NUMBER	DATE	CAUSE	BURIAL / MEMORIAL		1914*
AB LZ/631	HENRY, J 13/07/15	KIA	HELLES MEMORIAL		
AB LZ/132	HEWSON, AG 13/07/15	KIA	HELLES MEMORIAL		
STOKER1 SS106916	HICKLING, J 13/07/15	KIA	HELLES MEMORIAL		1914*
AB TZ/230	HINDHAUGH, R 13/07/15	KIA	HELLES MEMORIAL		
PO CH/201112	HISCOCK, E 13/07/15	KIA	HELLES MEMORIAL		1914*
AB C4/2507	HOWARD, DR 13/07/15	KIA	HELLES MEMORIAL		1914*
AB TZ/135	HOY, J 13/07/15	KIA	HELLES MEMORIAL		
AB CZ/1950	JAMIESON, L 13/07/15	KIA	HELLES MEMORIAL		
AB M3/221	JARRETT, HB 13/07/15	KIA	HELLES MEMORIAL		1914*
AB KW/98	JONES, ET 13/07/15	KIA	HELLES MEMORIAL		
AB KW/189	KITSON, J 13/07/15	KIA	HELLES MEMORIAL		
AB MZ/330	KORTENS, ER 13/07/15	KIA	HELLES MEMORIAL		
PO DEV/204218	LANGWORTHY, G 13/07/15	KIA	HELLES MEMORIAL		1914*
AB CZ/2270	LAWSON, J 13/07/15	KIA	HELLES MEMORIAL		
SUB LT	LINTOTT, W 13/07/15	KIA	HELLES MEMORIAL		
AB LZ/617	LONG, HJ 13/07/15	KIA	HELLES MEMORIAL		
STOKER1 SS106096	MACKINNON, A 13/07/15	KIA	HELLES MEMORIAL		1914*
LS M3/169	MAGUIRE, JB 13/07/15	KIA	HELLES MEMORIAL		1914*
AB CZ/1613	McLEOD, WS 13/07/15	KIA	HELLES MEMORIAL		
AB CZ/1620	McMILLAN, A 13/07/15	KIA	HELLES MEMORIAL		
AB CZ/101	McNISH, D 13/07/15	KIA	HELLES MEMORIAL		
AB CZ/1800	MILNE, M 13/07/15	KIA	HELLES MEMORIAL		

RANK/RATING	NAME				
NUMBER	DATE	CAUSE	BURIAL / MEMORIAL		1914*
STOKER1	MINSHALL, J				
SS101964	13/07/15	KIA	HELLES MEMORIAL		1914*
AB	MOUL, FJ				
T1/233	13/07/15	KIA	HELLES MEMORIAL		
AB	MUDGE, E				
TZ/1427	13/07/15	KIA	HELLES MEMORIAL		
AB	NELL, F				
KW/230	13/07/15	KIA	HELLES MEMORIAL		
STOKER1	O'KEEFFE, J				
SS101961	13/07/15	KIA	HELLES MEMORIAL		1914*
AB	PARKER, J				
MZ/335	13/07/15	KIA	HELLES MEMORIAL		
AB	PETRICHER, JO				
CZ/1523	13/07/15	KIA	HELLES MEMORIAL		
AB	PINKNEY, T				
TZ/76	13/07/15	KIA	HELLES MEMORIAL		
STOKER1	REYNOLDS, A				
SS106596	13/07/15	KIA	HELLES MEMORIAL		1914*
SUB LT	RICE, EV				
	13/07/15	KIA	HELLES MEMORIAL		
STOKER1	RIGGS, J				
SS108215	13/07/15	KIA	HELLES MEMORIAL		1914*
AB	ROBERTS, SA				
LZ/20	13/07/15	DOW	HELLES MEMORIAL		
LS	SCOTT, A				
SS101544	13/07/15	KIA	HELLES MEMORIAL		1914*
AB	SCULLION, A				
CZ/2716	13/07/15	KIA	HELLES MEMORIAL		
AB	SHARPLES, R				
KW/203	13/07/15	KIA	HELLES MEMORIAL		
AB	SINCLAIR, AH				
CZ/74	13/07/15	KIA	HELLES MEMORIAL		
SUB LT	SMYTH, BW				
	13/07/15	KIA	HELLES MEMORIAL		
AB	SOUTHWELL, JH				
TZ/1433	13/07/15	DOW	HELLES MEMORIAL		
AB	STONEHAM, FJ				
S3/327	13/07/15	KIA	HELLES MEMORIAL		
AB	STRANG, W				
CZ/2098	13/07/15	KIA	HELLES MEMORIAL		
AB	TERNENT, JW				
TZ/1787	13/07/15	KIA	HELLES MEMORIAL		
CPO	THOMAS, JF				
DEV/142191	13/07/15	KIA	HELLES MEMORIAL		1914*

RANK/RATING	NAME			
NUMBER	DATE	CAUSE	BURIAL / MEMORIAL	1914*
AB	THOMSON, AC			
C3/2578	13/07/15	KIA	HELLES MEMORIAL	1914*
AB	TURNS, S			
T6/212	13/07/15	KIA	HELLES MEMORIAL	
AB	WATTS, WL			
LZ/68	13/07/15	KIA	HELLES MEMORIAL	
AB	WELLINGTON, SN			
LZ/714	13/07/15	KIA	HELLES MEMORIAL	
AB	WHITE, CB			
TZ/2042	13/07/15	KIA	HELLES MEMORIAL	
AB	WILL, A			
CZ/628	13/07/15	KIA	HELLES MEMORIAL	
LT COL	EVELEGH, EG			
	14/07/15	KIA	SKEW BRIDGE CEMETERY	1914*
AB	HANNAH, W			
CZ/1352	14/07/15	DOW	LANCASHIRE LANDING CEMETERY	
LS	EDWARDS, A			
SS108287	15/07/15	DOW	LANCASHIRE LANDING CEMETERY	1914*
AB	FERGUSON, W			
TZ/2245	15/07/15	KIA	HELLES MEMORIAL	
AB	McRAE, C			
CZ/2288	15/07/15	DOW	LANCASHIRE LANDING CEMETERY	
AB	RICKS, ACJ			
BZ/24	15/07/15	DOW	SKEW BRIDGE CEMETERY	
STOKER1	SPRATT, T			
DEV/298606	15/07/15	DOW	LANCASHIRE LANDING CEMETERY	1914*
AB	ADDISON, A			
CZ/2256	16/07/15	DOW	EAST MUDROS MILITARY CEMETERY, LEMNOS	
AB	GILLON, JW			
TZ/3691	16/07/15	DOW	EAST MUDROS MILITARY CEMETERY, LEMNOS	
PO	COMLEY, L			
M4/3	18/07/15	DOW	PLYMOUTH NAVAL MEMORIAL	1914*
STOKER1	OWENS, D			
SS105590	19/07/15	DOW	PLYMOUTH NAVAL MEMORIAL	1914*
SUB LT	STARTIN, FHJ			
	19/07/15	DOW	LANCASHIRE LANDING CEMETERY	
AB	LOCKHART, J			
CZ/237	23/07/15	DOW	CHATBY WAR MEMORIAL CEMETERY, EGYPT	
STOKER1	BOWMAN, AE			
SS100786	06/08/15	DOW	PORT SAID WAR MEMORIAL CEMETERY, EGYPT	1914*

9

THE END-GAME AT GALLIPOLI:

15 JULY 1915 – 9 JANUARY 1916

In the aftermath of the Action of Achi Baba Nullah, the problem of command in what was left of Nelson Battalion was acute. Not only had Lieutenant Colonel Evelegh been killed but several senior officers had been wounded. Lieutenant Commander Tom Price, who had been wounded in the arm at Anzac on 1 May and had only rejoined from the convalescent camp in Egypt about three days before the battle, had been shot through the arm again and was invalided back to England in HS *Asturias* three days after the battle.[97] Lieutenant Commander Henry Andrews, who had only been promoted on 1 July, received a serious bullet wound in the leg on 14 July. He was evacuated to Egypt, invalided to England and was not fit again for active service until the middle of 1916.[98] Lieutenant Commander John Nicol, shot in the left leg in the Third Battle of Krithia on 5 June, had returned from hospital to Gallipoli with Lieutenant Commander Price and, on 14 July, he was made CO Nelson Battalion by Divisional Order. He remained in command for five days until a new, permanent CO was appointed but only survived a further two weeks on the peninsula before falling ill with enteric fever. He was sent to hospital and then on to Malta.[99] The wounded, invalided (and nominal 2i/c), Lieutenant Commander Primrose, had left the RND and had been appointed to HMS *Excellent* for sea service on 28 July. All five of the Nelson lieutenant commanders were, therefore, *hors de combat* before the end of July 1915.

Only five lieutenants and sub lieutenants of Nelson Battalion had survived the 13 July battle unscathed. All but one of these would fall sick and be invalided home over the following weeks. The Nelson Field State Report of fighting strength after the battle shows six officers and 386 ORs, the low point of the entire campaign, eighty per cent down on officers and sixty per cent down on ORs. On 17 July the dwindling band of officers was strengthened by a small draft of one lieutenant[100] and five new sub lieutenants. Four of the new sub lieutenants were ex-ratings.[101] However, only two of these sorely needed officer reinforcements survived the campaign, three being invalided sick in

October and one dying in action in December. With them came a reinforcement draft of 108 ORs.

The new CO of Nelson Battalion was to be Lieutenant Colonel Norman Ormsby Burge RMLI (known to family and friends as 'Nob'), who assumed command on 19 July. He had been serving at Gallipoli as a Major and 2i/c of the Divisional Cyclist Company, which was becoming the expert bombing unit of the division, given the lack of opportunity for action bicycling. Just before joining Nelson Battalion Burge had been in temporary command of the Howe for two weeks. Nine years younger than Lieutenant Colonel Evelegh, he had joined the Corps in February 1895 on leaving RNC Greenwich. In 1904 he had taken up an appointment as Captain of Marines in the pre-Dreadnought battleship HMS *Triumph*, where the first CO of Nelson Battalion, Commander Bridge, would also serve as a lieutenant a couple of years later. (*Triumph* had been torpedoed off Gaba Tepe at the end of May.) He also served in HMS *Victorious*[102] as a captain and, later in the decade, he served twice in HMS *Berwick*, an armoured cruiser. When not at sea his appointments were with Portsmouth Division RMLI. In 1912 he had been Superintendent of the RM School of Signalling at Gosport. Burge had been promoted to major in early 1914 after spending nearly thirteen years as a captain, half of that time spent at sea. When the RND first formed he was a company commander in Portsmouth Battalion, moving to the Divisional Cyclist Company when it formed in December 1914. He was awarded the 1914 Star for his service in Belgium with Portsmouth Battalion.

Lieutenant Colonel Burge recorded in his diary his appointment to Nelson battalion:

> Monday July 19th. I got a signal appointing me OC Nelson, temporarily of course . . . reported myself to Mercer [GOC 1st Brigade] about 7pm. He told me the whole Battn. wanted reorganising and as we were going to lose 100 stokers (who were also all in one company), it meant reorganising from top to bottom as a reinforcing draft had also turned up. So I've spent the week at that – a vile week with a howling red-hot wind you can't face for dust.

Norman Burge's forecast that he would only be temporarily in command of Nelson Battalion was wide of the mark. Commanding the Nelsons for a total of fourteen months, he would be the battalion's longest-serving CO.

At divisional level, in late July and early August, reorganization had also become, yet again, essential, not only because of the recent heavy losses in battle and to sickness but also because 300 RFR stokers had been recalled for duty in the Fleet. Nelson Battalion lost seventy-two stokers in this recall and they left for Mudros at very short notice on 26 July. The diarist Able Seaman Albert Wilson was among those invalided sick to Egypt in early August.[103] The first step in the re-shaping of the RND was to reduce the RM Brigade to two battalions by combining Chatham Battalion with Deal (as 1st RM) and Portsmouth Battalion with Plymouth (as 2nd RM). A few days later, on 2 August, the division was reduced to just two brigades: Hood Battalion moved from the 2nd Brigade to join Nelson, Drake and Hawke in the 1st Brigade and the remaining battalions, Howe, Anson, 1st RM and 2nd RM formed the 2nd Brigade.

As July drew to a close Lieutenant Colonel Burge described the conditions suffered by his new command and the pressing need to get the men away for the proper rest and recuperation which would never be granted:

> Sat July 24th. Strong rumours the whole Naval Division is to go to some island for rest and reorganisation. Heaven knows we want it badly enough – the 29th Divn. have been away so we certainly deserve to go. And it's hard work here in rest camp – the men are employed on arduous working parties all day. Got inoculated against cholera on Wed. Gave me a terrific tummy ache and felt rotten for 2 days.
>
> Sun July 25th. Hot wind still blowing and programme changed each day – we are always being told to go somewhere and do something (the Nelsons) and just before starting it's changed. Trying to get as many men as possible through inoculation but as it's voluntary it's mighty hard to persuade them.
>
> Mon July 26th. A nice day – very hot but not so much dust as usual. We've been expecting the Turks to make that big attack every day or night now. It hasn't come off yet – I wish it would because as soon as it's over there's more chance of our getting away. The betting is on Mitylene, which people who've been there say is delightful. Shady coves (places not people), trees, babbling brooks, lemons. Ye Gods, one can hardly bear to think of it.

A week later there was still no relief or proper rest and the island of Mitylene was still a mirage:

> Sun August 1st. Nothing doing except working parties and dust and flies.

In mid-August the RND moved to a new sector of the Helles front, taking over the left of the line between Krithia Nullah and Gully Ravine from 29th Division. They would remain there until early December. The two RND brigades alternated in the new front line throughout the next months, changing over at weekly intervals. The trenches were in a parlous state and subject to heavy Turkish shelling and bombing. The opposing trenches were very close and, in places, joined to each other, barricades being the only obstacle. These were fought over fiercely at regular intervals, but these encounters represented small-scale fighting in comparison with what had gone before in Hunter-Weston's set-piece massacres. The firing-line activities consisted of wiring, bombing, shelling, machine-gunning and pushing forward barricades, saps and trenches. If the trenches were close enough explosive bombs and less lethal tins of bully-beef could be fired at the Turks using early-pattern trench mortars and catapults. The CO would be an active participant in these activities when Nelson Battalion was in the firing line. He even managed to get himself hung up on the barbed wire in no-man's-land in the middle of the night. He commented that untangling himself quietly was not helped by the empty bully-beef tins which had been scattered in front of the Nelson's parapet.

The Divisional War Diary noted, shortly after the RND took over their new line on 16 August, that

> the sick list generally increased during the week – probably owing to stench in the firing line as very many dead [from a battle on 6 August] are still unburied in front of our trenches.

On 20 August 1,300 RND reinforcements arrived but it was noted that the 212 ORs drafted to Nelson Battalion were 'ill-trained and of inferior physique'. This draft included a lieutenant and four more sub lieutenants for Nelson Battalion, but all but two of these would fall sick and be lost to the battalion before the campaign ended.[104] The newcomers boosted the fighting strength of the battalion to sixteen officers and 599 ORs. The frustrations created by the conditions on the peninsula and the poor quality of these replacements from England caused Lieutenant Colonel Burge to give up on his diary, which by this time had filled about one third of an Army Field Message Book. On 29 August his final entry reads:

> Quite impossible to go on with diary. New draft would occupy remainder of this book. Undersized, untrained, undisciplined, weedy youths of 14–17. Dreadful !!!

Colonel Burge was so disappointed with this draft that he applied to the Staff for waterproof sheets for his war babies. He also included in a list of winter comforts for them seaside buckets and spades, night lights and books of fairy tales. His wry sense of humour was, fortunately, matched by that of the staff officer responsible for taking action on his demands.

The Battalion Quartermaster, Lieutenant Town, went to hospital in Alexandria in late August and his post was taken by Lieutenant James Gates RM. In early September Nelson Battalion seems to have been split in half for a spell in the trenches, with two companies attached to 2nd Brigade, and at this time the Adjutant, Lieutenant Carpenter, left and was replaced by Sub Lieutenant David Galloway. Another 'quite satisfactory' draft of some 800 officers and men for the RND arrived from England in late September, but these new arrivals would barely keep pace with the losses, nearly all to disease. For the Nelson Battalion this draft included another eight new sub lieutenants, five of them ex-ratings.[105] On 23 September more field promotions were needed to replace sick officers and Chief Petty Officers Charles Hosking, of

'C' Company, and Charles Reed, both long-serving Nelson senior rates, were commissioned.[106]

Lieutenant Commander Henry R. Robson of Hawke Battalion moved over to become 2i/c Nelson on 22 September.[107] Such was the level of sickness and injury amongst the RND commanders during the second half of 1915 that he and other senior officers seem to have been moved frequently between battalions. The last three months on Gallipoli were to be particularly turbulent for the command of Nelson Battalion.

For the RND the months of August to December on the peninsula did not feature a series of desperate major battles like those that had punctuated May to July and which had caused such terrible attrition, not least to Nelson Battalion. Nevertheless, more than forty Nelsons would die as a result of the final months of the campaign. It was now that the pandemic of enteric diseases really began to take its toll and nearly half of the deaths in this period would be from sickness, peaking in September and the first half of October. Lieutenant Commander Wilfred Miall-Green,[108] who had come to Nelson Battalion from Benbow in June, had since been twice evacuated ill. On 20 September he died of infection on passage to England on HS *Aquitania*. The return of rains in mid-September and the cooler weather of Autumn only slowly eased the deep-seated problems of disease. On 2 October the Divisional War Diary reported that

> The health of the division has improved though the sick list is still high and 418 men have been evacuated during the week.

In the following week 395 men were evacuated. On 16 October:

> The weather has been fine and cool and there has been some decrease in the sick list, 331 being evacuated during the week.

At this time the effective strength of the RND was only about 3,200 (at full strength eight battalions should have been about 8,000 men) and these evacuations represented a very high percentage of the force. For Nelson Battalion the numbers recorded sick were 132 in September, 262 in October and were still at 190 in November: for those three months the total of 584 sick compares with only eighteen killed or wounded. Even in January 1916 the number of Nelsons falling sick was still more than eighty. An illustration of the operational effect of large numbers of experienced men falling sick appears in a letter that Colonel Burge wrote to his family on 11 October. He reported that, while in the front line from 6 to 13 October, Nelson Battalion was down to about 500 men and that 400 of them, the men of the last two drafts, had never been in the fire trenches before.

The arrival, on 15 October, of two territorial battalions of the London Regiment to reinforce the RND was helpful to manpower. However, the increasingly frequent thunderstorms flooded the trenches and the muddy conditions were making life extremely unpleasant. The task of the working parties to restore collapsed trenches and parapets was greatly increased and the movement of rations and stores was made much more difficult. 21 October saw the arrival of another seven new Nelson officers[109] who, on the following day, had

> a wretched day and night, rain and cold wind. Some of the trenches became muddy and everyone very uncomfortable.

Lieutenant Colonel Burge fell sick and went to hospital on 23 October and Lieutenant Commander Robson took over the command of Nelson Battalion. Burge was invalided off the peninsula to Egypt a few days later and would not return for more than two months. On 29 October Lieutenant Commander Arthur 'Oc' Asquith came over from the Hood in temporary command. Asquith was, in turn, relieved as CO of Nelson on 1 November by Lieutenant Commander Edward Nelson also loaned from the Hood. Thus, for the first time, did Nelson command the Nelson!

A marine biologist by profession, Edward Nelson had served in that capacity on Scott's fatal polar expedition in 1910–1912 and was in the search party that had found the bodies of Scott and his companions. Captain Scott recorded in his diary that Nelson had 'a habit of methodical neatness' and noted him to be 'an exceedingly capable lecturer; he makes his subject clear and is never too technical.' Scott's wife, Kathleen, however, considered Nelson to be a playboy whose behaviour when ashore in England left him looking permanently tired. During the Antartic expedition his nicknames had been 'Marie' and 'Brontë' – it is not known whether they were carried forward to his naval career. Six months earlier, as a lieutenant, Edward Nelson had been in charge of the cutter that took Freyberg on his diversionary swim in the Gulf of Saros on the night of 25/26 April. Nelson was Adjutant of the Hood Battalion in early July 1915 and he had temporarily assumed command of the Hood from 21 July to 19 August when his new CO, Commander Bernard Freyberg, was wounded by a shell.

During his three days in command Asquith seems to have gained a poor impression of Nelson Battalion. His military biographer quotes him as writing that the Nelson was 'the biggest in numbers, the rawest in composition, and the worst in discipline . . . it would be interesting to try to pull Nelson together.' Nevertheless, he found the 'Nelson throne . . . very comfortable.'[110] Given that Nelson had taken by far the highest casualties, particularly amongst its officers, of any of the naval battalions, had suffered from a lack of continuity of senior leadership and had been reinforced with poor material from England, perhaps Asquith's critical assessment is hardly surprising.[111] Another lieutenant commander from Hawke Battalion was also temporarily attached to the Nelson: William A.P. Lane was a Nelson company commander from mid-December until he was shot in the hand and evacuated two weeks later.

One month later, on 22 November, Nelson Battalion received from England more badly-needed reinforcements, which 'arrived satisfactory and well-equipped'. This November draft only included one sub lieutenant, the last new officer to join the battalion on Gallipoli.[112] A week later the peninsula was struck by a terrible period of cold weather, but the Nelson Battalion, indeed the RND, seems to have come through this reasonably well, as the Divisional War Diary records:

> There have been some 20 cases of frost-bite – otherwise the men stood the cold wonderfully well and so far no great increase in sickness has resulted.

However, even as this wintry weather eliminated the problem of flies, the Nelson Battalion Medical Officer (MO), Surgeon Henry Parker, who had done so much for the battalion's sick and wounded for seven months, was himself falling ill with dysentery. Fortunately, after only a week in hospital on Mudros he would be able to return to his duties.[113] A couple of weeks later the other Nelson MO, Surgeon Alexander Gow, who had been with the battalion since November 1914 and had shared Surgeon Parker's task, would also leave to join the division's 2nd Field Ambulance.

The overall balance between the losses to the battalion from battle and sickness and the gains from incoming reinforcements can be observed from the Nelson Field State Reports of fighting strength over the last six months of the campaign. These show that the average strength for officers and ORs during the period was around sixteen officers and 530 ORs, both little more than half of the war establishment. They also show how reinforcements barely kept up with the inexorable losses. (See page 78)

Lieutenant Commander Nelson, still acting as Nelson Battalion commander on loan from Hood, was transferred to Nelson Battalion and promoted to the rank of Temporary Commander on 29 November 1915. In October he had been ill with jaundice and just before the turn of the year he was again sick, with pyrexia. Lieutenant Commander Arthur Asquith again came over from the Hood to take command for five days. Commander Nelson was evacuated to hospital in Malta and did not return to Nelson Battalion for a month, by which time the evacuation of the MEF from Gallipoli was over and the battalion was on Lemnos. Reverted to lieutenant commander, he was appointed 2i/c Nelson on his return. Lieutenant Colonel Burge did not return from hospital to re-assume command of the Nelson until 1 January 1916.

The severe weather was also to be behind the move of the RND back to the right of the Helles line in early December. There the Senegalese and colonial troops of the French Corps were unable to stand the change to a winter climate and they were withdrawn from Gallipoli. The RND brigades moved into some 2,000 yards of former French trenches, eventually taking over the whole of the French sector in preparation for the evacuation of the MEF from the

NELSON BATTALION FIELD STATE REPORTS,
JULY – DECEMBER 1915

WAR ESTABLISHMENT

OFFICERS	ORS
30	977

Date	Fighting Strength		
4 July	16	664	
11 July	17	674	
18 July	6	386	After 13 July battle
25 July	13	501	July reinforcements
1 August	11	432	Stokers depart 26 July
8 August	11	422	
15 August	11	410	
22 August	16	599	August reinforcements
29 August	15	550	
5 September	14	491	
12 September	12	413	
19 September	13	410	
26 September	24	565	September reinforcements
3 October	23	564	
10 October	21	521	
17 October	20	517	
24 October	21	628	October reinforcements
31 October	20	594	
7 November	16	544	
14 November	15	526	
21 November	14	462	
28 November	15	500	November reinforcements
5 December	17	536	
11 December	20	596	
18 December	19	609	
25 December	18	615	

peninsula. Nelson Battalion had lost ten ORs in fighting on the left of the front and they would lose another thirteen men during their time in the former French sector. Among these was the last Nelson officer to be killed in action in the campaign, Sub Lieutenant Bernard Kenny, in the week before Christmas.[114] Losses of senior NCOs were also serious in this period. Chief Petty Officer Edward Jones[115] was killed on 18 November and Chief Petty Officer Thomas McLaughlin[116] on 28 December. Wet winter weather now set in with a vengeance, a torrential rainstorm on 20 December causing 'more damage than a month's shelling'. Christmas Day was passed in bivouacs, with singing and band performances enlivening an otherwise normal day of Turkish shelling. The battalion performed its last tour of duty in the front-line trenches over the turn of the year, from 29 December to 1 January, temporarily commanded again during this period by Lieutenant Commander Asquith, who handed command back to Lieutenant Colonel Burge when he returned from hospital as the Nelsons came out of the line. The last Nelson to die on Gallipoli was Able Seaman Joseph Bowles, who was killed during shelling of the Nelson bivouacs on 4 January 1916, just four days before the end.[117] Seven Nelsons were wounded in this strafe by the Turkish artillery, which included the usual 'iron rations' from the large Turkish gun nicknamed 'Asiatic Annie', and Lieutenant Colonel Burge himself had a narrow escape by diving into his hole in the ground just in time.

The evacuation of the Nelsons from Gallipoli was achieved without accident or incident. The battalion was not involved in the manning of the trenches on the last night and, when the final arrangements and evacuation date were decided, 559 Nelsons and other units in bivouac were among the first away from the peninsula on the night of 8/9 January. These 2,000 men fell in at 5.45 pm and marched away with perfect timing, all the bivouacs being clear by 6.20 pm. At 'V' Beach they embarked for Lemnos. Lieutenant Colonel Burge had been appointed to a vital task at Skew Bridge as the Officer-in-Command of the final rendezvous for the RND evacuation, all units reporting to him as they withdrew to 'V' Beach. From 7.00 pm until 2.30 am he checked through the last RND men, first those who had held the firing line and then the men setting the trench-blocks, mines and booby-traps. He sailed for Imbros in the destroyer HMS *Grasshopper* at 3.30 am together with 400 Plymouth marines of the beach defence party. The Plymouth marines had been the first ashore on Gallipoli and were the last to leave. *Grasshopper* was the last ship away from 'V' Beach. Burge rejoined his battalion on Lemnos forty-eight hours later after a short detour to Imbros.[118]

Even after Nelson Battalion had been evacuated to the safety of Lemnos, the Gallipoli campaign continued to take its toll, with one rating dying of his wounds in Egypt in mid-January and another, who had been invalided at the end of November, dying in England of paratyphoid fever in February. The very last Nelson victim of the fighting on Gallipoli was Petty Officer Arthur Hunt, who had been wounded and taken prisoner by the Turks during the action on 13 July 1915. Five months later the American Embassy in Constantinople reported him as being in a hospital in that city. Arthur Hunt was later a prisoner in the town of Yozgat in central Anatolia and he died there of enteritis and malaria on 12 June 1916.[119]

Nelson Battalion lost 276 officers and men killed, missing or dead of disease as a result of their operations with the MEF. Dead officers numbered twenty-three; senior NCOs (chief petty officers and petty officers) seventeen. Many hundreds more were wounded or struck down by disease. Some returned to fight, many others were maimed and discharged as medically unfit.

Comparisons are invidious when surveying the total RND casualties in the MEF of more than 7,500 officers and men[120], but it is very clear that Nelson Battalion came off by far the worst of all the naval battalions. Their 277 dead compare with around 240 for Anson and Howe, about 230 for the Hood, about 210 for Collingwood, about 145 for Drake and about 125 for Hawke. A mere handful were lost to Benbow, who saw little action before disbanding. In the RM battalions, only Portsmouth took a greater loss than did Nelson. It would appear that Nelson Battalion bore over seventeen per cent of the RND officer deaths and more than ten per cent of the deaths among ORs. Looking only at the naval battalions, Nelson suffered some twenty-five per cent of the officers and eighteen per cent of the ORs dead.[121] The 'decimation' of Collingwood Battalion on 4 June 1915, with over 180 killed in a single day, was a tragedy more often quoted than the fifty per cent greater losses suffered by the Nelson Battalion in the course of the campaign.

Two Nelson ratings were awarded the Distinguished Service Medal at Gallipoli[122]:

Petty Officer J. McGrath, C1/1616   Stoker 1 E. Brown, SS211837

The following officers and men of Nelson Battalion were mentioned in despatches[123] by the Commander-in-Chief, General Sir Ian Hamilton, for their service during the Gallipoli campaign:

Lieutenant Colonel N.O. Burge RMLI	Lieutenant Colonel E.G. Evelegh RMLI (kia)
Lieutenant Commander E.W. Nelson	Lieutenant Commander H.C. Evans (kia)
Lieutenant R.J. Carpenter RMLI	Lieutenant E.M. Sharer
Lieutenant R.H. Tepper	Sub Lieutenant E.V. Rice (kia)
Sub Lieutenant F.H. Startin (kia)	Petty Officer G. Langworthy, Dev/204218 (kia)

Petty Officer C.R. Barker, LZ/337[124]

LS J. Dursley, Dev/300239

Able Seaman E. Thomas, MZ/172

Stoker 1 H. Lowe, SS/107035

General Sir Charles Monro, General Hamilton's successor as CinC MEF, mentioned the following Nelsons in his despatches[125]:

Lieutenant D Galloway (HQ 1st Bde)

Lieutenant HD Lamont-Fisher

Lieutenant JA Gates RMLI

Lieutenant REL Davies

Sub Lieutenant FW Sowerby

Chief Petty Officer JC Thompson, C2/1801[126]

Chief Petty Officer WJ Mason, M7/5

Petty Officer EB Barrett, M5/21[127]

Petty Officer TO Jones, Dev/SS/107315

Petty Officer J Corrigan, M3/163

Several other Nelson ratings were awarded certificates by the GOC RND 'for zeal and devotion to duty'.

NELSONS KILLED OR MORTALLY WOUNDED AT HELLES, OR DIED OF DISEASE, FROM MID-JULY 1915 TO THE END OF THE MEF CAMPAIGN.

RANK/RATING NUMBER	NAME DATE	CAUSE	BURIAL / MEMORIAL	1914*
AB CZ/236	CAIRNS, J 21/07/15	DOW	LANCASHIRE LANDING CEMETERY	
AB TZ/99	ASH, J 08/08/15	SICK	CAIRO WAR MEMORIAL CEMETERY, EGYPT	
AB TZ/44	POOLE, R 23/08/15	SICK	PIETA MILITARY CEMETERY, MALTA	
AB CZ/3453	MELVILLE, AMcG 30/08/15	DOW	LANCASHIRE LANDING CEMETERY	
AB WZ/128	PHILLIPS, L 04/09/15	SICK	PLYMOUTH NAVAL MEMORIAL	
AB SZ/21	SHORT, WC 06/09/15	KIA	SKEW BRIDGE CEMETERY	
AB CZ/17	DAVIDSON, T 10/09/15	SICK	GIBRALTAR (NORTH FRONT) CEMETERY	
AB TZ/3503	TEMPLE, DG 15/09/15	SICK	MALTA NAVAL CEMETERY	
LT CDR	MIALL-GREEN, WS 20/09/15	SICK	PORTSMOUTH NAVAL MEMORIAL	
AB TZ/4249	LAMPORT, TF 22/09/15	SICK	CHATHAM NAVAL MEMORIAL	
AB M5/148	EDGE, TJ 24/09/15	SICK	EAST MUDROS MILITARY CEMETERY, LEMNOS	1914*
AB WZ265	GREENHOUSE, J 25/09/15	SICK	PLYMOUTH NAVAL MEMORIAL	
STOKER1 SS105871	OWENS, W 07/10/15	SICK	MALTA NAVAL CEMETERY	1914*
AB CZ/1984	MILNE, W 11/10/15	SICK	CHATBY WAR MEMORIAL CEMETERY, EGYPT	
AB WZ/392	SMITH, E 12/10/15	SICK	PIETA MILITARY CEMETERY, MALTA	
AB CZ/2925	MILNE, T 08/11/15 EGYPT	SICK	CHATBY WAR MEMORIAL CEMETERY,	
AB LZ/1588	WEYMAN, CR 09/11/15	DOW	PINK FARM CEMETERY	

RANK/RATING	NAME			
NUMBER	DATE	CAUSE	BURIAL / MEMORIAL	1914*
AB	MacNULTY, J			
KX/478	15/11/15	SICK	EAST MUDROS MILITARY CEMETERY, LEMNOS	
AB	FERRIER, J			
CZ/4138	17/11/15	KIA	TWELVE TREE COPSE CEMETERY	
AB	COXON, TA			
TZ/4343	18/11/15	KIA	TWELVE TREE COPSE CEMETERY	
CPO	JONES, E			
C5/1744	18/11/15	KIA	REDOUBT CEMETERY	1914*
AB	DUDDEN, GW			
LZ/1320	23/11/15	KIA	REDOUBT CEMETERY	
AB	COULTHARD, TE			
TZ/1522	24/11/15	SICK	FLIMBY CEMETERY, CUMBERLAND	
AB	HAMILTON, W			
CZ/4008	29/11/15	SICK	CHATBY WAR MEMORIAL CEMETERY, EGYPT	
AB	EDGAR, AE			
TZ/4228	06/12/15	DOW	SKEW BRIDGE CEMETERY	
LS	KELLY, FA			
WZ/4	18/12/15	KIA	REDOUBT CEMETERY	
AB	GREENER, J			
KX/85	19/12/15	KIA	REDOUBT CEMETERY	1914*
AB	JONES, E			
WZ/195	19/12/15	KIA	REDOUBT CEMETERY	
SUB LT	KENNY, BW			
	19/12/15	KIA	HELLES MEMORIAL	
AB	JONES, WJ			
WZ/261	20/12/15	DOW	LANCASHIRE LANDING CEMETERY	
PO	KILLIP, JR			
M3/218	21/12/15	KIA	HELLES MEMORIAL	1914*
AB	CRAGGS, W			
MZ/309	22/12/15	KIA	HELLES MEMORIAL	
AB	DOVE, TE			
KX/45	23/12/15	SICK	SKELTON & BROTTON CEMETERY, YORKS	1914*
CPO	McLAUGHLIN, T			
CZ/245	28/12/15	KIA	HELLES MEMORIAL	
AB	STRACHAN, JG			
CZ/5228	31/12/15	ACCIDENT	REDOUBT CEMETERY	
AB	BOYD, R			
CZ/4251	01/01/16	DOW	LANCASHIRE LANDING CEMETERY	
AB	WATSON, FF			
TZ/5139	03/01/16	DOW	LANCASHIRE LANDING CEMETERY	
AB	BOWLES, J			
CZ/4395	04/01/16	KIA	SKEW BRIDGE CEMETERY	

RANK/RATING NUMBER	NAME DATE	CAUSE	BURIAL / MEMORIAL	1914*
AB TZ/3431	SHOBROOK, P 14/01/16	DOW	CHATBY WAR MEMORIAL CEMETERY, EGYPT	
AB MZ/96	HOLMES, V 01/02/16	SICK	SOUTHPORT (DUKE STREET) CEMETERY, LANCS	
AB WZ/1510	THOMAS, T 11/06/16	SICK	PLYMOUTH NAVAL MEMORIAL	
PO M3/214	HUNT, AV 12/06/16	SICK	BAGHDAD (NORTH GATE) WAR CEMETERY, IRAQ	1914*

10

LICKING THE WOUNDS – THE LEMNOS GARRISON:

10 JANUARY – 16 MAY 1916

The Nelson Battalion that left Gallipoli for Lemnos in early January 1916 was totally changed from that which had gone shore at Anzac Cove in late April 1915. The extent of that change can be gauged from another examination of the composition of the battalion's officer corps. The nominal list of those on the Gallipoli peninsula on the last days had comprised:

Commanding Officer	Lieutenant Colonel Norman O. Burge, RMLI
2nd in Command	*[Lieutenant Commander Edward W Nelson had been evacuated and was in hospital on Malta from 1 January 1916. He would not return as 2i/c until late January]*
Adjutant	A/Lieutenant Hedley T. Ely RNVR *[Replacing A/Lieutenant David Galloway, who had been transferred to HQ 1st Brigade as Staff Captain.]*
Lieutenant RNVR	Cyril A. Truscott *(Acting)* Charles S Hosking *(Acting)* George K. Turnbull *(Acting)*

Sub Lieutenant RNVR		
	Arthur Hobbs	Bernard Dangerfield
	Robert Ritson	Sydney Flowitt
	David Francis	John Stephens
	Eric W. Squires	John E. Greenwell
	Leonard Spain	John G. Coburn
	James H. Brothers	James A. Woodgate
	Edward J.B. Lloyd	Edmund Langstreth

Paymaster RNVR	John E. Macintyre

Quartermaster	Lieutenant James A. Gates, RMLI
Surgeon	Henry B. Parker, RN

It is evident that the company commanders, who had all been lieutenant commanders earlier in the campaign, are now acting lieutenants or even sub lieutenants. This would remain the pattern for the future. Only two officers on the list (Hosking and Hobbs) had fought through the entire Gallipoli campaign and both of these were former Company CPOs who had been commissioned in the field. Nine of the officers are ex-ratings. There was only one officer (Dangerfield) left of the July 1915 draft. The two remaining members of the August 1915 draft (Ely and Truscott) were, after only four months, among the senior officers in the battalion. The September draft of eight sub lieutenants was down to six and two officers of the intakes of October and November had been lost to the battalion through sickness. Sub Lieutenant Ritson had been temporarily attached from Hood Battalion in November and would return there immediately after the evacuation. Except for the Surgeon and the Paymaster, not one of the Nelson officers who sailed with the MEF from Avonmouth ten months earlier remained– all were dead or had been invalided home, wounded or sick.

A similar review of all the ORs who passed through Nelson Battalion at Gallipoli would be a daunting task. However, the precise composition of No.4 Platoon of 'A' Company at the start of the campaign is known from the diary of the author's father. The fate of these fifty men and their Platoon Sub Lieutenant gives a snapshot of a typical platoon which first went ashore at Anzac Cove.

After Nelson Battalion was landed on 29 April 1915 to relieve the hard-pressed ANZACs, nine members of this 51-strong platoon were killed or mortally wounded in the fighting for Baby 700 and The Chessboard on 2 and 3 May, including the Platoon Officer, Sub Lieutenant G.P. Cooke, and one of the Platoon Petty Officers. A further seven ratings were wounded in the fighting at Anzac. Of these, three had wounds which did not require repatriation and they later rejoined the Nelsons at Helles, while four, including the author's father, were evacuated to Egypt and then invalided to England. The platoon casualty rate of killed and wounded (sixteen out of fifty-one) during the two weeks on the Anzac front was, therefore, a little over thirty-one per cent. Only one of those killed at Anzac, Able Seaman Jack Scrowther, is in a marked grave at Beach Cemetery.

After the move from Anzac a further seven members of this platoon were killed in nearly eight months of fighting on the Helles sector. Thirteen others were wounded, this total of twenty casualties representing another forty per cent of the original fifty-one. However, for the thirty-eight members of the platoon who survived Anzac to fight on at Helles the twenty dead and wounded represented a casualty rate of over fifty-two per cent. Only one of those killed at Helles, Able Seaman William Short[128], is in a cemetery – he is 'believed to be buried' at Skew Bridge where he has a Special Memorial. In addition, twenty-three ratings were recorded as sick while at Helles, mainly of dysentery and fevers. Many men were sick and wounded or killed while at Helles. Of the platoon's wounded and sick at Helles, twenty-two had to be invalided to England. Only eight of the original fifty-one members of the platoon were still serving at Gallipoli with Nelson Battalion at the evacuation from Helles on 9 January 1916. Of those eight survivors, there was not one single rating who had not been either sick or wounded, or both, during his time fighting ashore.

To summarize the Gallipoli campaign for this platoon: of the fifty-one original members, sixteen men (thirty-one per cent) were killed or mortally wounded in action there. If they were not among the killed, the probability of their only being wounded was forty per cent. Their chance of being killed or wounded in action was about seventy per cent. Their probability of surviving on the Gallipoli Peninsula through the eight-month campaign until the withdrawal in January 1916 was about fifteen per cent. These few long-term survivors were absolutely certain to have suffered wounds or disease, but they had not been ill enough to merit invaliding to England, although most had been evacuated from the peninsula for treatment, usually at Mudros or in Egypt. Only fourteen members of this platoon went on to serve in the British Expeditionary Force (BEF) with the RND but four of them would be commissioned, three in the RND and one into the Army.

Immediately after landing at Mudros Nelson Battalion received another infusion of seven new sub lieutenants from home: James Cowan, Harold V.S. Johnson, Albert P. Mecklenburg, Percival Batchelor, Arthur P. Taylor, John H. Emerson and Arthur K. Smithells. Five of these officers were ex-ratings.[129] Sub Lieutenant Frederick J. Dean was also appointed to Nelson at this time but he was immediately re-appointed to the Royal Naval Air Service (RNAS) as an Observer.[130]

On 10 January the rear parties of the RND disembarked at Mudros, where Nelson Battalion had already moved into tented lines. They now formed part of the garrison of the Greek island of Lemnos, a fairly undemanding task according to Jerrold:

> the routine consisted of a certain amount of police work, the examination of persons passing in and out of the small area in occupation of the garrison, the mounting of numerous guards and pickets and the search for hostile snipers whenever someone threw a cartridge into the incinerator. The greater proportion of the garrison was employed on none of these duties, and carried out company, or battalion training.[131]

Parades, inspections, firing on the ranges and field exercises occupied the working days. For the officers (who could travel on horseback) and, much less frequently, the ORs the tedium of the routine could be broken by excursions across the island to Greek villages, especially to the hot baths at Therma.[132] Inter-battalion sports and band concerts were organized. At the end of January Lieutenant Commander Edward Nelson returned from hospital and took up his appointment as 2i/c Nelson Battalion. On 5 February the Nelsons moved out of their tents, which were taken over by the Divisional Train, and into more comfortable, hutted accommodation which had recently been vacated by No.3 Canadian Hospital. At the end of February a further draft of reinforcements for the RND arrived from England, including another seven sub lieutenants for Nelson Battalion,[133] but in March another three officers would be invalided home, sick. Training continued through March and early April while the future of the RND was being debated at the highest level. On 22 March a field exercise in battalion attack and defence was carried out between the Nelson and the Hood. The Divisional War Diary reports that 'Unfortunately a heavy rainstorm during the night seriously interfered with operations.' James Hilton of the Hood complained that his men had to bivouac in the field while the Nelsons marched back to their huts.

The four months on Lemnos provided the opportunity for leave to be given, mainly for those who had served lengthy periods on Gallipoli. Officers took passage back to England. The ORs who were granted leave had to content themselves with Malta. On 26 February command of Nelson Battalion had been passed temporarily to Lieutenant Commander Henry Robson of the Hawke when Lieutenant Colonel Burge returned to England on leave. Lieutenant Commander Nelson went home with him. Lieutenant Colonel Burge returned on 30 April but his 2i/c would be in England for three months, not rejoining Nelson until the end of May, by which time the battalion was in France.

On 29 March there was another exodus of ratings from the RND when the battleship HMS *Canopus* sailed for home taking with her a large number of RNVR ratings who were volunteers for sea service. Lieutenant Leonard Spain of Nelson Battalion was appointed in charge of the RND party for the passage home. Two of the eight survivors of No.4 Platoon, 'A' Company were among them.[134] On the following day Nelson Battalion was inspected by General Paris and a week later he accompanied Vice Admiral de Robeck on an inspection of the whole division. Decision time for the RND came in mid-month: on 16 April the division was placed under the Army Act. The War Office now had operational command. Preparations were set in hand for an early embarkation and work began to re-shape the battalion for operations with the BEF in France.

Two more sub lieutenants joined the battalion in late April.[135] In the following weeks suitably qualified officers were being transferred to join the newly-forming Brigade Machine Gun Companies (MGC). Included in the latter group from Nelson Battalion were Sub Lieutenants James H. Brothers and

James D. Black who were transferred to the 2nd Bde MGC, which became 189 Brigade MGC in France.[136] Sub Lieutenant Arthur Hobbs was transferred to the RND Base Depot at Calais in anticipation of the division's move to France and would not be part of the Nelson fighting strength in future.

The first RND battalions embarked for France on 7 May. On Tuesday 16 May 1916 Nelson Battalion embarked in HMT *Ionian* in Mudros Bay. She was lying alongside HMT *Franconia*, the liner that had brought the battalion out from England fifteen months earlier, but there would be few people on the present battalion strength who would have been one of her passengers. Only six men out of the fifty-one who had sailed out in *Franconia* as part of No.4 Platoon of 'A' Company would depart in the *Ionian*. Hood Battalion and units of the Divisional Engineers and Train also embarked in *Ionian* for the passage to France. Lieutenant Colonel Burge was OC Troops and the Nelson Adjutant, Lieutenant Ely, was made Ship's Adjutant. On the evening of that day the *Ionian* sailed for France, taking Nelson Battalion to join the BEF.

They left behind at Mudros one Nelson Battalion rating. Able Seaman Thomas Thomas[137] was left on the Depot Battalion strength and was transferred to hospital in Malta later in May, suffering from a gastric ulcer. He was invalided to England in HS *Rewa*, but died on board of his ulcer and a gastric abscess. He was buried at sea on 11 June 1916. The last Nelson casualty of the MEF, Able Seaman William Hutchinson, died of his wounds in September 1916.

'AND I THOUGHT OF ALL THE GRAVES BY DESOLATE TROY,

AND THE BEAUTY OF MANY YOUNG MEN NOW DUST,

AND THE LONG AGONY, AND HOW USELESS IT ALL WAS.'

From 'Proem' by Richard Aldington (1892–1962)

11

TRAINING TO BE REAL SOLDIERS – NELSON BATTALION JOINS THE BEF:

17 MAY – 4 OCTOBER 1916.

On the eve of the RND's transfer to France each battalion had submitted a list of officers to the HQ.[138] The Nelson Battalion list contains thirty-one names but not all of these officers were present on Lemnos.

Commanding Officer	Lieutenant Colonel Norman O. Burge, RMLI
2nd in Command	Lieutenant Commander Edward W. Nelson, RNVR *[On leave in England]*
Adjutant	Lieutenant Hedley T. Ely, RNVR
Lieutenant Commander RNVR	Henry R. Robson *[Temporarily attached from Hawke Battalion]*
Lieutenant RNVR	Lieutenant David Galloway *[Acting. Still in post at HQ 1st Brigade as Staff Captain. He would rejoin Nelson Battalion on 24th May in France.]* Cyril A. Truscott Charles S. Hosking *(Acting)* George K. Turnbull *(Acting)*

Sub Lieutenant RNVR		
	Bernard Dangerfield	Percival Batchelor
	Edwin L.A. Dyett	Harold R. Pearson
	Edward J.B. Lloyd	Alan L. Ball
	William D. Redmond	James Cowan
	Francis E. Rees	Eric W. Squires
	Sydney Flowitt	William D. Walker
	Albert P. Mecklenburg	Arthur P. Taylor

John E. Greenwell	Harold V.S. Johnson
Leonard S. Gardner	Herbert S. Strickland
John H. Emerson	David Francis
Arthur K. Smithells	

Quartermaster   Lieutenant James A. Gates, RMLI

Surgeon   Henry B. Parker, RN

The Nelson's Paymaster, John E. Macintyre RNVR, had now been transferred to the Divisional Staff as Field Cashier. He would remain with the RND until April 1918, serving first in the RND Base Pay Office, Rouen, and then at Blandford. Two other Nelson officers were on detached duty: Lieutenant Spain with the RNVR sea draft and Sub Lieutenant Stephens, serving with the Depot Battalion, Mudros. Both of these officers rejoined in France in June. These thirty-two then formed the initial officer corps of Nelson Battalion as part of the BEF.

The uneventful five-day passage from the Aegean to Marseilles provided some time for relaxation, including a sports afternoon organized by Lieutenant Commander Robson, who was still temporarily attached to the Nelson. The embarked troops had few duties other than to provide large numbers of men to keep a look-out for enemy submarines. Given that most of the look-outs had probably never seen a submarine, it was inevitable that the voyage was punctuated by frequent false alarms. Malta was abeam at midday on 19 May and two days later, on the evening of 21 May, the *Ionian* made her way into harbour at Marseilles, the Hood band playing, appropriately, 'The Marseillaise'. On the following afternoon the troops disembarked and marched, led by the Hood Band, through enthusiastic, welcoming crowds to the station. There they boarded the trains which would take them north to the RND assembly area near Abbeville at the seaward end of the River Somme.

The train journey took two days, travelling up the Rhone Valley to Lyons, north to Dijon, then turning north-west and passing south and west of Paris. The French people gave them a warm welcome at most places they stopped and Red Cross nurses passed food and drink onto the train. Passing through Amiens, the trains then followed the south bank of the Somme to Pont Rémy, where the troops detrained on the evening of 24 May. There the Nelson Battalion was met by the 2i/c, Lieutenant Commander Nelson, and they were marched, in a steady downpour, for eight miles through the Picardy countryside to their billets in the village of Huppy about five miles south of Abbeville. At least in Huppy, well behind the front, the men's billets in stables, barns and empty cottages were generally intact. The billets they would later occupy to the east would be considered palatial if they were roofed.

The move to the BEF in France coincided with yet another reorganization of the RND's brigades. In an attempt to retain three brigades of sailors and marines, it was hoped to form new battalions (2nd Hood, 2nd Drake, 2nd Hawke and 2nd Anson) by splitting some of the battalions in France and forming new ones from the reserves available at Blandford. Lieutenant Commander Tom Price, wounded on Gallipoli with the Nelson, was appointed as 2i/c of 2nd Drake Battalion at Blandford. A new 1st Brigade was to be formed, comprising 1st and 2nd Drake and 1st and 2nd Hood Battalions, commanded by an Army officer, Brigadier General C.L. McNab (Royal Sussex Regiment), who took up his appointment on 28 May. Nelson Battalion was moved to a new 2nd Brigade with Howe and 1st and 2nd Hawke Battalions under the command of another Army officer, Brigadier General L.F. Phillips DSO (60th Rifles), who assumed command on 27 May. The 3rd Brigade, comprising 1st and 2nd Anson and 1st and 2nd RM, was now the only one commanded by an RND 'old hand', Brigadier General Charles N. Trotman CB RMLI, who had been an RND Brigade GOC since Antwerp. The Nelson's Brigade GOC throughout the Gallipoli campaign, David Mercer, had been promoted and appointed Adjutant-General Royal Marines. However, these new brigade arrangements were short-lived and never came to full fruition because the RND reserves at Blandford were insufficient in numbers to make up four new battalions and also sustain the existing ones. The Navy List of July 1916 gives a breakdown of this transitory organization. It is somewhat at variance with that given by Jerrold in the Divisional History.

The shuffling of battalions and brigades would continue throughout the early weeks in France but by the end of June 1916 realism had won: the '2nd battalions' were disbanded and the RND had assumed the organization that would endure until early 1918. The reorganization was announced by General Paris at a Divisional Conference on 1 July and over the next few days Nelson Battalion came together again with Drake, Hawke and Hood as 2nd Brigade under Brigadier General Phillips. Brigadier General Trotman handed over Anson, Howe and the two RMLI battalions to Brigadier General H.E.S. Prentice DSO (Highland Light Infantry) and they were formed into 1st Brigade. Brigadier General Trotman moved over to become the RMLI GOC of the four Army infantry battalions which would join the RND as its third brigade. The first Army units in the RND were 7/Royal Fusiliers, 4/Bedfordshire Regiment, 10/Royal Dublin Fusiliers and 1/Honourable Artillery Company. With the reorganization came new identities. Army formation numbers were adopted: 1st Brigade became 188 Infantry Brigade; 2nd Brigade became 189 Brigade; the newly attached Army battalions formed 190 Brigade; and the RND became the 63rd (Royal Naval) Division. The first operation order to carry the title of the new 189 Brigade was issued on 24 July.

Brigadier General Phillips inspected Nelson Battalion at Huppy in the forenoon of 30 May but the battalion would have only nine days there before being ordered to begin training in the Pas-de Calais area for trench warfare

BEF-style. There had been no suitable training area around Huppy and the week had been spent carrying out route marches, training grenadiers (bombers) and testing the new issue of rifles on a thirty-yard firing range. Marching out of billets at 5.30 am on 3 June, the battalion entrained at Pont Remy and, after a long-delayed departure, finally left in the early afternoon for Bryas, about thirty-two miles to the north-east, arriving there in the early evening. It would be 10.00 pm before they entered their new billets in the village of Beugin after a seven-mile march. More than seventeen hours with just haversack rations gave rise to complaints. These were reinforced when it was found that the new billets were in a filthy condition and the latrines and refuse pits had not been covered by the previous battalion.

Nelson Battalion had now entered the training area of IV Corps of First Army and its fighting strength was reported as twenty-five officers and 735 ORs. Training for fighting in France now ramped up. New weapons came into the RND including Stokes mortars and Lewis and Vickers machine guns. For the first time in its fighting history the RND was being properly equipped. New tactics had to be learned in a short time. Dedicated Divisional Artillery (2nd Northumbrian RFA: 223, 315 and 317 Field Artillery Brigades) was a concept unknown to those who had fought at Gallipoli and the procedures of infantry had to be modified accordingly. Lectures, specialist training, weapon firing and route marches filled a very busy two weeks based on Beugin. On 17 June Nelson Battalion moved five miles east to billets at Verdrel, near Fresnicourt-le-Dolmen. They were now only about six miles behind the front line in the Angres-Souchez sector, which ran north-south just to the west of the mining town of Lens. Intensive training continued from Verdrel but the battalion now had the added task of providing working parties in support of the front. Units were also being sent to Army units in the front line to learn from the experienced troops, coming under the orders of the brigades of 47th Division to which they were attached for on-the-job training. This period saw the first Nelson death with the BEF when Able Seaman Joseph Pigott[139] was killed in action on 25 June. The Nelsons remained at Verdrel for two weeks. During June Lieutenant Spain and Sub Lieutenant Stephens rejoined the battalion and, a sign of the changes taking place in the new operational environment, Sub Lieutenant Greenwell was posted to 189 Brigade Trench Mortar Battery.[140]

On 1 July (the first day of the Somme offensive) the battalion moved out of billets and into the 'Angres II' sector of the front line for the first of their tours of duty, although this was still a part of their training and introduction to the BEF routines. They entered the trench system in the afternoon and relieved 22/London Regiment. By 7.00 pm the handover was complete with two Nelson companies in the front line, one in reserve and one attached to the battalion on their right flank. The routine, continuous repair and maintenance work on the front line and support trenches, was interspersed by exchanges of fire with the German lines. The first such occurred on the first full day in the line, 2 July, when the Germans opened up on the Nelson trenches with minenwerfers (mortars) and rifle grenades and caused significant damage. The reply came on the following morning when the Nelsons opened up rapid fire on the German trenches at 9.45 am with Stokes mortars, medium trench mortars and rifle grenades, 'with the occasional salvo of shrapnel'.[141] For an hour in the small hours of 4 June the German lines were again swept with Lewis guns, Stokes mortars and rifle grenades. On the evening of that day the Nelsons were relieved by 22/Londons, bringing to an end their first blooding in the trenches of France. The battalion withdrew back to their billets at Verdrel for the night. The casualties of that first seventy-two hours in the trenches of France had included three men killed in action, one dead of wounds and seventeen wounded.

There had also been another accidental death during the period in the trenches. A Court of Enquiry was convened by Lieutenant Colonel Burge at Villers-au-Bois on 7 July

> for the purpose of investigating and reporting on the death of TZ/2161 LS(HG) Proctor [sic], TH and the wounding of TZ/5736 [sic] AB Little, D, both of 'A' Co., Nelson Battalion.

Lieutenant Commander Galloway was President and Sub Lieutenants Lloyd and Dyett were members of the enquiry.[142] It was tragically apparent that yet another lesson of war had been learned the hard way. Able Seaman Little, who had received a wound over the left eye in the incident, stated:

> I was returning from the trenches with about 20 other men, among whom was PO [sic] Procter who had found a nose cap (I think a fuse and detonator) in the trenches today. He showed it to some artillery men in a doorway and one of them screwed the nose cap off and tried to take something out. The explosion then occurred and I was carried into the house.

This introduction to the new fighting environment had emphasized the changes from the conditions that they had been forced to endure at Gallipoli. Jerrold noted:

> The 'line' in France was a revelation to us poor amateurs from the East; dirty, unplanned, badly wired, with trenches shallow and badly-sited, it really frightened us until we realised that the vast military machines on both sides stopped dead two miles behind their respective fronts. At Gallipoli we held our trenches; there was nothing else to hold. There were no reserves and no room for manoeuvre. Neither side could afford to allow the other elbow room.[143]

It would be another twenty days before the battalion would go back into the trenches. Meanwhile, large numbers of officers and men (more than half of

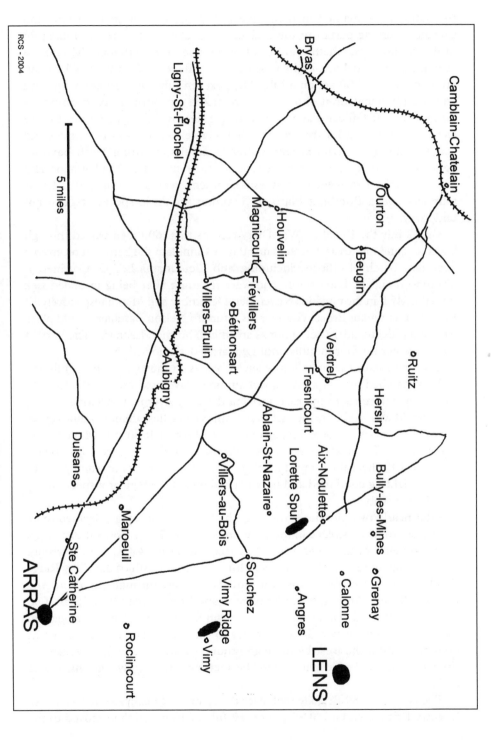

Camblain-Chatelain

Bryas

Ligny-St-Flochel

5 miles

Ourton

Houvelin

Magnicourt

Beugin

Frévillers

Villers-Brulin

Béthonsart

Verdrel

Fresnicourt

Ablain-St-Nazaire

Lorette Spur

Aix-Noulette

Ruitz

Hersin

Bully-les-Mines

Aubigny

Villers-au-Bois

Souchez

Grenay

Calonne

Angres

LENS

Duisans

Maroeuil

Ste Catherine

Vimy Ridge

Vimy

ARRAS

Roclincourt

4. Angres-Souchez Sector and IV Corps Training Area.

the battalion) remained in their billets at Verdrel, close to the front, and provided working parties to the 2nd and 47th Divisions – the continuing lot of the infantryman whether in or out of the line. The battalion HQ and the remainder moved back eight miles to the village of Camblain-Châtelain arriving there at 6.00 am on 6 July. The next ten July days, generally fine and warm with occasional showers, were taken up with more training. A Canadian Staff Officer came over from the nearby village of Pernes to give lectures on scout and patrol work to all available Nelson officers. Snipers and scouts among the ORs received their specialist training, with bayonet fighting and other classes of instruction for the remainder. The battalion HQ was reorganized to meet its new establishment, which now included Lewis Gunners and a Bombing Platoon. Training for these specialists also got underway.

On 12 July the Battalion War Diary records that '600 men passed through baths', a quite rare treat. On the same day at Camblain the battalion received a large new batch of officers, including Sub Lieutenants E.V.G. Gardner, J. Thompson and E. Langstreth, who were rejoining after being invalided sick from the MEF in the previous November, December and March respectively.[144] For Sub Lieutenant Ernest Gardner his return to Nelson Battalion would place him alongside his elder (but junior as an officer) brother, Leonard. They would serve together for four months until Leonard's death in action.

Two days later the battalion received orders to move and on 15 July the Nelson marched out on a warm, wet summer day back towards the front to Coupigny, ten miles to the east, arriving there for overnight billeting at 4.30 pm. Jerrold was struck by the fact that in this village 'less than two miles back, not a pane of glass had been broken or ever was broken during the whole course of the war'.[145] The next day saw a two-mile march in the early evening to billets at 'Fosse 10' where they stayed for three days. Specialist training and practice bayonet fighting continued and the men had one of the regular inspections by the MO for scabies.

After nearly two months of training, the Division was at last deemed to be competent to take its place in the front line and on 17 July General Paris took over command of the Angres-Souchez sector from the GOC 47th Division. The new line of responsibility ran south north, from north of the Vimy Ridge (held by the Germans) across the Souchez River, through the destroyed mining village of Angres, towards Calonne and Bully to the west of Lens. Old mine workings and slag heaps were the main features of the northern part of the sector, changing to a flat river valley to the south. The whole sector was dominated from the west by the high ground of the Lorette Spur which the French Army had won back from the Germans in bloody fighting a year earlier.

The Nelson's 189 Brigade took over the southern Souchez sector from 141 Infantry Brigade and at 10.30 pm on 19 July Nelson Battalion moved to the woods near Aix-Noulette (Bois Noulette or Noulette Wood) to relieve the 19/Londons as the Brigade Reserve. This marked the beginning of the series of five rotational tours into the front line which the battalion would undertake over the next two months. During this period Nelson and Hawke Battalions would alternate every six or seven days, relieving each other in the forward trenches. Douglas Jerrold, as Adjutant of Hawke Battalion, remembered the Nelson and Hawke routine of this period well. When out of the trenches the battalions were in reserve in Noulette Wood 'within a mile of the first line, where we lived in huts as safely as at Blandford', or manning the Lorette Spur, which

> provided 'billets' for a company after a week in the trenches, the 'billets' consisting of dirty dug-outs looking out on decayed and flooded trenches. They all faced the wrong way and could have been blown to pieces in a minute.

Conditions were better at nearby Ablain St. Nazaire,

> where there was the remains of a village destroyed in the fighting for the Lorette Spur [where] we were also undisturbed and could even bathe in a pleasant stream, having anticipated modern fashion and built ourselves a bathing pool.[146]

The routine for taking over at the front would generally see an advance party of company commanders with their senior NCOs and perhaps an NCO per platoon moving forward on the evening of the first day to begin the relief, with the battalion Lewis gun detachments being the first to hand over. Dusk on the following day would see battalion guides leading the troops forward to execute the full relief which would take about three or four hours to complete. The battalion being relieved would pass to the rear in the small hours of the morning.

The first trench tour for the Nelsons was from 26 to 31 July in the 'Souchez II' sector, a period characterized by hot summer weather by day and very misty nights. The tour was fairly quiet with the days filled by the usual work on the trenches. On the last day, as advance relieving parties from Hawke were arriving, the Nelson War Diary records:

> Slight annoyance by minenwerfer. Retaliation from 18th Bde. Time of opening fire from time ordered through liaison officer 5'30" [5½ minutes].

Hawke Battalion completed the relief just before midnight on 31 July and the Nelsons went to the rear to become the Brigade Reserve in Noulette Wood. They had suffered one man killed (on 27 July) and two wounded. Douglas Jerrold recorded a somewhat jaundiced view of trench activity in the Angres-Souchez sector:

The only casualties occurred when trench-mortar experts decided to have a little target practice. This was hotly resented because owing to the limited range of their guns they had to fire from our reserve trenches. After firing they retired into a dug-out, while the Germans 'retaliated' on us, and honour demanded that a subaltern, a sergeant and a half dozen men should stand up and pretend to enjoy it. If the retaliation went on long enough the company commander had to appear, and if the worst came to the worst some one from battalion headquarters had to express the requisite curiosity by getting shot at himself.[147]

The few days out of the line were occupied with the inevitable working parties but every man was able to bathe at least once and new shirts were issued. Some junior officers were sent back to Base to understudy in the Quartermaster's department or learn the workings of 1st Line Transport. While the battalion had been in the line Sub Lieutenant James Woodgate, who had been invalided home sick from Mudros, rejoined and was attached to the 189 Brigade Light Trench Mortar Battery. On 6 August it was time to relieve the Hawke Battalion and the Nelsons were again in the line by midnight on that day. This turned out to be the most active and dangerous of the Nelson tours of duty at Souchez II. The first full day, 7 August, was spent clearing trenches which had been damaged by German bombardment. At 6.00 pm some seven to ten rounds were fired from a minenwerfer and two of the Nelson's medium trench mortars were knocked out. Trench mortars and artillery retaliated. Overnight wiring parties and patrols went out into no-man's-land and the next day the German attack was repeated, mortally wounding Petty Officer A.P. Wedel[148] who died of severe rifle grenade wounds two days later at the field ambulance. A Nelson sniper, equipped with a telescopic sight, shot an enemy sniper – a feat which was repeated the next day. On 10 and 11 August the two sides engaged in exchanges of minenwerfer and artillery. During one of these duels one of our own trench mortars fell short into the Nelson trenches, killing two men and wounding three others. At midnight on 11–12 August the relief by the Hawke Battalion was complete and the Nelsons again went back to Noulette Wood. The casualty list this time stood at fifteen: one rating killed in action, two dead of wounds and twelve men wounded.

Only three days were spent at Noulette Wood before the battalion marched, on the wet evening of 14 August, the three miles to the Lorette Spur arriving at 11.30 pm. There they relieved Drake Battalion, the Nelson HQ setting up in Ablain-St.Nazaire. Then it was back into the routine of working parties for three more days. On 18 August it was time to move back to 'Souchez II' sector to relieve Hawke Battalion and just after midnight the turnover was complete. This tour, from 19 to 24 August, was not quiet, with exchanges of mortar fire, artillery and rifle grenades the order of each day, but, mercifully, casualties were minimal. The Hawke Battalion was again in position by 11.30 pm on 24

August and the Nelsons withdrew to the reserve position on the Lorette Spur, counting themselves fortunate to have suffered only one man wounded.

The last days of August were sultry and wet but working parties were still in demand. On the last day out of the line there was a thunderstorm and heavy rain, which meant that no work could be done. The Nelson War Diary notes that, while at Ablain, nightly patrols of officers were started to prevent lights and smoking in the open, a sensible precaution as the Nelson HQ was shelled on 27 August, although no damage or casualties resulted. On 28 August a draft of 150 reinforcements arrived, including four petty officers and seven leading seamen. Three men were retained as HQ signallers and the remainder were posted to companies. 30 August was relief day, and another wet one. The Nelsons were in the line and the Hawkes were out just after midnight. The earlier rain and a showery spell between 31 August and 5 September meant that work on trench drainage took priority, as waterlogged trenches would make life total misery. This penultimate tour in the line at 'Souchez II' ended at midnight on 5–6 September and the battalion moved back to the Lorette Spur. One man had been killed and two wounded.

Overnight on 6–7 September the Nelsons moved back to billets at Noulette Wood, where the MO again hunted for scabies, the men went through the baths and new shirts were issued. 12 September saw Nelson Battalion move forward again to relieve the Hawke. Handover was completed by 10.30 pm. This would be the battalion's last tour in the trenches of the 'Souchez II' sector and it followed the familiar five-day routine of 'patrols, listening posts, strafes and wiring'. Seven men were wounded in this period, one of whom later died. 18 September was spent handing over to 8/Lincolnshire Regiment of 37th Division who were taking over the Calonne-Angres-Souchez sector from the RND. The relief was completed at 1.00 am on 19 September and Nelson Battalion marched back the eight miles to the billets at Verdrel which they had vacated in early July, arriving at 5.00 am. The six tours in the Angres-Souchez front line had cost Nelson Battalion twelve ORs dead and forty wounded.

There would be only one day to rest at Verdrel because the battalion was under orders to move back to the IV Corps training area. On 20 September the Nelsons marched eight miles to Magnicourt-en-Comté arriving at noon to take up billets there and in nearby Houvelin. The next day the battalion MO conducted his periodic search for scabies mites, there was a kit inspection and, for the first time, the Nelson War Diary records that there was a 'make-and-mend'. 'Hands to make and mend clothes', a period for personal administration and no work (usually called a 'make-and-mend') was one of the many naval traditions practised by the RND, probably to the despair of Army officers. Nelson Battalion spent a full week based around Magnicourt, the days filled with company training and range firing. It was during this period that the Nelson's MO, Surgeon Henry Parker, broke his left thigh in an accident and was invalided to England via 20th General Hospital at Camiers. He had been with the battalion since January 1915 and would not return. His replacement, Surgeon Ernest F. Cox RN, would join Nelson battalion from 1st Field Ambulance after the RND had moved south in early October. Lieutenant Geoffrey F. Gilbert also joined at this time. He had been in the July reinforcement but went sick on arrival in France. He would be invalided home, again sick, before the November battle on the Ancre. Geoffrey was the brother of Robert and Wilfred Gilbert who had both served with the Nelsons at Gallipoli where Wilfred was killed and Robert wounded.

The week of training around Magnicourt culminated in a full day of brigade training on 27 September, at the end of which Nelson Battalion marched four miles east through Frévillers to billets in Béthonsart. Another six days training based around Béthonsart started with a two-day tactical exercise in open warfare at brigade level on 28 and 29 September and the month ended with a ten-mile brigade route march. Like all such marches, it consisted of fifty minutes on the march and a ten-minute rest at the roadside in each hour. The men of the Nelson would become well-experienced in this method of moving across the country.

As October 1916 opened, Nelson Battalion was completing company training and live bombing practice and preparing to move to a new war front, the Somme. There the British and German Armies had been locked in combat since the slaughter of 1 July 1916. In the darkness of 2.50 am on the morning of 4 October the battalion paraded at Béthonsart and then marched away through the night. Passing south through the village of Villers-Brûlin and then west to the entraining station of Ligny-St. Flochel, they covered nearly eight miles in about three hours, arriving around dawn.

NELSONS KILLED OR MORTALLY WOUNDED DURING OPERATIONS IN THE ANGRES-SOUCHEZ SECTOR, FROM 17 JUNE TO 19 SEPTEMBER 1916.

RANK/RATING NUMBER	NAME DATE	CAUSE	BURIAL / MEMORIAL	1914*
AB TZ/5517	PIGOTT, J 25/06/16	KIA	TRANCHEE DE MECKNES CEMETERY, AIX-NOULETTE	
AB TZ/4396	GOMERY, WF 04/07/16	DOW	BARLIN COMMUNAL CEMETERY EXTENSION	
LS TZ/2161	PROCTER, TH 04/07/16	ACCIDENT	BULLY GRENAY COMMUNAL CEMETERY, BRITISH EXTENSION	
PO KW/129	THORPE, JF 04/07/16	KIA	TRANCHEE DE MECKNES CEMETERY, AIX-NOULETTE	
PO TZ/2495	WILKES, HM 04/07/16	KIA	TRANCHEE DE MECKNES CEMETERY, AIX-NOULETTE	
AB TZ/6669	WORNER, WV 04/07/16	KIA	TRANCHEE DE MECKNES CEMETERY, AIX-NOULETTE	
AB SZ/199	MORLEY, H 27/07/16	KIA	LIEVIN COMMUNAL CEMETERY EXTENSION	
PO WZ/140	WEDEL, AP 10/08/16	DOW	BARLIN COMMUNAL CEMETERY EXTENSION	
AB TZ/7533	KENNEDY, J 11/08/16	KIA	BOIS-DE-NOULETTE BRITISH CEMETERY, AIX-NOULETTE	
AB CZ/5183	SMALL, WC 12/08/16	DOW	BARLIN COMMUNAL CEMETERY EXTENSION	
AB CZ/4302	STIRLING AJ 31/08/16	KIA	BOIS-DE-NOULETTE BRITISH CEMETERY, AIX-NOULETTE	
AB LZ/4906	KING, AJ 19/09/16	DOW	BARLIN COMMUNAL CEMETERY EXTENSION	

12

FORGING A REPUTATION THE HARD WAY – FIGHTING ON THE ANCRE:

5 OCTOBER – 31 DECEMBER 1916.

The War Diary for 4 October records that the trains south left Ligny later that morning taking thirty-four officers and 809 ORs of Nelson Battalion. Their destination at Acheux-en-Amiénois was only a little over twenty miles south, but the journey would take the whole day, with trains for the whole division moving slowly because of a breakdown on the railway. Nelson Battalion de-trained at 6.30 pm and, in a heavy downpour, marched to hutted and tented billets in Acheux Wood. The RND now formed part of V Corps of the Fifth Army. It would be eleven days before Nelson Battalion would be back in the front line and, meanwhile, there was a lot to learn about the new area of oper-ations.

Douglas Jerrold considered the relatively quiet front line around Lens, which they had just left, 'a battlefield *manqué*' – not quite the real thing. In contrast, his memory of the RND's new sector on the Somme was

> a God-forsaken battleground created by earnest Staff officers . . . slightly hysterical about their still incomplete labours. An atmosphere of over-elaborated brusque inefficiency pervaded the hinterland of slaughter. Too many men, too many officers, far too many generals, and a thousand times too many jacks-in-office, RTOs, Town Majors, APMs, Traffic Control Officers, Laundry Officers, Liaison Officers, Railway Experts and endless seas of mud.[149]

Nelson Battalion had three days at Acheux, the first of which was taken up with camp cleaning, bathing and, a special luxury, cinema in the evening at the YMCA. The next two days were spent back in the training routines, including instruction in bayonet fighting. An incident on Saturday, 7 October illustrates that bayonet training was not without its dangers. Sub Lieutenant Lloyd was conducting platoon training, in which his ratings were 'practising in pairs the exercise of an unarmed man depriving the armed enemy of his rifle'. Able Seaman Hendrie rushed forward to disarm Able Seaman Nelson and managed to knock off his opponent's bayonet scabbard and then impale his arm on the naked bayonet. The subsequent Court of Enquiry found the wounding to be accidental.[150]

On 8 October the Nelsons marched to new billets in Mailly Wood but found, on arrival, that there was no accommodation for them. They marched on to Englebelmer four miles to the east and close behind the front line on the west bank of the River Ancre. They would become very familiar with these billets over the next five weeks. From Englebelmer, parties from the battalion would make familiarization visits to the new front line. On 10 October the War Diary notes that instruction was given on communications between aircraft and infantry: the observations from aircraft were assuming increasing importance for battlefield intelligence and for artillery accuracy. For the next five days the demands for working parties multiplied until almost the whole of the Nelson's manpower was engaged, giving little time for rest before going into the line. The heavy rains of early October had collapsed the trenches and filled shell-holes waist-deep. The work to restore the quagmire that was the front line was unceasing and the weather was getting colder.

On 14 October the wounding of General Paris would result in the unpopular Major General Cameron D. Shute DSO, an Army general, taking over as GOC RND. His arrival only served to highlight the different traditions of the RND which sat uneasily with the Army's way of doing things.

On 16 October the Nelsons moved forward from Englebelmer to relieve the 13/Royal Sussex Regiment in the Auchonvillers sector for just 24 hours. The handover was complete by 1.30 pm but the battalion was in for a baptism of fire, with heavy German artillery fire on the trenches which resulted in one rating being killed[151] and ten wounded. On the following day Nelson Battalion was relieved by 8/Argyll and Sutherland Highlanders. The relief was completed by 2.00 pm and the men marched back to billets in Englebelmer. The wet autumnal weather on the Ancre was now beginning to turn decidedly wintry. Two working parties were provided out of Englebelmer and the battalion was then marched across to Mesnil in preparation for another spell in the line. They would only be there for one overnight stay before moving out but

> Mesnil was cold. It always was; it was the only place we ever struck in all our wanderings where any kind of comfort was utterly impossible. There was nowhere to sleep, nowhere to sit, nowhere to look and nowhere to walk.[152]

Nelson Battalion would have two more tours in the front line before the major assault planned for November. The first of these began on 21 October, another cold day, when the battalion moved up into the Hamel sector to relieve Hawke Battalion. The relief was completed at 1.30 pm and the rest of the day was

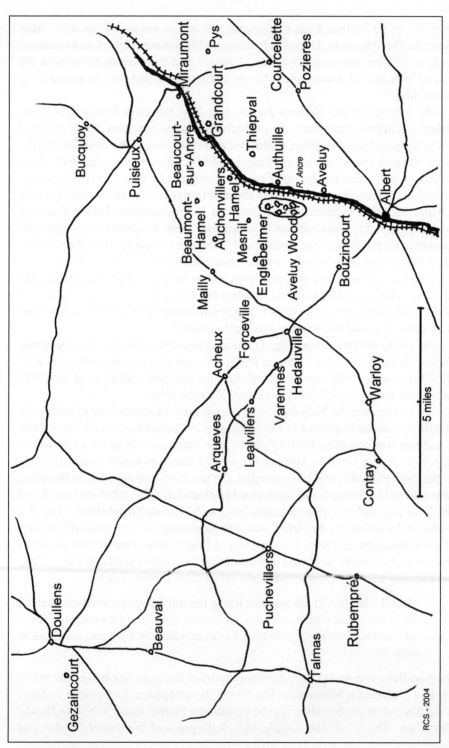

5. Area of Operations on the River Ancre

RCS - 2004

spent in digging new trenches. Hood and Drake Battalions provided working parties of four officers and 100 men to assist in this task. The following two days in the line were cold, dull and wet. British artillery was firing in an attempt to cut the enemy wire, but otherwise the War Diary considers it was 'fairly quiet'. Patrols were sent out and the Germans made life uncomfortable by firing tear gas shells. This is the first record of the men of the Nelson coming under attack by chemical weapons. On 24 October the Hawke Battalion came forward again as the relief and the Nelsons marched back to Englebelmer. Fairly quiet or not, those 72 hours in the line had resulted in the deaths of eight junior ratings. Among them was Able Seaman Fred Robson[153], who was one of the veterans of the original 'A' Company, No.4 Platoon, in which the author's father served at Gallipoli. Fourteen men of that platoon had survived some or all of the Gallipoli campaign to fight in the BEF. Fred Robson was the first of six of those survivors who died in France, two with Nelson Battalion, one with the Drake and three with Howe.

Five days in Englebelmer saw the start of the battalion's preparations for the coming offensive on the Ancre, the first of these days consisting of a full kit inspection and a rare 'make-and-mend'. On the morning of 27 October Brigadier General Phillips inspected the battalion and on the following day the Nelsons turned out on parade in full fighting order for an inspection by Lieutenant Colonel Burge. These few days immediately behind the line also saw continuing demand for working parties as the battlefield was being prepared.

On 30 October the Nelsons were on the move again, marching first to shelters at Varennes for the night and then on to Puchevillers in the Corps rear area on the following day. They were now in billets some twelve miles from the front line and would stay there for four days of relative rest. The highlight of this period was an inspection by the new GOC, General Shute, on 3 November. He already had a low opinion of his new division of sailors and had reported them as unfit to go into action. He had been due to inspect on the previous day and the men had been kept on parade in a freezing downpour for several hours until the inspection was postponed. His opinion of Nelson Battalion at this inspection is unrecorded but his wishes as to how the coming battle should be fought were made very clear.

On 5 November the recent route march was retraced, first to Varennes for the night and then, having provided working parties on the roads totalling 290 men during the day, the battalion marched back to Englebelmer on the following evening. One day was allowed to draw breath and then the Nelsons were back in the front line at Hamel on 8 November. This tour would last forty-eight hours and was characterized by repeated German shelling with gas, high explosive and shrapnel shells during the hours of darkness. When the Nelsons were relieved by 1/RMLI from 188 Brigade on the evening of 10 November they were lucky to march back to their Englebelmer billets with only two dead and a handful of wounded to show for their stay in the line. A total of eleven ORs of Nelson Battalion had been killed or mortally wounded during the month of preparation for the Battle of the Ancre.

The Adjutant, Sub Lieutenant Emerson,[154] had issued Nelson Battalion Order No.50, which covered the operational aspects, on 25 October and this was followed two days later by Order No.51 detailing the administrative arrangements for the coming battle.[155] Final orders only arrived from the higher command on 10 November.

Over the previous month of constant training and endless working parties in worsening weather the fighting strength of ORs across the RND had been seriously reduced. The average RND battalion fighting strength was now probably dropping towards 500 and the men were exhausted even before going into action.[156] However, on the eve of battle the number of Nelson officers was at a reasonable level:

Commanding Officer	Lieutenant Colonel Norman O. Burge, RMLI
2nd in Command	Lieutenant Commander Edward W. Nelson, RNVR
Adjutant	Sub Lieutenant John H. Emerson
Lieutenant Commander RNVR	David Galloway

Lieutenant RNVR	Cyril A. Truscott	Leonard Spain
	Bernard Dangerfield	Sydney Flowitt
	Frank D. Purser	

Sub Lieutenant RNVR	Percival Batchelor	Edmund Langstreth
	Edwin L.A. Dyett	James R. Savary
	Edward J.B. Lloyd	Alan L. Ball
	William D. Redmond	James Cowan
	George A. Reddick	Eric W. Squires
	William D. Walker	Frederic W. Chardin
	Albert P. Mecklenburg	Arthur P. Taylor
	Ernest V.G. Gardner	Ernest W. Cashmore
	Leonard S. Gardner	Herbert S. Strickland
	David Francis	Douglas R.G.P.
	Arthur K. Smithells	Alldridge

Francis E. Rees *[attached 189 Bde LTM Batty]*
James A. Woodgate *[attached 189 Bde LTM Batty]*

Quartermaster	Lieutenant James A. Gates, RMLI
Surgeon	Ernest F. Cox RN

On 11 November the War Diary shows the Nelsons 'resting' at Englebelmer, insofar as any real rest could be had in barns, shacks and cellars in freezing weather. The following day was designated 'Y Day' for the coming battle. The battalion 2i/c, Lieutenant Commander Nelson, remained in the rear with those officers and men who were to remain in reserve during the initial attack. The rest of the battalion moved forward to Mesnil at 4.00 pm and ninety minutes later, after darkness had fallen, the men, probably about 400 strong, moved to the forward trench lines in preparation for the following morning's assault on the German trenches in front of Beaucourt-sur-Ancre. There, in the freezing cold and darkness of a November night the Nelsons were to lie down on the open ground behind Roberts Trench, the second in the British line, in readiness for 'Z Day', 13 November 1916.

In accordance with battalion orders the men were in fighting order, comprising greatcoats worn with the skirts hooked back. Over this they wore a haversack on their back containing one iron ration and one ration for 'Z-Day'. Each man carried in addition: four sandbags (two each side under the belt and tied); two gas helmets; waterproof sheet and mess tin on the back of the belt. One Very light and one flare were carried in the left pocket and each man had two Mills grenades as well as his rifle and ammunition. Wire cutters were also issued and the men who carried these wore a yellow arm-band. The battalion runners were lightly equipped with a rifle, bayonet and fifty rounds of ammunition and these men wore a blue armlet with a white stripe. The battalion orders stated:

> The very strictest orders are to be issued to the men that they must lie perfectly still when it begins to get light on the morning of 'Z Day', as observation will probably result in heavy losses before the attack begins. Men will be awakened without noise at 5am. The success of the whole operation depends on an entire absence of noise and movement after daybreak.

And so, for about ten hours the men of the RND lay in the open on the frozen mud 'in the petrifying cold that comes before a November dawn . . . freezing in the coldest dawn in history'.[157] In front of the Nelsons and holding the front line trenches were their old chums of the Hawke Battalion, with whom they had done tour and tour about over the previous months. They were under orders to leapfrog each other in the coming advance and would share the same perils. The Nelson Battalion formed up in four waves immediately in rear of the Hawke, close up to the bank behind Roberts Trench. Each wave, spread over a frontage of about 300 yards, consisted of four platoons, one platoon from each company in order A,C,D and B from left to right. The plan called for the first wave of Nelsons to move forward 150 yards behind the last wave of the Hawkes and for the second wave of Nelsons to be just ten yards behind the first. The third and fourth waves would follow at forty-yard intervals. It was

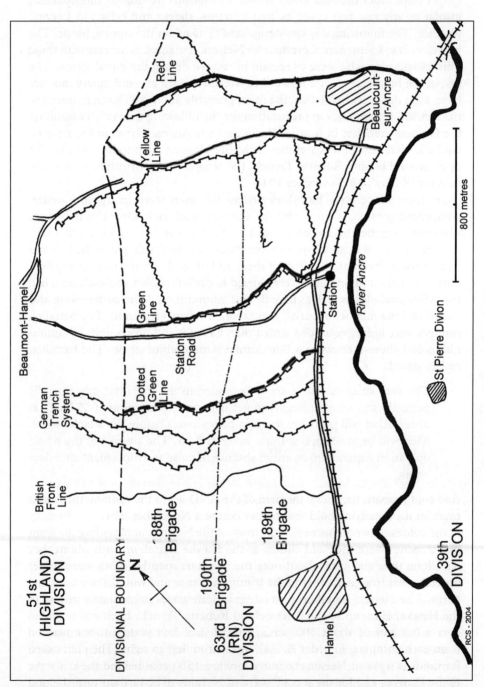

6. Battle of the Ancre – the RND's objectives.

not to be so simple. As dawn approached a dense, freezing mist settled over the battlefield.

The plan of attack upon which the Nelson Battalion troops and the rest of the RND were embarked was ambitious and dangerous. The German lines in front of Beaucourt-sur-Ancre and Beaumont-Hamel had withstood four months of British attempts to take them since the first day of the Battle of the Somme and the defences had been greatly strengthened over time. The front-line system alone consisted of three lines of trenches and there were further fortified lines behind these. The plan required the assaulting battalions to leap-frog over each other as they took successive German lines. These had been designated, in the order they would be encountered:

> *DOTTED GREEN LINE* – the third line of the German front line trench system, on a ridge crest.
>
> *GREEN LINE* – another fortified line atop the next ridge crest.
>
> *YELLOW LINE* – the next fortified line (Beaucourt Trench) immediately in front of the village of Beaucourt.
>
> *RED LINE* – the final RND objective beyond Beaucourt.

In 189 Brigade sector, on the right of the RND front, Hawke would capture the first objective, the *DOTTED GREEN LINE.* Nelson would then pass through and capture the *GREEN LINE,* the last two waves clearing up any dug-outs or pockets of resistance left behind along the Station Road running from the railway line beside the River Ancre to Beaumont-Hamel (this road was designated the *DOTTED BLUE LINE*). Hawke would then leap-frog Nelson and take the *YELLOW LINE* at Beaucourt, with Nelson closing up behind. The Nelson would then leap-frog Hawke to take the *RED LINE* where the Brigade would consolidate against the inevitable German counter-attack. On the right of Hawke and Nelson, Hood and Drake Battalions would execute a similar assault along the north bank of the Ancre. The battalions in the lead would have to keep close up to the British creeping barrage.

On 189 Brigade's left, the battalions of 188 Brigade would carry out a similar attack, with 1/ and 2/RMLI on the far left of the RND front and Howe and Anson on their right, passing through each other to the successive objectives. Spread across the rear of the RND front were the four Army battalions of 190 Brigade who would move forward to consolidate the positions captured by the other two brigades.

The full course of the RND's battle for Beaucourt has been fully described elsewhere.[158] This narrative will confine itself to the fate of the men of Nelson Battalion who went forward on that cold mid-November morning. As the British barrage opened up at 5.45 am the men moved forward through the mist in almost total darkness and with visibility near to zero. How they managed to move their freezing bodies after hugging the ice-covered ground unprotected for ten hours is a mystery.

Douglas Jerrold, the Hawke Battalion Adjutant, was waiting in the forward trenches to follow up the advance with his CO. He had a close view of the Hawkes and Nelsons advancing to their fate:

> The massed artillery of two armies was raining down on the narrow quarter of a mile from the front line where we were standing to the German front line. Every variety of shell was dropping but we only saw the lines of infantry, first of our own men, then of the Nelson Battalion, disappearing into the mist in perfect order and sequence. Any barrack square in Christendom would have been dignified by such an exhibition of precision. Here, for hundreds of simple and Christian men, was their hour of opportunity. Here all grievances were forgotten and all enmity healed. "They went like Kings in a pageant to the imminent death." I shall never see a sight more noble. I was, you see, in the front row of the stalls. Eight lines of men passed me so closely that I could see every expression on their faces as they faded into the mist, and among all those men walking resolutely to wounding or death, I saw not one expression of fear or regret, or even of surprise.[159]

The Nelson War Diary takes up the narrative:

> Owing to dense fog, last wave of Hawke Battn., which by programme should have been 150 yards ahead of our first wave, could not be seen. The German barrage was negligible but heavy machine-gun fire opened upon us at about the time our 4th wave crossed our original front line. We suffered a considerable number of casualties unfortunately losing a high percentage of officers. The first two waves advanced and, keeping in touch with the barrage, arrived at the steep banks situated between the German 3rd Line and STATION ROAD known as the TERRACES. Very considerable opposition was met but after hand-to-hand fighting with bombs and bayonet the remainder advanced to STATION ROAD. Dugouts here were cleared with little opposition and the advance continued to *GREEN LINE* without difficulty.

What this brief summary does not make clear is that the number of men of Nelson and Hawke who survived the passage of the German front lines was very small indeed. Nearly all the Nelson officers had become casualties before the German third line was crossed. The losses to machine-gun fire had been massive, and were to be even worse for the Nelson third and fourth waves as they followed up. The cause of the problem was a very large fortified redoubt situated in the German second line to the left-centre of the line of advance of Hawke and Nelson. The deep redoubt was disguised as a trench and was heavily reinforced with concrete. Half a dozen machine guns, complete with their crews, could be brought up into action from deep dug-outs by means of elevators. The guns had a field of fire of 360°, so troops to the rear were equally vulnerable. The tragedy was that the attacking battalions were totally unaware of its existence until they were mown down by its guns. Practically untouched by the British artillery, its formidable firepower was rapidly brought into action once the barrage had passed overhead. The Nelson and Hawke continued to press their attack into the storm of lead but all eight waves of men took terrible casualties. Douglas Jerrold, who was to become a casualty of this fortress together with his CO, was later to say of this obstacle:

> General Shute's explanation . . . was that the 'strongpoint' . . . had been overlooked by our own battalion in the mist . . . The real lesson was that the 'strong-point' *ought* to have been overlooked, and that our attack should have taken the lines of least resistance to the left and the right of it.[160]

Jerrold is less than fair to General Shute, who made clear in his Report of Operations[161] his opinion on dealing with such enemy strongpoints:

> Troops are always inclined to reinforce when a portion of the attack is held up. This only increases casualties. The opposite should be the course followed. Push in between strong-points and so surround them. They are bound to surrender in time if all efforts to relieve them are beaten back.

Nevertheless, the immediate threat from the men of Nelson and Hawke surrounding the redoubt probably prevented its firepower being concentrated on the left flank of Hood and Drake Battalions and on the right flank of Howe and Anson and perhaps made the task of those battalions that bit easier. The Nelson War Diary continued:

> Meanwhile the 3rd and 4th waves encountered very heavy enfilading machine-gun fire and, suffering very heavy casualties, lost cohesion and direction and, except for small detached parties, ceased to exist as a fighting force. Battalion HQ passed our original front line at about 6.30 am and advanced into 'no man's land' and there encountered very heavy enemy fire from close range. It afterwards transpired that a proportion of the German front line system was still holding out. In front of this stronghold the CO and Adjutant were both killed.

Lieutenant Colonel Burge had gone forward with Sub Lieutenant Emerson, his Adjutant, (as had the CO and Adjutant of Hawke Battalion who were both wounded) to take charge of the Nelsons under fire from the redoubt. Both battalions lost their commanders at about the same time. The two battalion Surgeons also went forward together to tend the wounded around the redoubt. Surgeon Cox survived unscathed but his companion from the Hawke was killed. Brigadier General Phillips' Report on Operations[162] singled out the actions of Lieutenant Bernard Dangerfield, the Signals Officer of Nelson Battalion, at this point in the battle

> [Dangerfield] did excellent work in rallying parties of men who had lost their officers in an endeavour to organise an attack against a strong point. This officer also did very good work in running a line out to the HQ of Nelson Battalion although he was already slightly wounded in the hand.

He was rewarded with the Military Cross. The redoubt, however, was too strong to be taken by infantry, no matter how well led.

Those Nelsons who had managed to get past the German redoubt unscathed had pressed on forward to the *GREEN LINE* on the ridge beyond Station Road. The Nelson War Diary estimates that this body of men was about 100 strong (about twenty-five per cent of the Nelson Battalion attacking force). In reality it was probably a mix of Hawkes and Nelsons, the organization in battalions and waves having broken down completely under the withering fire of the redoubt. Around late morning, these remaining troops

> continued the advance on the barrage lifting and occupied a position in the *YELLOW LINE*. Here they found that they were out of touch on either flank. After information had been received that troops were holding the *YELLOW LINE* just west of Beaucourt this party moved after dusk to position on the left [of] and in touch with these troops.

After some four hours of horrendous fighting a small body of Nelsons, mostly from the first two waves, had reached the *YELLOW LINE*, about 150 yards south-west of Beaucourt, at around noon under the command of Sub Lieutenant Ernest Gardner.[163] The troops on their right were of Hood and Drake Battalions under Lieutenant Colonel Freyberg. These battalions, on the right of the line, had been spared the worst of the attentions of the machine guns in the German redoubt and had made somewhat faster progress forward but still suffering heavy casualties. They had reached the YELLOW LINE about ninety minutes earlier than the remnants of Nelson and Hawke and there they consolidated for the rest of the day, digging in and bringing all the troops who had made it that far forward into one composite unit under Freyberg's command. Sub Lieutenant Gardner had made contact with Lieutenant Colonel Freyberg by 5.00 pm and the Nelsons were directed to dig in on the Hood's left flank and extend the line. After darkness had fallen, Lieutenant Truscott brought forty to fifty reserve men forward to reinforce the small number of Nelsons and, as senior officer, took over command from Sub Lieutenant Gardner, who was the only Nelson officer remaining in the action. However, the number of Nelsons in the force in front of Beaucourt was now so small that, as the Nelson War Diary succinctly puts it:

From this time the Battalion ceased to exist as an identity.

Nelson Battalion, as a cohesive unit, may have played no further part but the Nelson War Diary records for 14 November that 'A considerable number of our men took part in the advance on and capture of Beaucourt' under Lieutenant Colonel Freyberg. He commanded, with outstanding courage that brought him a Victoria Cross, a composite attacking force of surviving Hoods, Drakes, Nelsons, Hawkes and 1/HAC. These RND troops were reinforced by men of 13/King's Royal Rifles from 11 Infantry Brigade. Beaucourt was taken in style in the dawn light and hundreds of Germans surrendered to Freyberg's force. The redoubt which had been such a killer of the men of Nelson and Hawke Battalions was also mopped up on that morning, the Nelson War Diary laconically reporting:

> That morning the stronghold in the German front line system surrendered on the advance of a tank.

Some hundreds of German troops (reports vary between 200 and 600; 400 is probably a good figure) surrendered from the protected depths of this single position.

The rest of 14 November, the day of the capture of Beaucourt, was spent consolidating the gains in the new front line until, between 1.00 and 2.00 am on the next day, the exhausted 189 Brigade was relieved and withdrew to the safety of the fateful ex-German strongpoint. Later on 15 November, at 10.15 am, as 37th Division relieved the RND, what was left of Nelson Battalion withdrew back to billets at Englebelmer for a short stop to pick up the battalion rear party and then marched on a couple of miles to Hédauville. From there, in the evening, a convoy of lorries took the exhausted Nelsons five miles to the rear where they entered billets at Arquèves.

For them the Battle of the Ancre was over. The first day of fighting had cost Nelson Battalion 114 officers and men killed; on the next two days the remnants of the battalion would see another nine ORs killed in action or dying of wounds. Over the following month another thirteen men would die from the wounds they had received in action, making a total of 136 deaths. The Nelsons had seen their Commanding Officer, Lieutenant Colonel Burge, killed together with nine of their junior officers. The elder of the Gardner brothers, Leonard, was killed.

Killed in action:-
Sub Lieutenants D.R.G.P. Alldridge, A.L. Ball, E.W. Cashmore, J.H. Emerson, D. Francis, L.S. Gardner, E. Langstreth, G.A. Reddick, E.W. Squires.[164]

All of the other nine Nelson officers who went into the attack had been wounded and only two of them remained at duty:

Wounded and invalided home:-
Lieutenant Commander D. Galloway[165], Lieutenant S. Flowitt[166], Sub Lieutenants E.J.B. Lloyd[167], A.K. Smithells,[168] F.W. Chardin[169], J.R. Savary[170], A.P. Mecklenburg[171].

Wounded and remained at duty:-
Lieutenant B. Dangerfield, Sub Lieutenant E.V.G. Gardner

From its fighting strength, the battalion had lost, killed or wounded, fourteen of twenty-five sub lieutenants, including the Adjutant, and four of nine officers of lieutenant's rank or above. For the ORs, the Nelson War Diary estimated twenty-four killed, 197 wounded, 120 missing and one gassed. Today's figures for the ORs dead are 125, of whom eighteen died of wounds. Those officers and men with no known grave, commemorated on the Thiepval Memorial, number forty-six. The RND historian recorded that, of those who went forward on 13 November, only 100 men of the Nelson remained uninjured.[172] This battle also saw the last deaths of Nelson Battalion veterans of Antwerp: the Commanding Officer, one petty officer and four able seamen who died had served in that operation just over two years earlier.

Three officers and eight ORs of Nelson Battalion were awarded medals for gallantry in the Battle of the Ancre. The Military Cross was awarded to:

Sub Lieutenant E.V.G. Gardner – 'For conspicuous gallantry in action. He showed great courage and initiative in keeping his men together and continuing the attack at a critical time. He personally carried out several valuable reconnaissances under heavy fire.'[173]

Lieutenant B. Dangerfield – 'For conspicuous gallantry in action. He established and maintained communications under very heavy fire. Later he carried out a dangerous reconnaissance and led a considerable number of men forward who were held up.'[174]

Sub Lieutenant A.P. Mecklenburg – 'For conspicuous gallantry in action. Although twice wounded, he rallied his men close in front of a strongly held enemy position and, charging through, broke up all opposition and reached his correct objective.'[175]

The first Military Medals for gallantry for men of the Nelson were awarded[176] to:

A/Petty Officer G. Price[177]   A/Petty Officer T. Matthew[178]

Able Seaman J. Alder[179]   Able Seaman R.W. Foster[180]

Able Seaman J. Fox[181]   Able Seaman J. McLeod[182]

Able Seaman D. Nixon[183]   Corporal J. Vernon[184]

1. Lt Col Edmund Evelegh, RMLI, CO Nelson Battalion November 1914 to July 1915, as a captain in 1905. © *Royal Marines Museum*

2. Lt Col Evelegh, *(left)* and the Rev Robert Primrose, Battalion Chaplain *(right)*, at Blandford Camp, before embarking for Gallipoli.

7. Surgeon Charles Taylor, the first Medical Officer of Nelson Battalion, at Blandford Camp

8. Sub Lt Harold Treves at Blandford Camp in late 1914. Promoted to Lieutenant on Christmas Eve 1914, he served at Gallipoli as 2i/c of 'C' Company under Lt Cdr Nicol until mortally wounded in late May 1915.

9. Lt John Nicol at Blandford Camp in late 1914. He commanded 'C' Company at Gallipoli as a Lt Cdr and was temporarily Nelson Battalion CO after Lt Col Evelegh was killed in July 1915.

10. Surgeon Alexander Gow at Blandford Camp in late 1914. He looked after the wounded and sick of Nelson Battalion for most of the Gallipoli campaign.

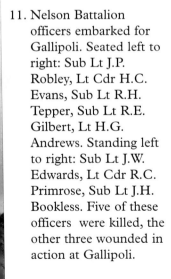

11. Nelson Battalion officers embarked for Gallipoli. Seated left to right: Sub Lt J.P. Robley, Lt Cdr H.C. Evans, Sub Lt R.H. Tepper, Sub Lt R.E. Gilbert, Lt H.G. Andrews. Standing left to right: Sub Lt J.W. Edwards, Lt Cdr R.C. Primrose, Sub Lt J.H. Bookless. Five of these officers were killed, the other three wounded in action at Gallipoli.

18. Able Seaman Alfred Oswald Hall, LZ/346, of 'A' Company, who died in HS *Gascon* on 3 May 1915 of wounds received in the attack on Baby 700 at Anzac. He was buried at sea. *Gascon* carried many of the Nelson wounded to Alexandria.

19. Two RND junior ratings in full battle kit at Blandford, mid-1915. The man on the left is John Tweddle, TZ/1987 who, as a Nelson Petty Officer, was Mentioned in Despatches in November 1917.

20. Petty Officer John Tweddle. Cross-posted to Hawke Battalion, he died of wounds on 22 March 1918, the second day of the German's Spring offensive.

21. Petty Officer John Tweddle, on leave with his family in December 1917, shortly after being Mentioned in Despatches.

22. A group of Nelson Battalion ratings, probably at Betteshanger Camp in October/November 1914.

23. Digging roads at Bandford Camp in late 1914. Nelson Battalion was the first to enter the camp and this photograph, taken by Lt Nicol, probably shows Nelson ratings at work soon after it opened.

24. Nelson Battalion ratings training with semaphore flags. Location unknown. Late 1914 or early 1915.

25. A group of Nelson Battalion petty officers at Blandford on 26 February 1915, two days before they embarked with the MEF. The only one identified is Petty Officer Henry M. Burgoyne, M3/162, who was killed in France with 188 Brigade MG Co in November 1916.

26. Sports day in HMT *Franconia* on passage between Malta and Lemnos, early March 1915. Pillow-fighting on a spar rigged over a canvas bath.

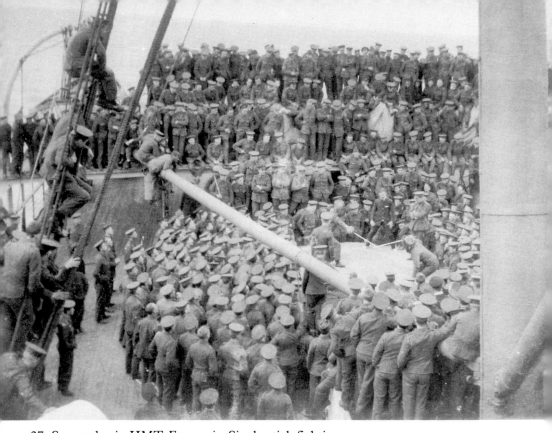

27. Sports day in HMT *Franconia*. Single stick fighting.

28. Musketry practice in the trenches at El Kantara, Egypt.

29. Practising boat landing drill in Trebuki Bay, Skyros, April 1915.

30. Nelson Battalion learning boat-handling in Trebuki Bay, Skyros, April 1915. The light cruiser HMS *Doris* is in the backround.

31. Nelson Battalion resting during field training ashore on Skyros, April 1915.

32. Nelson Battalion advancing in artillery formation on Skyros, April 1915.

33. Nelson Battalion mustered in HMT *Minnetonka* to be briefed by Lt Col Evelegh about the impending landings on Gallipoli.

34. Cap badge of the Nelson Battalion.

35. Nelson Battalion camp in Acheux Wood. Probably taken in early October 1916 after the move south from Angres-Souchez.

36. Nelson Battalion on the march in the Somme area.

Sub Lieutenant D Francis, killed on 13 November, and Able Seaman Henry Denver, TZ/2944, were among those cited for distinguished and gallant services and devotion to duty in the despatches of the CinC BEF, Field Marshal Sir Douglas Haig.[185]

At Arquèves the men of Nelson Battalion had just two days to lick their wounds before moving on. They were reunited with their spare kit, which had been stowed in an unused billet at Englebelmer before the battle, and had the unpleasant task of sorting out the possessions of their dead comrades for return to the next-of-kin. The long list of casualties had to be collated, reports made, signals sent and letters written by officers to wives and parents of the dead. In the afternoon of 16 November the whole of 189 Brigade went on parade on the outskirts of Arquèves. The GOC, Brigadier General Phillips, addressed his brigade, expressing his pride and congratulating them on their performance at Beaucourt. He had been clearly distressed at the losses endured in the battle by his men. Of all the congratulatory messages passed down to battalions, from the King down through the CinC and GOCs of Army, Corps and Division, only that of Brigadier General Phillips contained words which deplored the heavy casualties suffered.

On 18 November the survivors marched away from Arquèves to Gézaincourt, eight miles to the north-west, for an overnight stop before going on to billets at Candas. There on the afternoon of 20 November Nelson and Drake battalions were inspected by General Shute and the Commander-in-Chief, Field Marshal Sir Douglas Haig. On 21 November they were on the road again, marching ever westward, eleven miles to Domqueur on the first day, five miles to Oneux on the second day, ten miles to Grand Laviers, just west of Abbeville, on the third day. Finally, on 24 November the battalion marched the final thirteen miles to their destination, Le Champ Neuf, on the north bank of the mouth of the River Somme. The Nelsons were now on the English Channel some fifty miles behind the front on the Ancre, having marched some fifty-five miles in seven marching days. The last day's march had been the longest and the 189 Brigade War Diary noted that

> The march was a long one, most units not reaching their destination until 3pm, but on this day less men fell out than on any of the preceding days although the march was further than any of the others.

From 25 November Le Champ Neuf was to be the Nelson's training base for the next seven weeks over the turn of the year. The whole brigade was based in the area west of the town of Rue for rest, reorganization and training. On the first day Nelson Battalion received a reinforcement draft of 143 ORs, with a further ninety-two on the following day. On 26 November the battalion commanders, adjutants and company commanders gathered in the school-house at St Firmin, where Brigadier General Phillips held a brigade conference to learn the lessons from the recent battle and to carry these forward as the

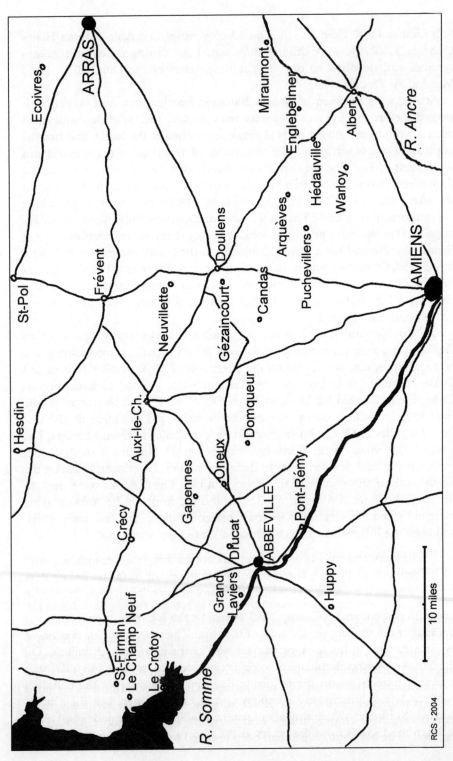

7. Picardy – Pas de Calais – Somme.

RCS - 2004

10 miles

principles to be followed in the training period just beginning. The last days of November were spent in training: bayonet fighting, arms drill, ceremonial drill, route marches and lectures filled the forenoon of each day. The afternoons were all devoted to compulsory games. On 30 November Brigadier General Phillips inspected the battalion transport and billets.

With the death of Lieutenant Colonel Burge in action, Lieutenant Commander Edward Nelson had been appointed to command Nelson Battalion and he was promoted to Commander on 14 November. His place as 2i/c was taken by Lieutenant Leonard Spain who was made an acting lieutenant commander on the same date. Sub Lieutenant James Cowan was appointed the new Adjutant in place of Sub Lieutenant John Emerson who had died alongside his battalion commander at Beaucourt. In early December Commander Nelson acted as Brigade Commander while Brigadier General Phillips took ten days leave in England.

Lieutenant Colonel Burge's death in action was a grievous loss not just to Nelson Battalion and the RND but also to the Royal Marines. It is clear from letters that he wrote to his family that 'Nob' was a man with a great sense of humour who saw it his duty to jolly his men along when times where hard. He said of himself that he had a 'semi-automatic, bogus cheeriosity' but, in truth, there does not seem to have been much that was bogus about the man. His obituary in *The Globe and Laurel* recalled with affection that:

> In the wardroom he was always a most popular messmate, the life and soul of whatever was going on and especially to the fore in any theatricals, for which he had great talent . . . .. Those privileged to see some of his letters were intensely interested in the vivid descriptions and humorous stories of the striking scenes of those months, when he seemed always cheery and able to see the humorous side of every hardship . . . a valuable and zealous officer . . . the very best of messmates and cheeriest of companions. His thoughtfulness for the welfare of others made him a general favourite.'[186]

As the year moved into December, the comprehensive training programme continued. The Nelson War Diary records company drill, specialist training, arms drill, bayonet fighting, route marches, firing practice, wiring, advancing by waves and taking up positions in the dark. Practice trenches were dug in the training area and used for attack and defence. Meanwhile, new drafts of reinforcements continued to arrive from England, twenty-seven ORs on 1 December, forty-three on 5 December, 151 on 14/15 December and sixteen more on 27 December. By the end of December Nelson Battalion had received a transfusion of more than 470 new ratings. These late-1916 drafts included the first ratings entered into the RND from the Army under the newly introduced system of conscription – ratings whose service number had an 'R' prefix.[187] The battalion, which had been reduced to a fighting strength of four lieutenants and seven sub lieutenants, had also received eighteen new officers to replace those killed and wounded on the Ancre.[188] This draft included five newly commissioned men who were the first Nelson officers to have passed through one of the Officer Cadet Battalions which had been set up across the country. Prior to this, new officers for the RND were sent direct to Crystal Palace for their officer training. Former ratings continued to be a good proportion of newly-commissioned officers.

Among the new officers was an outstanding man who would rise rapidly to become one of the heroes of the RND, Lieutenant Archibald Buckle. Mobilized as an RNVR London Division petty officer on the outbreak of the war, he had served at Antwerp with Drake Battalion before being commissioned in December 1914. His fighting career as an officer was about to start with Nelson Battalion and he would be awarded the Distinguished Service Order on no less than four occasions and be Mentioned in Despatches four times before the end of the war.[181] His first contact with Nelson Battalion was in August 1916 when he acted as the Conducting Officer for a draft of Nelson ratings from England to France.

Sporting activities continued to break up the training routine. Hood Battalion took the brigade cross-country championship despite a Nelson runner being first man across the finishing line. Nelson also made it to the brigade soccer final at St Firmin, but were beaten by Drake.

This month also saw the bravery of officers and ratings in the November battle being recognized, with citations for Military Medals being presented to Leading Seaman Fox and Able Seaman McLeod on 13 December and for the Military Cross to Sub Lieutenant Gardner a week later. On a sadder note, a Court of Enquiry was convened on 27 December to investigate the accidental shooting of Able Seaman W.J. Bell. He had been shot in the chest in the course of the battle on 13 November and had died of his wounds on 30 November.

The low point of the whole of 1916 must, however, have been the trial by court martial of Sub Lieutenant Edwin Dyett on 26 December – Boxing Day. He was charged with 'deserting His Majesty's Service' on 13 November 1916 during the Battle of the Ancre. An alternative, lesser charge of 'Conduct to the prejudice of good order and Military discipline' was also raised. The trial, under the presidency of the GOC 18th Division RA, was held at Nelson Battalion HQ at Le Champ Neuf. The members of the court were mostly Army officers but included one RND officer from 4/Bedfords of 190 Brigade. The naval member of the court was a major of Marines from 2/RMLI. The Prosecutor was one of Dyett's fellow Nelson officers, Sub Lieutenant Herbert Strickland. Dyett's defence (such as it was) was provided by Sub Lieutenant Cecil V. Trevanion from Hawke Battalion. Witnesses for the Prosecution from Nelson Battalion included Commander Nelson, Lieutenants Truscott and Dangerfield and Sub Lieutenant Ernest Gardner

The background to and progress of the controversial trial of Sub

Lieutenant Dyett have been covered in great detail in books by Leonard Sellers[190] and others. The story will not be re-told here. Suffice to say that Dyett was ordered forward from the battalion reserve and, in circumstances of admitted confusion, claimed to get lost. Thereafter his movements were to the rear of the battle area and he played no part in the combat operations. He was found guilty of desertion and sentenced to death but with a recommendation by the Court for mercy. That recommendation was supported by GOC RND but not by higher commanders. On 2 January 1917 Field Marshal Haig confirmed the death sentence. On 3 January the proceedings and confirmed sentence of the court martial were forwarded to the Commanding Officer of Nelson Battalion, together with instructions to inform Sub Lieutenant Dyett of the outcome. However, records show that Commander Nelson had taken himself off to England on leave on 28 December, leaving Lieutenant Commander Spain in acting command. To proceed on leave on the day after a court martial had sentenced one of his junior officers to death might be considered an extraordinary display of self-interest (or indifference) on the part of a Commanding Officer. Commander Nelson did not return to the battalion from his New Year break until 9 January. In his absence Sub Lieutenant Edwin Dyett was shot at dawn on Friday, 5 January 1917 in the nearby village of St Firmin. His body now rests in the CWGC cemetery at Le Crotoy.[191] Opinion will continue to be divided about the penalty inflicted on Dyett and, indeed, on all the death sentences in the First World War. The view through the telescope of hindsight is bound to be distorted. It is clear that Edwin Dyett's conduct during the Battle of the Ancre was far below that which might have been expected of him. The verdict of his peers, who tried him and had themselves been subject to similar battle strains, was clear and it ill behoves the modern reviewer to question the values they applied and the judgements that they handed down nearly a century ago. Some shortcomings in the justice handed down by the Army have been highlighted and it has also been suggested that the execution of Edwin Dyett may have been illegal because the approval of the Admiralty was not sought. This author cannot fault the verdict of Dyett's court martial. The sentence was that demanded by military law in 1916 (the RND was subject to the Army Act) and was reviewed and confirmed at the highest level.

At the end of 1916 it could truly be said that Nelson Battalion, indeed the whole RND, had been transformed into the 'real soldiers' of the title of Chapter 11 and had, as in the title of this Chapter, forged a reputation as a fighting force of great skill, guts and determination in the face of daunting opposition. The scale and courage of their advance on the Ancre was inspiring and the number of prisoners taken there was the greatest since the beginning of trench warfare in late 1914. This was probably a great surprise to their divisional GOC, General Shute, whose earlier low opinion of the RND had scarcely been hidden. For Nelson Battalion this reputation had been earned at the cost of 162 officers and ORs dead and perhaps 250 wounded since arriving in France seven months earlier. As at Gallipoli in 1915–16, the numbers of Nelson Battalion dead during the months with the BEF in 1916 were the highest of the naval battalions of the RND, although Anson and Hawke, who had shared with Nelson the attentions of the German machine-gunners in the strongpoint in front of Beaucourt, suffered comparable losses.

NELSONS KILLED, MORTALLY WOUNDED OR DIED OF DISEASE FROM 16 OCTOBER TO 31 DECEMBER 1916, INCLUDING THE BATTLE OF THE ANCRE

RANK/RATING NUMBER	NAME DATE	CAUSE	BURIAL / MEMORIAL	1914*
AB TZ/1436	SCOTT, G 16/10/16	KIA	AUCHONVILLERS MILITARY CEMETERY	
AB SZ/442	BISHOP, JE 22/10/16	KIA	HAMEL MILITARY CEMETERY, BEAUMONT-HAMEL	
AB LZ/4359	LAYZELL, JW 23/10/16	KIA	HAMEL MILITARY CEMETERY, BEAUMONT-HAMEL	
AB CZ/4624	McGARTLAND, W 23/10/16	KIA	HAMEL MILITARY CEMETERY, BEAUMONT-HAMEL	
AB TZ/46	ROBSON, F 23/10/16	KIA	HAMEL MILITARY CEMETERY, BEAUMONT-HAMEL	
AB TZ/1833	BECKHAM, R 23/10/16	KIA	HAMEL MILITARY CEMETERY, BEAUMONT-HAMEL	
AB WZ/845	GILLARD, EW 23/10/16	KIA	HAMEL MILITARY CEMETERY, BEAUMONT-HAMEL	
AB LZ/4063	HINSON, A 23/10/16	DOW	VARENNES MILITARY CEMETERY	
AB BZ/3514	WORRALL, W 24/10/16	DOW	COUIN BRITISH CEMETERY	
AB KX/79	PATTERSON, H 10/11/16	KIA	KNIGHTSBRIDGE CEMETERY, MESNIL-MARTINSART	1914*
AB TZ/339	McKENRY, J 10/11/16	DOW	VARENNES MILITARY CEMETERY	
AB CZ/4032	ADAMS, J 13/11/16	KIA	ANCRE BRITISH CEMETERY, BEAUMONT-HAMEL	
AB TZ/8514	BARNFIELD, F 13/11/16	KIA	ANCRE BRITISH CEMETERY, BEAUMONT-HAMEL	
AB M6/189	BILLINGTON, JW 13/11/16	KIA	ANCRE BRITISH CEMETERY, BEAUMONT-HAMEL	1914*
AB CZ/5216	BUCHAN, D 13/11/16	KIA	ANCRE BRITISH CEMETERY, BEAUMONT-HAMEL	
LT COL	BURGE, NO 13/11/16	KIA	HAMEL MILITARY CEMETERY, BEAUMONT-HAMEL	1914*

Rank/Rating Number	Name Date	Cause	Burial / Memorial	1914*
LS CZ/3510	BURT, AB 13/11/16	KIA	ANCRE BRITISH CEMETERY, BEAUMONT-HAMEL	
AB TZ/6626	CADMAN, J 13/11/16	KIA	ANCRE BRITISH CEMETERY, BEAUMONT-HAMEL	
AB CZ/5196	CAMPBELL, D 13/11/16	KIA	ANCRE BRITISH CEMETERY, BEAUMONT-HAMEL	
SUB LT	CASHMORE, EW 13/11/16	KIA	ANCRE BRITISH CEMETERY, BEAUMONT-HAMEL	
AB C1/2530	CATTRAN, EC 13/11/16	KIA	ANCRE BRITISH CEMETERY, BEAUMONT-HAMEL	1914*
PO CZ/3102	CHALMERS, H 13/11/16	KIA	ANCRE BRITISH CEMETERY, BEAUMONT-HAMEL	
AB WZ/948	CHARLES, WH 13/11/16	KIA	ANCRE BRITISH CEMETERY, BEAUMONT-HAMEL	
AB WZ/127	CHARLES, WJ 13/11/16	KIA	ANCRE BRITISH CEMETERY, BEAUMONT-HAMEL	
PO CZ/1734	CONNOR, J 13/11/16	KIA	ANCRE BRITISH CEMETERY, BEAUMONT-HAMEL	
AB TZ/137	COUCH, A 13/11/16	KIA	ANCRE BRITISH CEMETERY, BEAUMONT-HAMEL	
AB CZ/2473	DAVIDSON, R 13/11/16	KIA	ANCRE BRITISH CEMETERY, BEAUMONT-HAMEL	
PO M3/203	DAVIS, KB 13/11/16	KIA	ANCRE BRITISH CEMETERY, BEAUMONT-HAMEL	1914*
SUB LT	EMERSON, JH 13/11/16	KIA	ANCRE BRITISH CEMETERY, BEAUMONT-HAMEL	
AB BZ/1280	EVERETT, WB 13/11/16	KIA	ANCRE BRITISH CEMETERY, BEAUMONT-HAMEL	
AB CZ/536	FARQUHARSON, JC 13/11/16	KIA	ANCRE BRITISH CEMETERY, BEAUMONT-HAMEL	
AB KX/38	FERGUSON, R 13/11/16	KIA	ANCRE BRITISH CEMETERY, BEAUMONT-HAMEL	1914*

RANK/RATING	NAME		
NUMBER	DATE	CAUSE	BURIAL / MEMORIAL

LS	FLETCHER, JM		
CZ/495	13/11/16	KIA	ANCRE BRITISH CEMETERY, BEAUMONT-HAMEL
AB	FLETT, W		
CZ/1738	13/11/16	KIA	ANCRE BRITISH CEMETERY, BEAUMONT-HAMEL
AB	FOSTER, J		
TZ/5915	13/11/16	KIA	ANCRE BRITISH CEMETERY, BEAUMONT-HAMEL
SUB LT	GARDNER, LS		
	13/11/16	KIA	ANCRE BRITISH CEMETERY, BEAUMONT-HAMEL
PO	GRAHAM, GS		
CZ/4271	13/11/16	KIA	ANCRE BRITISH CEMETERY, BEAUMONT-HAMEL
AB	GRIFFIN, S		
LZ/1620	13/11/16	KIA	ANCRE BRITISH CEMETERY, BEAUMONT-HAMEL
AB	HARLAND, HC		
TZ/4382	13/11/16	KIA	ANCRE BRITISH CEMETERY, BEAUMONT-HAMEL
AB	HAY, R		
CZ/4182	13/11/16	KIA	ANCRE BRITISH CEMETERY, BEAUMONT-HAMEL
AB	HENDERSON, J		
CZ/7405	13/11/16	KIA	ANCRE BRITISH CEMETERY, BEAUMONT-HAMEL
AB	HOLLOWAY, E		
TZ/6634	13/11/16	KIA	ANCRE BRITISH CEMETERY, BEAUMONT-HAMEL
AB	HUNTER, D		
CZ/4202	13/11/16	KIA	ANCRE BRITISH CEMETERY, BEAUMONT-HAMEL
AB	HUNTER, J		
CZ/4978	13/11/16	KIA	ANCRE BRITISH CEMETERY, BEAUMONT-HAMEL
AB	HUNTLEY, CR		
TZ/3290	13/11/16	KIA	ANCRE BRITISH CEMETERY, BEAUMONT-HAMEL
AB	JEPSON, T		
TZ/5976	13/11/16	KIA	ANCRE BRITISH CEMETERY, BEAUMONT-HAMEL
LS	JOHNSON, EJ		
TZ/4295	13/11/16	KIA	ANCRE BRITISH CEMETERY, BEAUMONT-HAMEL
AB	JONES, JE		
WZ/315	13/11/16	KIA	ANCRE BRITISH CEMETERY, BEAUMONT-HAMEL

RANK/RATING NUMBER	NAME DATE	CAUSE	BURIAL / MEMORIAL
AB CZ/4793	KEMP, D 13/11/16	KIA	ANCRE BRITISH CEMETERY, BEAUMONT-HAMEL
SUB LT	LANGSTRETH, E 13/11/16	KIA	ANCRE BRITISH CEMETERY, BEAUMONT-HAMEL
LS MZ/306	LAURIE, J 13/11/16	KIA	ANCRE BRITISH CEMETERY, BEAUMONT-HAMEL
AB CZ/5622	LYONS, J 13/11/16	KIA	ANCRE BRITISH CEMETERY, BEAUMONT-HAMEL
AB CZ/4558	MacKENZIE, AG 13/11/16	KIA	ANCRE BRITISH CEMETERY, BEAUMONT-HAMEL
AB CZ/4974	McGOWAN, T 13/11/16	KIA	ANCRE BRITISH CEMETERY, BEAUMONT-HAMEL
AB CZ/4248	McSAVENEY, J 13/11/16	KIA	ANCRE BRITISH CEMETERY, BEAUMONT-HAMEL
AB TZ/5181	MERRYWEATHER, WP 13/11/16	KIA	ANCRE BRITISH CEMETERY, BEAUMONT-HAMEL
AB BZ/790	MORRISH, GH 13/11/16	KIA	ANCRE BRITISH CEMETERY, BEAUMONT-HAMEL
AB TZ/3656	PARKER, T 13/11/16	KIA	ANCRE BRITISH CEMETERY, BEAUMONT-HAMEL
AB CZ/6358	PATERSON, JB 13/11/16	KIA	ANCRE BRITISH CEMETERY, BEAUMONT-HAMEL
SUB LT	REDDICK, GA 13/11/16	KIA	ANCRE BRITISH CEMETERY, BEAUMONT-HAMEL
LS TZ/4294	RENNER, WJ 13/11/16	KIA	ANCRE BRITISH CEMETERY, BEAUMONT-HAMEL
AB TZ/8945	RICE, P 13/11/16	KIA	ANCRE BRITISH CEMETERY, BEAUMONT-HAMEL
AB BZ/3338	RICHARDSON, H 13/11/16	KIA	ANCRE BRITISH CEMETERY, BEAUMONT-HAMEL
AB MZ/293	ROWEN, AH 13/11/16	KIA	ANCRE BRITISH CEMETERY, BEAUMONT-HAMEL

RANK/RATING	NAME		
AB WZ/1599	SERRETTE, WB 13/11/16	KIA	ANCRE BRITISH CEMETERY, BEAUMONT-HAMEL
AB KW/247	SKIPPINS, CW 13/11/16	KIA	ANCRE BRITISH CEMETERY, BEAUMONT-HAMEL
AB TZ/5335	SMILES, J 13/11/16	KIA	ANCRE BRITISH CEMETERY, BEAUMONT-HAMEL
AB LZ/698	SMITH, L 13/11/16	KIA	ANCRE BRITISH CEMETERY, BEAUMONT-HAMEL
SUB LT	SQUIRES, EW 13/11/16	KIA	ANCRE BRITISH CEMETERY, BEAUMONT-HAMEL
AB TZ/4327	STOCKS, JE 13/11/16	KIA	ANCRE BRITISH CEMETERY, BEAUMONT-HAMEL
AB BZ/4015	TEBBUTT, F 13/11/16	KIA	ANCRE BRITISH CEMETERY, BEAUMONT-HAMEL
LS TZ/1777	TUCKER, EJ 13/11/16	KIA	ANCRE BRITISH CEMETERY, BEAUMONT-HAMEL
LS TZ/2387	WALKER, JH 13/11/16	KIA	ANCRE BRITISH CEMETERY, BEAUMONT-HAMEL
AB BZ/4302	WANN, P 13/11/16	KIA	ANCRE BRITISH CEMETERY, BEAUMONT-HAMEL
AB TZ/8537	WEATHERILL, A 13/11/16	KIA	ANCRE BRITISH CEMETERY, BEAUMONT-HAMEL
AB TZ/5256	WILLIAMSON, A 13/11/16	KIA	ANCRE BRITISH CEMETERY, BEAUMONT-HAMEL
AB TZ/3580	WILLIS, M 13/11/16	KIA	ANCRE BRITISH CEMETERY, BEAUMONT-HAMEL
AB SZ/45	WYATT, S 13/11/16	KIA	ANCRE BRITISH CEMETERY, BEAUMONT-HAMEL
PO CZ/2016	McDONALD, D 13/11/16	KIA	CAYEUX MILITARY CEMETERY
AB CZ/5051	PATRICK, W 13/11/16	DOW	MARTINSART BRITISH CEMETERY
SUB LT	ALLDRIDGE, DRGP 13/11/16	KIA	THIEPVAL MEMORIAL

RANK/RATING	NAME		
NUMBER	DATE	CAUSE	BURIAL / MEMORIAL
AB	ANDERSON, T		
TZ/2486	13/11/16	KIA	THIEPVAL MEMORIAL
AB	AXE, GF		
TZ/4575	13/11/16	KIA	THIEPVAL MEMORIAL
SUB LT	BALL, AL	13/11/16	
		KIA	THIEPVAL MEMORIAL
LS	BELL, S		
TZ/223	13/11/16	KIA	THIEPVAL MEMORIAL
AB	BOYLE, B		
CZ/4611	13/11/16	KIA	THIEPVAL MEMORIAL
AB	BREAKWELL, L		
TZ/5358	13/11/16	KIA	THIEPVAL MEMORIAL
AB	BUTTERS, R		
CZ/3073	13/11/16	KIA	THIEPVAL MEMORIAL
AB	CALDWELL, R		
CZ/5045	13/11/16	KIA	THIEPVAL MEMORIAL
AB	CARR, CTG		
TZ/5182	13/11/16	KIA	THIEPVAL MEMORIAL
AB	COOK, A		
TZ/3473	13/11/16	KIA	THIEPVAL MEMORIAL
AB	CUNNINGHAM, D		
CZ/5450	13/11/16	KIA	THIEPVAL MEMORIAL
AB	CUNNINGHAM, J		
CZ/1034	13/11/16	KIA	THIEPVAL MEMORIAL
AB	DAVIS, WC		
LZ/4406	13/11/16	KIA	THIEPVAL MEMORIAL
AB	DAVISON, RW		
TZ/1326	13/11/16	KIA	THIEPVAL MEMORIAL
SUB LT	FRANCIS, D		
	13/11/16	KIA	THIEPVAL MEMORIAL
AB	GIBBONS, J		
TZ/78	13/11/16	KIA	THIEPVAL MEMORIAL
AB	GRAHAM, WL		
TZ/3302	13/11/16	KIA	THIEPVAL MEMORIAL
AB	HALL, H		
TZ/5103	13/11/16	KIA	THIEPVAL MEMORIAL
LS	HATTERSLEY, F		
KW/272	13/11/16	KIA	THIEPVAL MEMORIAL
AB	HENDRY, A		
CZ/3104	13/11/16	KIA	THIEPVAL MEMORIAL
AB	HENRY, DA		
LZ/4213	13/11/16	KIA	THIEPVAL MEMORIAL
AB	HODGE, RT		
CZ/4053	13/11/16	KIA	THIEPVAL MEMORIAL
AB	HODGES, GWF		
SZ/385	13/11/16	KIA	THIEPVAL MEMORIAL

RANK/RATING NUMBER	NAME DATE	CAUSE	BURIAL / MEMORIAL
LS TZ/1928	HUGHES, E 13/11/16	KIA	THIEPVAL MEMORIAL
AB CZ/4114	HUTTON, D 13/11/16	KIA	THIEPVAL MEMORIAL
AB TZ/4229	IRVING, JR 13/11/16	KIA	THIEPVAL MEMORIAL
AB TZ/5209	JENNISON, H 13/11/16	KIA	THIEPVAL MEMORIAL
AB TZ/365	LAMBERT, GF 13/11/16	KIA	THIEPVAL MEMORIAL
AB CZ/2232	LILLIE, WGD 13/11/16	KIA	THIEPVAL MEMORIAL
AB CZ/394	MacMASTER, H 13/11/16	KIA	THIEPVAL MEMORIAL
AB TZ/7542	MARTIN, H 13/11/16	KIA	THIEPVAL MEMORIAL
AB TZ/7093	McAULIFFE, E 13/11/16	KIA	THIEPVAL MEMORIAL
AB TZ/3365	PEEL, S 13/11/16	KIA	THIEPVAL MEMORIAL
AB BZ/792	PRICE, RP 13/11/16	KIA	THIEPVAL MEMORIAL
AB WZ/1404	REES, T 13/11/16	DOW	THIEPVAL MEMORIAL
AB TZ/2230	SANDERSON, W 13/11/16	KIA	THIEPVAL MEMORIAL
AB TZ/4366	SCHOFIELD, JE 13/11/16	KIA	THIEPVAL MEMORIAL
AB CZ/370	SIMPSON, A 13/11/16	KIA	THIEPVAL MEMORIAL
AB WZ/1502	SPARKES, CO 13/11/16	KIA	THIEPVAL MEMORIAL
AB MZ/331	THOMSON, W 13/11/16	KIA	THIEPVAL MEMORIAL
AB LZ/4171	TRUBSHOE, A 13/11/16	KIA	THIEPVAL MEMORIAL
AB CZ/7290	WILLIAMSON, L 13/11/16	KIA	THIEPVAL MEMORIAL
AB TZ/2617	WOOD, GP 13/11/16	KIA	THIEPVAL MEMORIAL
LS LZ/120	MARDEN, LG 14/11/16	DOW	PUCHEVILLERS BRITISH CEMETERY
AB CZ/4307	SANDERSON, D 14/11/16	DOW	PUCHEVILLERS BRITISH CEMETERY
AB CZ/6377	STEWART, A 14/11/16	KIA	THIEPVAL MEMORIAL

RANK/RATING NUMBER	NAME DATE	CAUSE	BURIAL / MEMORIAL
AB WZ/1474	WILLIAMS, ET 14/11/16	KIA	THIEPVAL MEMORIAL
AB TZ/7294	BRADSHAW, GA 14/11/16	KIA	VARENNES MILITARY CEMETERY
AB TZ/8118	DICK, JT 15/11/16	KIA	ANCRE BRITISH CEMETERY, BEAUMONT-HAMEL
AB TZ/7435	GRAHAM, G 15/11/16	KIA	ANCRE BRITISH CEMETERY, BEAUMONT-HAMEL
AB TZ/4481	STABLES, J 15/11/16	DOW	CONTAY BRITISH CEMETERY
AB CZ/3724	MacFARLANE, A 15/11/16	DOW	VARENNES MILITARY CEMETERY
AB WZ/1327	BOWDEN, WG 17/11/16	DOW	CONTAY BRITISH CEMETERY
AB CZ/5094	AINSLIE, W 18/11/16	DOW	CONTAY BRITISH CEMETERY
AB WZ/1342	LEWIS, T 18/11/16	DOW	CONTAY BRITISH CEMETERY
LS BZ/662	ROWE, CH 18/11/16	DOW	CONTAY BRITISH CEMETERY
PO TZ/59	LEGG, W 18/11/16	DOW	ST SEVER CEMETERY EXTENSION, ROUEN
AB CZ/6585	KENDALL, R 19/11/16	DOW	ST SEVER CEMETERY EXTENSION, ROUEN
LS CZ/1421	JOHNSTONE, S 20/11/16	DOW	ST SEVER CEMETERY EXTENSION, ROUEN
AB WZ/383	FOWLER, A 21/11/16	DOW	ETAPLES MILITARY CEMETERY
AB CZ/1436	BELL, WJ 30/11/16	ACCIDENT	BOISGUILLAUME COMMUNAL CEMETERY
AB CZ/2641	MALCOLM, A 30/11/16	DOW	ETAPLES MILITARY CEMETERY
AB WZ/1258	MORRIS, A 01/12/16	DOW	BOISGUILLAUME COMMUNAL CEMETERY
AB BZ/737	BENNETTS, H 04/12/16	DOW	ST SEVER CEMETERY EXTENSION, ROUEN
AB TZ/5757	EMMS, GT 08/12/16	SICK	ETAPLES MILITARY CEMETERY
AB CZ/2331	WYPER, J 20/12/16	DOW	GLASGOW (EASTWOOD & SIGHTHILL) CEMETERIES
AB TZ/7530	SCANLON, JV 22/12/16	SICK	LE CROTOY COMMUNAL CEMETERY

13

BEYOND BEAUCOURT – THE ATTACKS TOWARDS MIRAUMONT:

1 JANUARY – 19 MARCH 1917.

The new year saw training continue at Le Champ Neuf for another two weeks in dry, cold weather. The individual, specialist and company training came together on the training areas at St Firmin and Vercourt in practice attacks at battalion and brigade level on 2 and 3 January. The end of the training period saw troops being re-briefed on trench discipline and routines and undergoing gas helmet drill as they prepared to return to the front line on the Ancre. The routine progress of this training had been interrupted on Friday 5 January when a firing squad of Nelson ratings was assembled for the execution of Sub Lieutenant Dyett at St Firmin. It is certain that this was a task to be avoided if at all possible. Dyett was tied to a stake, his eyes were bandaged and at 7.30 am the men of the Nelson fired from a trench at the identity disc over his heart.

A week later Nelson Battalion was on the road again, the return to the front beginning with a march of some sixteen miles to billets in the village of Drucat, just north of Abbeville. The weather broke on this first day of the march and it was a wretched plod to the east in heavy rain. The march continued over the next four days with overnight stops in Gapennes and Candas (two nights), arriving at Rubempré on 17 January having covered over fifty miles on the roads. Heavy snowfalls and gales had dogged each day of the march making every mile a miserable, cold experience. On the following morning motor buses arrived to move the Nelsons to the Ancre, taking them on to Lancashire Dump on the eastern fringe of Aveluy Wood, south of Mesnil. This base was on the western bank of the Ancre about three miles behind the front line at Beaucourt. From there the battalion marched straight into the line, taking over the Beaucourt left sub-sector from three battalions of 32 Infantry Brigade. That same afternoon this brigade had executed an attack towards Puisieux from what were to be the Nelson's lines and, hence, they found themselves relieving a large, mixed force of 6/Yorkshire, 6/Yorkshire & Lancashire, and 9/West Yorkshire Regiments. To add to the confusion, the relief was late because the buses bringing the Nelsons forward had been slow and there was great difficulty in locating the forward posts in the frozen quagmire which constituted the British front line. Eventually, after a very long day of travel and frustration, Nelson Battalion completed the relief at 2.00 am on 19 January.

The situation on the front beyond Beaucourt was, to say the least, uncomfortable. The forward posts were isolated shell-holes in the bottom of a valley. The ground had been rendered solid by the hard, biting frosts which had gripped the battlefield for over four weeks. The field was swept by German shell fire and any movement by day was immediately observed from the high ground on the ridge ahead, making provision of rations, indeed any daylight movement, a hazardous undertaking. The troops 'were condemned merely to freeze in silence till relief came' observed Jerrold.[192]

The battalion's return to the front line was marked throughout by heavy German shelling during which the men worked to push the forward posts further out. Two able seamen were killed on the first day in the line. Consolidation of the outposts and the front line system continued over the next three days. As heavy German artillery bombardment continued, with retaliatory British shelling passing overhead, the vigilance of one outpost near the Puisieux Road resulted in a German patrol of two men being shot. (The 189 Brigade War Diary describes them as 'two of the enemy who had apparently lost their way.') It was ascertained that they belonged to the 3rd Bavarian Reserve Regiment. The next day a German mail bag was found near the front line. The Germans were observed ahead in the Puisieux Road valley at ranges of between 200 and 1,000 yards. On 22 January, with artillery exchanges continuing apace, resulting in the deaths of six men, the Nelsons were relieved by their old friends from the Hawke Battalion. The relief was complete at 11.00 pm and Nelson Battalion moved back into the support lines as the brigade reserve. Their four days in the line had cost them fourteen dead, ten in action and four of wounds, including the first three of the conscripted 'R' ratings to die.

Five days were spent in the Beaucourt support lines and the whole battalion was engaged in providing working parties and carrying parties, those not so employed working on the maintenance of the reserve trenches. A full platoon was sent back to Varennes to assist at the casualty clearing station. On 27 January the Dublin Fusiliers of 190 Brigade moved into the support lines and completed their relief of Nelson Battalion by 8.00 pm. The Nelsons immediately marched, through the dark and cold of a winter's night, ten miles back to billets at Forceville, via Lancashire Dump, Bouzincourt and Hédauville, arriving well after midnight.

The fighting strength of officers in early February, as Nelson Battalion prepared for a large-scale battle for the first time in 1917, was:-

Commanding Officer	Commander Edward W. Nelson, RNVR
2nd in Command	Captain Houghton Griffiths (Army)
Adjutant	Sub Lieutenant James Cowan

Lieutenant RNVR

Cyril A. Truscott	Leonard Spain
Bernard Dangerfield MC	Archibald W. Buckle

Sub Lieutenant RNVR

Percival Batchelor	William D. Walker
Herbert S. Strickland	Ernest V.G. Gardner MC
Arthur P. Taylor	George W. Bloomfield
Arthur F. Wolfe	William A. Bowler
Dennis S. Brown	William Wellwood
Louis F. Hunt	Cecil A. Clerk
Ernest E. Wicks	Horace E. Fair

James A. Woodgate *[attached 189 Bde LTM Batty]*
Kenneth A. Hucklebridge *[attached 189 Bde LTM Batty]*

Quartermaster	Lieutenant James A. Gates, RMLI
Surgeon	Ernest F. Cox RN

Already the officer reinforcements of mid-December had been whittled down and the battalion was again below complement. Within a month of joining five of the new officers were in hospital or had been invalided home[193] and one had been transferred to the Army.[194] The 'old guard', who had fought with Nelson Battalion at Gallipoli were now down to four: Commander Nelson and Lieutenants Truscott, Dangerfield and Spain. One of the new officers, Sub Lieutenant Wolfe, had served at Gallipoli as a rating. Commander Nelson was now the only RNVR officer in command of a naval battalion of 189 Brigade, Army officers commanding the other three. On 18 January Lieutenant Spain, who had been acting as battalion 2i/c, was also replaced by an Army officer, Captain Houghton Griffiths. Commissioned from the militia in 1907, he had previously served with the Manchester Regiment and the West India Regiment and in Sierra Leone with the West Africa Regiment in 1914. He had fought later with 2nd Rajput Light Infantry in Mesopotamia, where he had been wounded.[195] Several Army officers were appointed to the naval battalions of the RND during General Shute's tenure as GOC, presumably to render more professional his command of amateur sailors-would-be-soldiers. Captain (Temp/Major) H.W. Barker, of 6/West Yorkshire Regiment, was also attached to Nelson Battalion in February. Senior Army NCOs were also posted in, often as Company Sergeant Majors.[196]

The RND was now working towards its next major engagement. This would be an attack on the trenches to which the Germans had retreated after the loss of Beaucourt. These were known as the Puisieux and River trenches and they ran up and across a ridge north of the River Ancre, opposite the south bank town of Grandcourt. These German positions commanded the British ground and straddled the line of advance east towards Miraumont. There were only four days at Forceville to prepare: personal kit had to be issued or mended, anti-gas respirators were tested at the Divisional Gas School, company training was carried out. On the last day of January the battalion was inspected by General Phillips and everyone had a session in the baths. At 11.00 am on 1 February the battalion paraded and marched back to the front line, stopping only for a midday meal and for tea. The winter of 1916–17 was the coldest of the war so far and the march back to the trenches was executed in weather that was bright and sunny but very cold and with a hard frost underfoot. The Nelsons were installed in the front line trenches by 10.30 pm, with 'D' Company forward, in outposts that were just frozen, water-filled shell-holes, and the other three companies in support. One hour later the first casualty occurred when a British shell fell short into one of the Nelson outposts, killing a junior rating.[197] The artillery batteries were informed. At midnight an artillery test was executed: 'Test F' required the laying down, on demand, of one round of shrapnel and this was achieved by a battery of 223 Brigade RFA in 3½ minutes.

Test barrages were laid down by the RND's supporting artillery during the evening of 2 February and the Germans replied in kind. That night saw final preparations for the attack, which was to be carried out by Hood Battalion on the right and Hawke Battalion on the left. Nelson Battalion was to be in close support. Their principal tasks were to move forward behind the attacking battalions, two Nelson companies consolidating a line of outposts running north from the Bois d'Hollande to a south-west to north-east trending trench called Artillery Alley. They would be reinforcements for the Hood and Hawke, if called for. The other two Nelson companies would move to the left flank, with one company securing Artillery Alley and back along that trench to the Puisieux Road. They would thus form a defensive flank on the left, northern boundary of the brigade's battlefield. However, the 189 Brigade orders did not call for the Nelson company in Artillery Alley to move as far forward as the junction with Puisieux Trench. To ready their positions for the assault, the Nelsons spent the night connecting existing trenches and outposts and digging new ones. On the following day, 3 February, German artillery was very active and casualties were sustained in the forward posts. After dark the assaulting battalions moved forward to their jumping-off line, just 300 yards from the German's forward Puisieux Trench. Everyone was in place by 10.40 pm and it seems that this had been achieved without the Germans' noticing. General Phillips described the conditions, in his Report of Operations, as being 'a full moon and a slight ground mist. It was freezing hard and the ground was like iron and covered with snow'.[198]

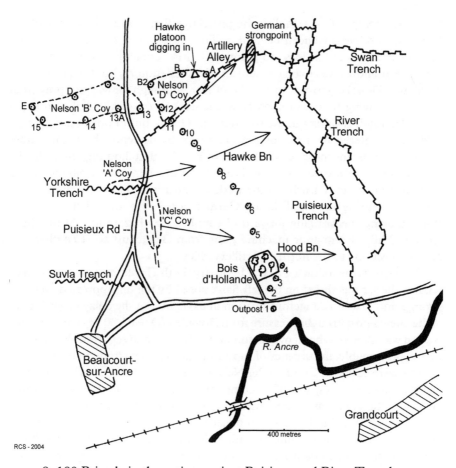

8. 189 Brigade in the action against Puisieux and River Trenches.

The British barrage went in precisely at 11.00 pm on 3 February and with great accuracy. The Hood and Hawke moved forward in a night assault on the German trenches and two companies ('A' and 'C') of the Nelson moved forward behind them to occupy the line of outposts north of the Bois d'Hollande ready to give support, if needed. The other two companies moved to consolidate the northern (left) flanking position along and to the north of Artillery Alley back across the Puisieux Road. The major problems encountered in the battle were caused by gaps which opened up between Hawke and Nelson on the left flank and (more seriously) between Hood and Hawke on the centre-right. These gaps allowed the enemy to move back and occupy, or remain in, some positions. The Nelsons encountered this problem near the eastern end of Artillery Alley. Here the Germans established a troublesome fire position which could bring machine guns to bear on both the

Nelsons, attempting to establish the protective flank, and on the rear of the Hawkes, who had advanced beyond it. The reason for the failure to consolidate the left flank at this forward point, with firm contact between Nelson and Hawke Battalions, was to be the subject of a later enquiry, but the findings are unknown. Douglas Jerrold, (a Hawke officer, although he was not present at this battle having been wounded at Beaucourt) spoke of a verbal plan being misunderstood, resulting in Nelson Battalion being out of position,[199] but no evidence is offered for this opinion. The post-battle report by Commander Nelson records an unexpected platoon of Hawke Battalion digging-in in the middle of the Nelson positions, well to the rear of where the battalions should have made contact. Clearly, in the darkness positions had been mistaken by someone. During the small hours German artillery pounded the Puisieux Road, making the bringing forward of supplies very hazardous. At first light General Phillips sent four machine guns from Beaucourt to strengthen the Nelson positions to the north of Artillery Alley.

Throughout the following day, 4 February, both Hawke and Nelson tried to remove the serious threat on the left flank posed by the unsuppressed German strongpoint. It was a dangerous mission in daylight, but the delay in getting rid of the enemy post brought pressure from Brigade HQ. At 3.30 pm Commander Nelson was invited to hand over command to his 2i/c and report to Brigade HQ where, presumably, the urgency of capturing the German strongpoint and other matters were stressed. Commander Nelson may also have been in trouble with his Brigadier for 'losing' one of his companies, which had withdrawn early without relief, the company commander having 'mis-read his orders'. The orders and reports of this battle were complicated, unnecessarily, by the practice of referring to battalions by number rather than by name (eg Nelson was No.3 Battalion) and to companies by number rather than by letter (eg Nelson 'D' Company was No.1 Company). However, this convention was not consistently used and some confusion may have ensued. Commander Nelson resumed command at 4.45 pm. While he was away at Brigade HQ a party of thirty-six Nelsons of 'D' Company went forward (taking with them sixteen men of the Hawke's mal-sited platoon) and took the German position after it had been reduced by Stokes mortars. The bombardment by the 189 Brigade mortar battery, which brought down fifty rounds on the Germans, was under the control of Leading Seaman Colin Wheeler, a former Nelson rating.[200] During the previous night he had broken up a bombing attack on Sub Lieutenant Gardner's 'B' Company with forty well-aimed Stokes rounds. He was awarded the Military Medal[201] and the Distinguished Conduct Medal for his outstanding conduct during this battle. The citation for his DCM states:

> For conspicuous gallantry and devotion to duty. He handled three trench mortars with marked ability and greatly assisted in clearing up a difficult situation. He set a fine example throughout.[202]

Sub Lieutenant Arthur Wolfe[203] and six Nelson ratings were killed in the fighting on 4 February. That night a team from 2nd Field Company, Royal Engineers, was moved forward to the captured position close to the juncture of Artillery Alley and Puisieux Trench and a strong point was constructed there to command the left flank. A Nelson patrol sent forward from this post eventually firmed up the contact with Hawke Battalion. At dusk two waves of the enemy, about seventy strong, were observed advancing from the north, but their advance was checked by a barrage from the RND's artillery and by rifle fire from the Nelson posts. The Germans were dispersed.

Thereafter, the situation on the left flank was relatively secure, with Hawke Battalion having pushed forward to take the northern end of River Trench. An intense German artillery barrage came down along the Nelson's lines at 9.00 pm but it was not followed up by a counter-attack. Further south, down the slope towards the Ancre, the battle was even more keenly fought, but eventually, by dusk on 5 February, the German lines were taken and consolidated by the Hood with reinforcements from Drake Battalion. For the Nelsons, holding the northern flank of the battlefield, casualties had continued throughout the day. That evening 189 Brigade's newly won positions were handed over to 190 Brigade, the 4/Bedfords taking over the portion of the line held by Nelson Battalion, who withdrew to the support lines by 10.00 pm. As this handover was taking place, a patrol of Howe Battalion entered Grandcourt, south of the river (the RND sector ran south of the Ancre at this time), and found it abandoned by the Germans. Their retreat east to the Hindenburg Line had begun at the instigation of the local German commander, Crown Prince Ruprecht. The early signs of German planning for this withdrawal had been evident for several weeks, but had not been picked up by Allied intelligence. If they had been, it is possible that the attacks towards Miraumont need not have been carried out and the attendant casualties might have been avoided.

The attack on Puisieux and River Trenches had cost Nelson Battalion an officer and eighteen ORs killed or dead of wounds, but in this battle it had been their friends in the Hawke who had borne the brunt of casualties, with Drake and Hood also suffering badly. For the wounded, who numbered nearly forty, evacuation from the battlefield probably had to wait until darkness fell and the freezing temperatures added the severe danger of frost-bite while lying out in the open. Typical among such casualties was Able Seaman Norman Richardson[204], who had received a gunshot wound to the calf but had to have his foot amputated because of frostbite.

Nelson Battalion spent the next five days in the support lines, the first day employed in cleaning up dug-outs which had been left in a filthy condition. The following three days continued the pattern of cold, bright, frosty weather and saw the whole battalion employed on working parties. On 10 February a Court of Enquiry was convened in the Hawke HQ at Englebelmer to investigate the reasons behind the gap in the fighting line which had opened up between the two battalions during the recent fighting. It would continue for three days. On the same day the two battalions exchanged places and the Nelsons moved back to billets at Englebelmer, with two companies being sent further back to Léalvillers to work for the Director of Transportation.

The next phase of the RND's push along the north bank of the Ancre towards Miraumont was to take place on 17 February, with 188 Brigade exploiting the gains made earlier in the month by 189 Brigade. Nelson Battalion would not be directly engaged in this attack but the two companies which had not already been detached back to Léalvillers would be placed at the disposal of GOC 188 Brigade to be employed as carrying parties for the period of operations. On 12 February these two companies were carrying out their back-breaking tasks in the support line behind 190 Brigade but on the following day they moved across the Ancre to Thiepval to work under the Royal Engineers and the battalion HQ moved back to Forceville. Temperatures were climbing somewhat in mid-February with a definite thaw setting in. Frozen mud gave way to liquid mud and the going across the battlefields became harder. The Nelson companies worked on their allotted tasks for another two days until, on 16 February, the eve of 188 Brigade's attack, the two Thiepval companies moved back across the Ancre to the old German front line system. Sub Lieutenant Crosland-Taylor was wounded with shell shock on this day but rejoined after two weeks treatment. For the duration of 188 Brigade's successful assault on the Sunken Road north of Baillescourt Farm the two Nelson companies provided the 'lifting and shifting' manpower essential to support the tempo of operations. On 18 February, with the conclusion of operations, they moved back to Thiepval and the routine of working parties resumed there and continued at Léalvillers.

At this time command of the RND passed from Major General Shute to Major General C.E. Lawrie, CB, DSO. The weather was now alternating between fine and misty days. The battalion HQ moved to Hédauville on 19 February. The working party routine continued, with a change of scenery on 23 February when the two companies at Léalvillers moved to Thiepval and the Thiepval companies moved to Varennes. 23 February also saw the arrival of eleven officers as reinforcements from England.[205] Three days later Nelson Battalion HQ and the companies from Varennes moved to a new camp (Spring Garden Camp) that had been set up at Pys on the south side of the Ancre and two miles south-east of Miraumont. This town had been occupied by 190 Brigade a couple of days earlier without a fight. The Nelsons arrived at Spring Garden Camp on 26 February to find that no tents had been erected and they were forced to spend the night in the gum boot store. The weather continued misty and damp over the next few days. The tents were erected the following morning and the working parties turned-to again, the two companies at Pys working for the Australians. The next day the two companies that had been based at Thiepval moved into Spring Garden Camp and the battalion was reunited for the first time in nearly three weeks.

On 27 February a Court of Enquiry was convened by General Lawrie to investigate whether any deserters from 1/RMLI, Howe or Anson Battalions could have passed information to the Germans before the attack ten days earlier. GOC Fifth Army had ordered a widespread investigation into this possibility. Lieutenant Colonel Lewis (who would later command the Nelson), at that time acting in command of 189 Infantry Brigade, presided and Major Barker of the Nelson was one of the two members of the Court. No evidence was found to implicate men of the three battalions.

As the year moved into March, Nelson Battalion continued to provide working parties in the areas taken over by the British advances of the previous month, mainly around Miraumont and Courcelette. They would have another eighteen days in Spring Garden Camp, which was steadily improved. The battalion 2i/c, Captain Griffiths, was invalided home on 8 March. He was suffering the painful after-effects of spending several hours in a frozen shell-hole where he had been trapped waist-deep in water in an earlier action.[206] Lieutenant Buckle was promoted to lieutenant commander a week later, but his record does not show him being made 2i/c. Routine orders in March announced the award of the Military Medal to Nelson ratings for their gallantry during the fighting towards Miraumont a month earlier.[207] The men so decorated were:

Petty Officer R.L. Barrie[208]   Leading Seaman A.J. Jupp[209]

Able Seaman J.R. Campbell[210]   Able Seaman W. Duthie[211]

Able Seaman A. Steele[212]

Petty Officer E Rennie was among those cited for distinguished and gallant services and devotion to duty in a despatch of Field Marshal Sir Douglas Haig sent on 9 April 1917.[213] Mentioned in the same despatch was Able Seaman James Inns, another Nelson man who had been transferred to 189 Brigade LTM Battery when the battalion arrived in France.[214]

On 15 March the battalion was put through the baths and thereafter another move was imminent. Sunday, 18 February, after church parade, was spent making the final preparations to leave Pys and on the following day the battalion marched out. The move to a new base would take a full week of route marching.

NELSONS KILLED, MORTALLY WOUNDED
OR DIED OF DISEASE
FROM 1 JANUARY TO 30 MARCH 1917,
INCLUDING THE ATTACK ON PUISIEUX
& RIVER TRENCHES

RANK/RATING NAME BURIAL / MEMORIAL	NUMBER	DATE		CAUSE
SUB LT	DYETT, ELA			
	05/01/17	EXECUTED		LE CROTOY COMMUNAL CEMETERY
AB	BUCKMASTER, W			
LZ/4324	19/01/17	KIA		HAMEL MILTARY CEMETERY, BEAUMONT-HAMEL
AB	HURST, G			
TZ/5098	19/01/17	KIA		THIEPVAL MEMORIAL
AB	WILLIAMS, J			
WZ/2398	20/01/17	KIA		HAMEL MILITARY CEMETERY, BEAUMONT-HAMEL
AB	SMART, CH			
R/273	21/01/17	DOW		VARENNES MILITARY CEMETERY
AB	COWIE, JW			
CZ/1202	22/01/17	KIA		THIEPVAL MEMORIAL
AB	HAMER, T			
R/64	22/01/17	KIA		THIEPVAL MEMORIAL
AB	PHILPOTT, F			
LZ/4283	22/01/17	KIA		THIEPVAL MEMORIAL
AB	SYMONS, A			
TZ/6400	22/01/17	KIA		THIEPVAL MEMORIAL
AB	VATON, EA			
LZ/5074	22/01/17	KIA		THIEPVAL MEMORIAL
AB	WALDEN, HJ			
BZ/887	22/01/17	KIA		THIEPVAL MEMORIAL
AB	ELLIOTT, DG			
R/304	23/01/17	KIA		THIEPVAL MEMORIAL
AB	ROBERTS, EM			
BZ/9058	24/01/17	DOW		MESNIL COMMUNAL CEMETERY EXTENSION
AB	MORFEE, PE			
R/25	25/01/17	SICK		VARENNES MILITARY CEMETERY
AB	ALLUM, JL			
LZ/4348	28/01/17	DOW		PUCHEVILLERS BRITISH CEMETERY
AB	NEEDHAM, A			
TZ/6680	01/02/17	POW		THIEPVAL MEMORIAL
AB	ALLBURY, RC			
R/351	02/02/17	KIA		ANCRE BRITISH CEMETERY, BEAUMONT-HAMEL

RANK/RATING NUMBER	NAME DATE	CAUSE	BURIAL / MEMORIAL
AB TZ/8508	FREEMAN, H 02/02/17	DOW	DONCASTER OLD CEMETERY
AB TZ/5253	LINTIN, A 03/02/17	KIA	THIEPVAL MEMORIAL
AB TZ/8868	THOMPSON, W 03/02/17	KIA	THIEPVAL MEMORIAL
LS TZ/3140	GEDDES, W 04/02/17	KIA	QUEENS CEMETERY, BUCQUOY
AB LZ/5264	HIBBERD, WN 04/02/17	KIA	THIEPVAL MEMORIAL
AB CZ/4191	JOHNSTONE, J 04/02/17	KIA	ANCRE BRITISH CEMETERY, BEAUMONT-HAMEL
AB CZ/2807	MATHEWSON, A 04/02/17	KIA	THIEPVAL MEMORIAL
AB BZ/9048	PARKES, CJ 04/02/17	KIA	SERRE ROAD CEMETERY NO.1
LS LZ/1788	PYM, JW 04/02/17	KIA	ANCRE BRITISH CEMETERY, BEAUMONT-HAMEL
SUB LT	WOLFE, AF 04/02/17	KIA	THIEPVAL MEMORIAL
AB LZ/1879	CLARK, HW 05/02/17	KIA	QUEENS CEMETERY, BUCQUOY
AB TZ/5357	CONSTABLE, EG 05/02/17	KIA	QUEENS CEMETERY, BUCQUOY
AB TZ/8189	GREENWOOD, WH 05/02/17	KIA	QUEENS CEMETERY, BUCQUOY
AB TZ/5359	PEET, GH 05/02/17	KIA	THIEPVAL MEMORIAL
LS LZ/2714	ROOKE, AW 05/02/17	DOW	VARENNES MILITARY CEMETERY
AB TZ/5370	VICKERS, H 05/02/17	DOW	AVELUY WOOD CEMETERY, MESNIL-MARTINSART
AB WZ/1551	WOOD, W 05/02/17	KIA	THIEPVAL MEMORIAL
AB LZ/4466	COOK, AA 06/02/17	DOW	VARENNES MILITARY CEMETERY
AB SZ/485	SPRATT, CT 12/02/17	SICK	GORING (ST MARY) CHURCHYARD, SUSSEX
AB CZ/2462	ROLLO, JD 14/02/17	DOW	VARENNES MILITARY CEMETERY
AB CZ/4796	CONNOLLY, A 15/02/17	KIA	THIEPVAL MEMORIAL

RANK/RATING NUMBER	NAME DATE	CAUSE	BURIAL / MEMORIAL
AB R/268	WAITE, HL 15/02/17	KIA	CONNAUGHT CEMETERY, THIEPVAL
AB CZ/6430	McLACHLAN, GMacG 19/02/17	SICK	MONT HUON MILITARY CEMETERY, LE TREPORT
AB R/353	WALKER, AO 14/03/17	SICK	PUCHEVILLERS BRITISH CEMETERY

14

ON THE ARRAS FRONT – SECOND BATTLE OF THE SCARPE – GAVRELLE:

20 MARCH – 25 APRIL 1917

Crossing the Ancre again, the men of Nelson Battalion marched south-west nine miles to Warloy-Baillon and into billets for the first night. Now well behind the front, the next three days would see them marching steadily to the north with overnight stops at Puchevillers and Neuvillette before going into billets for two nights in villages near Frévent. The battalion HQ with 'A' and 'C' Companies rested at Séricourt, while 'B' and 'D' Companies moved into billets at Honval. They had marched some thirty-five miles over four days and a general clean-up and foot inspection was the order of the day. The route march was resumed on 24 March with overnight billets at Valhuon and Westrehem before the battalion marched into camp at Annezin on 26 March after another twenty-five miles on the road. Annezin, about two miles west of the town of Béthune, would be the Nelson Battalion base for training before the next tour in the line. During this period Sub Lieutenant Herbert Siddle, who had missed the February fighting through sickness, and Lieutenant George Turnbull, who had been in England on duty since October, rejoined.

The RND was at first split up for the next phase of the British strategy. This was to be an attack on the German lines running from Givenchy-en-Gohelle (close to the Souchez sector of the line, near Lens, which had been the Nelson's introduction to the BEF in mid-1916), south through Vimy Ridge and to the east of Arras. 189 and 190 Brigades of the RND were attached to XIII Corps, which was being held in general reserve in the rear areas. 188 Brigade, however, had been attached to 5th Division of I Corps and in early April found itself on the front line to the west of Lens, while the Divisional Artillery was supporting the Canadians at Vimy. The initial attacks of the Battle of Arras took place between 9 and 12 April, but XIII Corps and its RND component remained in reserve throughout. For Nelson Battalion this meant twelve days in their base at Annezin, during which there was a period of work-up training, applying the lessons learned on the Ancre for the battles to come.

While the battalion was at Annezin a tragic death occurred when Able Seaman William Attwood, BZ/3156, killed himself on the night of 4/5 April. Attwood had a poor disciplinary record and had faced a Field General Court Martial (FGCM) a week earlier. He had been found guilty of

> Conduct to the prejudice of good order and military discipline in that he, in the field, on 19th March 1917, being a prisoner under escort, threw his rifle on the ground and discarded his equipment.

The court found him not guilty of using insubordinate language to a superior officer. He had been sentenced to three months' Field Punishment No.1. Public exposure of the prisoner was a part of this punishment and normally involved his being tied to a stake or a wagon wheel for up to two hours a day (often called 'crucifixion' by the soldiers), sometimes for one hour in the morning and one hour in the afternoon. Commander Nelson convened a Court of Enquiry on 5 April to enquire into the circumstances of Attwood's death. The Court heard evidence that Attwood had been a prisoner in the guardroom and that at around midnight a shot had been heard. The Petty Officer of the Guard discovered Attwood lying on his bed under a blanket with a rifle lying beside him, the muzzle close to his head, grasped by his right hand. He had been wounded by a bullet which entered near his nose and exited through the top of his head. A medical officer was on the scene within minutes and found Attwood to be still barely alive but he died on arrival at the nearest Casualty Clearing Station. Two weeks earlier Attwood had, at the request of Commander Nelson, been examined by the Nelson MO before he was tried. He found him to be mentally unstable but not of unsound mind. The Court of Enquiry was of the opinion that Attwood had shot himself and that he was of unsound mind at the time.[215] The question of how the prisoner in the guard-room came to be in possession of a loaded rifle was not resolved. All the sentries' rifles were accounted for. Able Seaman Attwood was 28 years old and came from Birmingham.

On 8 April the battalion was on parade at 9.30 in the morning, kit reduced to the minimum so that the force could move quickly, if required, to move forward from reserve. The Nelsons then marched five miles south to Ruitz, arriving there at noon, but they were unable to take over their billets for another five hours. There would be two full days at Ruitz with company commanders conducting training. Whilst there, the last new officer to join before the coming battle, Lieutenant William Mathew, would join the Nelson.[216] On the afternoon of 10 April, the second day of the battle to the east, the battalion was brought to two hours notice to move. In the event, they were not required and they were stood down before dark. On the following day the Nelsons paraded at 11.00 am and marched off through persistent, heavy rain for five hours, the

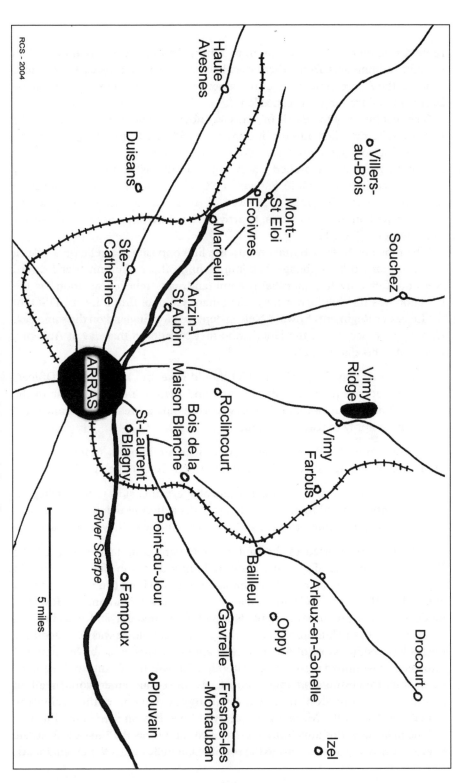

9. Operations around Arras and Gavrelle.

route taking them eight miles south to Villers-Brûlin. They were now back in the rear training area from where they had set off six months earlier to move south to the Ancre. The weather remained terrible on the next day at Villers-Brûlin and all training was cancelled.

The first phase of the Battle of Arras was now coming to its conclusion. XIII Corps was being called into the line and over 13 and 14 April the RND moved forward. Nelson Battalion passed their 'starting point' at Béthonsart at 11.00 am on 13 April and marched seven miles south-east towards Arras. They paused overnight at a camp known as 'X' Hutments in Ecoivres, south of Mont-St. Éloi and five miles north-west of Arras. At 8.00 am on the next day they marched on, north of Arras, to arrive in late afternoon at their new sector to the west of Gavrelle.

The move of Nelson Battalion into the line opposite Gavrelle on 14 April was also marked by a change of commanding officer. Commander Edward Nelson, after only five months in command, was relieved at noon, as the battalion was moving forward, by Lieutenant Colonel Frank Lewis, DSO, of the Leicester Regiment. Edward Nelson departed for England on the same day. Commander Asquith of the Hood, who met Nelson on that day at Aubigny, recorded in his diary that he

> lacks many qualities which a CO should have: but he knows his Officers and had reconnoitred this position; and there is no clearer case of the truth about not swapping horses when crossing a stream. I recommended him to apply to teach the Yanks.[217]

In contrast, the 189 Brigade clerk, Able Seaman Thomas Macmillan, was impressed by the new Nelson CO and described Colonel Lewis as

> a small wiry man, close to sixty years of age, rather slow in the intake, but indefatigable and totally devoid of fear. As a disciplinarian he was unsurpassed, and seemed to have all his officers in the hollow of his hand.[218]

Edward Nelson reverted to the rank of lieutenant commander and left the RND a month later. From his commissioning as a sub lieutenant on 23 September 1914 he had risen to command both the Hood (on two occasions) and Nelson Battalions and had been an acting Brigade Commander. However, he does not appear to have shone as a battle commander and, except for a mention in Sir Ian Hamilton's despatches after Gallipoli, he was not decorated for his leadership. Most of his command appointments arose by his stepping into dead or wounded men's shoes, although this was hardly unusual. Perhaps he was too much the academic scientist. His post-war career would see him resume his profession in marine biology to become the Scientific Superintendent of the Marine Laboratory at Nigg Bay on the Moray Firth.

The fighting in this area from 9 to 14 April (known as the First Battle of the Scarpe – the River Scarpe runs to the south of Gavrelle across the Douai Plain), had seen a highly successful advance of over three miles which had taken two of the three German defence lines between Arras and Gavrelle and Oppy. Gavrelle was a fortified village in the third German line and had not fallen to the recent advance. It was to be the objective of the RND in the Second Battle of the Scarpe planned for later in the month. 189 and 190 Brigades went straight into the line to relieve the 34th Division of XVII Corps. Nelson Battalion arrived at their holding point, the bridge on the Arras – Gavrelle road over the railway line south of the Bois de la Maison Blanche, at 3.45 pm. The RND HQ were in a dug-out close to this wood, which is near today's CWGC Bailleul Road East Cemetery. The company commanders immediately went forward to inspect the battalion's positions in the new battle area. The companies moved forward into the line at 7.30 pm and by 11.00 pm the relief had been completed. 190 Brigade was on the left and 189 Brigade on the right of the new sector. Nelson Battalion was on the left flank of 189 Brigade with 'A' Company forward.

The RND historian describes the situation in the sector as:

> unenviable . . . the new front line lay on the forward slope of the hill looking down into the plain of Gavrelle. On the crest of this hill was the captured German switch line from Fampoux through Point du Jour (a miniature fortress now in the 189th Brigade sub-sector) to Farbus, and our support troops in this line and our reserves on the reverse slope were screened from all observation. The position of the front-line troops was, however, deplorable. From the crest of the hill to the enemy's line in front of Gavrelle was a perfectly open belt of country, more than 3,500 yards in depth. Not only, therefore, our front line but our communications were at the mercy of an observant enemy who allowed no interval of immunity to ration and carrying parties, engineers, signallers and runners, on whose attentions the infantry in the trenches so implicitly rely.[219]

The action started on the following morning, 15 April, as 190 Brigade started to move forward towards the Oppy-Gavrelle line. The Nelsons moved forward on their left to conform. At noon 10/Dublin Fusiliers and 4/Bedfords attempted a frontal attack on Gavrelle, but they were strongly resisted by German machine guns and were heavily shelled. The German artillery also rained down on all the rear lines and continued, without a break, well into the evening. The Dublins and Bedfords were stopped in their tracks and withdrew. This unsuccessful attack by 190 Brigade cost Nelson Battalion its first casualties at Gavrelle: four killed and more than a dozen wounded, one mortally.

On the next day artillery exchanges continued, British guns bombarding Gavrelle and Oppy for six hours from noon. The Nelson War Diary notes that

'Several small enemy parties [were] seen and considerable train movement at Izel and Douai. At 4pm one of our planes was brought down, pilot and observer being wounded.'

At 1.00 am on 17 April 'B' and 'D' companies of Nelson Battalion attempted, under cover of darkness, to move forward to capture the German line and, optimistically, Gavrelle. It was not to be. The defences of Gavrelle were far too strong. 'B' company lost direction and the patrols which 'D' company pushed forward found heavy German barbed wire uncut, despite the artillery bombardment. Both companies withdrew and were back in their lines by dawn. After a 'quiet' day Hawke Battalion came forward to relieve the Nelsons, who retired to the reserve line west of the Bois de la Maison Blanche. They would have three days in the reserve, during which the inevitable working parties were called for, repairing roads and carrying stores. On 21 April Nelson Battalion moved forward to take over the front line from Hawke, receiving the benefit of an intense German barrage of gas shells as they approached the trenches and taking several casualties. The scene was now being set for a successful RND assault on Gavrelle. Throughout 22 April preparations were made, hampered during the early morning and forenoon by a heavy German bombardment during which four able seamen were killed and several wounded. The British heavy guns pounded Oppy, the German line in front of Gavrelle and the village itself. At 10.30 pm the Nelsons moved up to their battle positions in readiness for the assault at dawn on 23 April.

The battle plan called for 190 Brigade to move forward north of the Arras-Fresnes road (which formed the inter-brigade boundary) running west-east through Gavrelle, taking the German front line immediately north-west of the village (the *BLUE LINE*). They then had to form a defensive flank across the higher ground to the north of Gavrelle. Simultaneously, 189 Brigade were tasked to advance south of the Fresnes road through the *BLUE LINE*, on to the second objective (the *YELLOW LINE*), the road south from Gavrelle to Fampoux, and on to the third objective (the *GREEN LINE*) a German trench about 350 yards beyond Gavrelle. The 189 Brigade task was a demanding one which not only required them to take a heavily defended German line but also to fight their way through a village which had been devastated by shell-fire. Urban fighting is one of the most specialized military operations which requires great skill and tenacity on the part of an attacking force, ruined buildings and their cellars providing an ideal environment for snipers and hidden defenders. Such was the challenge facing the officers and men of Nelson Battalion who were drawn up on the left of 189 Brigade, with 4/Bedfords on their left and Drake Battalion on their right. Behind Nelson and Drake, the Hood Battalion was poised to follow up in support.

The Commanding Officers of both the Nelson and Hood Battalions were very new in post and before the attack Commander Asquith, CO Hood, had taken the opportunity to discuss the operation in detail with Lieutenant Colonel Lewis. Asquith noted in his diary that he was concerned about Lewis, an Army officer, new to the RND, who was an unknown quantity. Christopher Page notes:

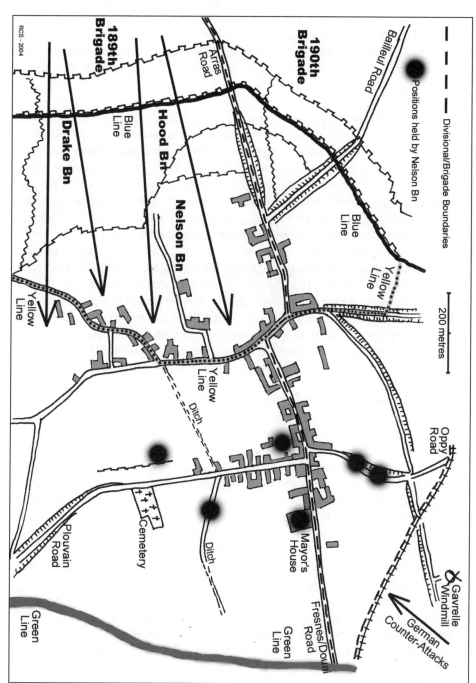

10. The Battle for Gavrelle.

He had heard, possibly from Commander Nelson . . . that Lewis was of questionable competence and a 'dug-out'. As his personal safety, and that of his entire Battalion, depended on Nelson Battalion's performance, his need to ensure that their CO understood exactly what was required is apparent. His concerns were unfounded; Lewis was an excellent officer.[220]

The British barrage opened up at 4.45 am on 23 April and crept forward towards Gavrelle, generating a maelstrom of dust and smoke, closely followed by Nelson Battalion moving in four waves with the Drakes on their right. The early progress by the assaulting troops of Nelson and Drake was good and the *BLUE LINE* of German defences west of the village was taken in fifteen minutes, together with a number of German prisoners. Hard on their heels, on the initiative of Commander Asquith, came the men of the Hood. The village ahead of them was a different proposition and was a nest of concealed machine-gunners and snipers. The number of casualties started inexorably to mount from continuous hand-to-hand fighting. The Nelsons pressed forward and they eventually reached the *YELLOW LINE* in the middle of the village, although by now the men of Nelson and Hood were almost inextricably mixed in the chaos of street-fighting. To complicate matters even more, men from the Bedfords, who should have been holding the flank north of the village, had also been drawn down into Gavrelle. Here, on the *YELLOW LINE*, the barrage paused and a vain attempt was made to make order out of the chaos before resuming the advance.

The renewed advance took the Hoods and Nelsons forward together to the approximate line of the Oppy-Gavrelle-Plouvain road but further advance to the *GREEN LINE* was impossible because of machine-gun and sniper fire. Ahead was a strong German garrison holding the Mayor's house and garden and this was not firmly in the hands of a party from the Hood until 7.00 am. By this stage, after just over two hours of bitter fighting, the line on the eastern edge of the village was held by a mixed force of Nelsons and Hoods with the Nelsons biased towards the northern flank. The Drakes were dug in further to the right on the line of the sunken road to Plouvain. The enemy forces on the northern flank remained a potent threat because the Bedfords had not been successful in getting a strong force forward to form the defensive flank on the high ground to the north. German counter-attacks from the north-east were pressed strongly against this sector where 189 and 190 Brigades were but tentatively in touch with each other. Through the day Nelsons were holding a line from a trench just west of the Rue de Plouvain opposite the cemetery and running north across the Arras-Douai road (the Brigade boundary) to a position in the sunken road which ran towards Oppy. A small party of Nelsons was also in the ditch south of the Mayor's garden.

The Germans brought down a constant, intense heavy artillery barrage on

Gavrelle throughout the daylight hours, causing many casualties. Colonel Lewis' sailors were under continuous enemy pressure at the north-east corner of the village and he authorized an SOS on two occasions between 4.00 and 5.00 pm. About 200 German troops made a concerted attack on the Nelsons, who came simultaneously under a heavy bombardment of minenwerfer. The RND's heavy artillery were asked to relieve the pressure with counter-battery fire.

As the day wore on it became obvious to the three battalion commanders that it would not be possible to move on to the *GREEN LINE* to the east of the village. Nelson Battalion went firm on a line from the Mayor's house, at the north-east corner of the village, north and west towards the Oppy Road, where they were barely in touch with the Bedfords, and they held the left flank together against the threat from the high ground to the north. Hood Battalion held the line south from the Mayor's house with Drake Battalion on their right.[221] In the evening came more reports of the enemy troops moving forward in small groups and a creeping artillery barrage was laid down 250 yards in front of the 189 Brigade line to clear the area. Although by dusk Colonel Lewis had managed to make contact on his left with two platoons of 4/Bedfords, they in turn were out of touch with the rest of the Bedfords so two platoons of Nelsons were diverted there to hold the line. Even so the northern flank situation remained precarious.

An invitation received by the battalion commanders, late in the day, from GOC 189 Brigade, to attempt a further advance, under a barrage to be timed by them, was tactfully declined and at dusk the line was redistributed. Howe Battalion came forward after dark and the Hood was withdrawn. Nelson Battalion then eased left to the north of Gavrelle, where the Bedfords' line was weakest. The fresh troops of the Howe came in on the line south from the main road to where the Drakes remained in their positions. They were all in for another punishing day ahead. At dawn the Germans were still pouring in rifle fire on the Nelsons from a ridge of high ground to the north surrounding the Gavrelle windmill and two additional Stokes mortars were brought up to shell some of the houses being used by snipers. The Nelson men were to take the brunt of attacks from German trenches north-east of the village on the morning of 24 April, starting with another barrage of minenwerfer and 5·9-inch artillery which was quietened by counter-battery fire called down from British 'heavies'. At one point during that afternoon a Nelson platoon holding the Mayor's House with a Lewis gun was forced to retire after direct hits from enemy artillery. The short Nelson War Diary entry for 24 April does less than justice to the fury of the Germans' response to the loss of Gavrelle and the tenacity of the RND's defence of their gains despite hours of continuous shelling:

> Enemy furiously bombarded Gavrelle from 10am to 3pm during which time he massed for attack and about 3.30pm assaulted our line in force.

At no point did he gain any success and suffered severely. We held our line intact throughout the night.

Just before dawn on 25 April, after forty-eight hours of continuous fighting and five days in the front line, Nelson Battalion was relieved by Howe Battalion as 188 Brigade took over Gavrelle. The exhausted Nelsons marched back by platoons to the oil factory at St Laurent-Blagny where they boarded buses which took them west beyond Arras to billets at Maroeuil. The next day was occupied with the, by now standard, post-battle routine of counting up those who were still around, seeing what kit they had left and reorganizing the men into a semblance of fighting companies. Letters to the next-of-kin of those killed were a major task for the Nelson officers.

On the eve of the battle for Gavrelle the fighting strength of Nelson Battalion's officers had again changed significantly since they fought in early February. There had been numerous comings and goings in the intervening ten weeks:-

Commanding Officer	Lieutenant Colonel Frank Lewis DSO *[Leicester Regt]*
2nd in Command	Major David Wilkie *[5/Black Watch]*
Adjutant	Sub Lieutenant James Cowan
Attached	Major H.W. Barker *[6/West Yorks.]*
Lieutenant Commander RNVR	Archibald W. Buckle

Lieutenant RNVR	Cyril A. Truscott	Leonard Spain
	George K. Turnbull	William C. Mathew
Sub Lieutenant RNVR	Percival Batchelor	William D. Walker
	Ernest V.G. Gardner MC	George W. Bloomfield
	Arthur P. Taylor	William A. Bowler
	Edmund J. Palmer	William Wellwood
	Holt C. Hewitt	Cecil A. Clerk
	Herbert A. Siddle	Horace A Cole
	Edward H. Smith	William A. Nicoll
	Charles V. Davis	Arthur D.H. Simpson
	Robert M. Macaulay	Robert H. Pawson
	James H. Anderson	

Winthrop J. Crosland-Taylor *[attached 189 Bde LTM Batty]*
James A. Woodgate *[attached 189 Bde LTM Batty]*
Kenneth A. Hucklebridge *[attached 189 Bde LTM Batty]*
Herbert S. Strickland *[detached to RND HQ for training]*

Quartermaster	Lieutenant James A. Gates, RMLI
Medical Officer	Captain F.R.H. Laverick, RAMC

Among the experienced company commanders, Lieutenant Bernard Dangerfield MC had left for England on 14 April on special leave. A month later he was discharged from the RND on transfer to the RNAS as an Observer.[222] Lieutenant Wilfred Webb and Sub Lieutenants Denis Brown and Louis Hunt had all returned to England in March to join the Indian Army, after barely three months with Nelson Battalion. Other junior officers had been invalided sick. The battalion had also lost its naval Surgeon, Ernest Cox who had been invalided with influenza in early February. He did not return and an Army doctor, Captain Laverick, was MO until a new naval surgeon joined in May.

After the battle for Gavrelle the command picture had changed again. The casualties among the Nelsons leading the assault through the ruins of Gavrelle had, once again, been terrible. On the first day alone fifty-nine officers and men are recorded as having fallen, including two company commanders, Lieutenants George Turnbull and Cyril Truscott, and two Sub Lieutenants, Holt Hewitt and Herbert Siddle. Another thirty-five died on the second day of fighting, including the 2i/c, Major David Wilkie.[223] Ten officers were wounded in the battle: Lieutenant Commander Buckle remained at duty; Sub Lieutenants Taylor,[224] Davis, Simpson, Smith, Macaulay, Nicoll, Cole and Anderson were invalided home; Sub Lieutenant Palmer died of his wounds on 27 April. Of the ten sub lieutenants who had joined two months earlier only one, Sub Lieutenant Pawson, now remained. Several senior rates of the Nelson companies also lost their lives: two CPOs and five POs fell or were mortally wounded in action. Among them was Petty Officer Horace Putland who, as an able seaman, had been in No.4 Platoon of 'A' Company at Anzac with the author's father.[225]

In the first two days of the battle for Gavrelle it was, yet again, Nelson Battalion which had sustained the largest number of deaths among the three naval battalions engaged. The Hood, following Nelson Battalion through the hell of street-fighting, had lost close to sixty and a larger number of officers. Drake Battalion, attacking over more open ground, lost just over eighty but fewer officers. The ninety-four Nelson battle losses on 23 and 24 April eventually rose to a final total of 111 officers and men who died as a result of the attack on Gavrelle, the last casualty of the fighting succumbing to his wounds five months later on 15 September in England. Only about a dozen of those who fell fighting in Gavrelle have known graves, a testimony to the severity of the German retribution which fell on the village. The names of eighty-one Nelsons are commemorated on the Arras Memorial to the Missing. Not since Gallipoli had so many Nelson men been buried in unknown graves. The numbers wounded in the incessant shelling, mortaring and sniping were very large.

The lion's share of the gallantry awards after Gavrelle went to Hood and Drake Battalions, only one officer from Nelson Battalion being deemed worthy of recognition. The Military Cross was conferred on:

<u>Sub Lieutenant W.J. Crosland-Taylor</u> – 'For conspicuous gallantry and devotion under heavy shell fire during several enemy counter-attacks. He not only tended the wounded in full view of snipers but he led back Lewis gunners, who had been driven from their posts, and his courage and example greatly helped to save a critical situation.'[226]

The Military Medal for gallantry in the field at Gavrelle was awarded[227] to fifteen ratings of Nelson Battalion, the highest number for any of the actions in which the battalion took part. The men so decorated were:

Chief Petty Officer A.J. Collins[228]	Petty Officer J. Marchant[229]
Petty Officer J. Tait[230]	A/Petty Officer J. Duncan[231]
Leading Seaman W. Dudley[232]	Leading Seaman C. Dockrill[233]
Leading Seaman A.R. Hamill[234]	Able Seaman W. Barnfather[235]
Able Seaman J.W. Candlish[236]	Able Seaman F.L. Chettle[237]
Able Seaman H. Hollis[238]	Able Seaman J.W. Inns[239]
Able Seaman C. Johnston[240]	Able Seaman J. Martin[241]
Able Seaman J.H. Spicer[242]	Able Seaman H.J. Webb[243]

The record of Nelson Battalion while at Gavrelle would be incomplete without recalling that three men were subject to trial by Field General Court Martial for desertion there.[244] Two of them were found guilty of desertion and sentenced to death.

Able Seaman William P. Reilly, TZ/5250, a Battalion HQ signaller, was charged with deserting during the attack on Gavrelle on 23/24 April. He was tried and sentenced to death on 8 May. However, the GOC First Army refused to confirm the finding of guilty and the death sentence of the Court. He directed that Reilly be released and relieved from all consequences of his trial. Effectively, therefore, Reilly was not guilty of the desertion charge or of any other charges. Captain Laverick, the Nelson MO, came in for very severe criticism for his treatment of Reilly, who had reported sick and was clearly unfit for battle. General Lawrie, GOC RND, commented in the court-martial papers that Captain Laverick had

> failed in his duties both in a Field Ambulance and as a Medical Officer in a Battalion and an adverse report on him is being forwarded.

The second man sentenced to death was Able Seaman Charles Rogers, TZ/7075, noted as a man of exceptionally low intelligence, who had gone missing in early May when the Nelsons were out of the line in billets at Roclincourt, from where they were sending working parties to the forward trenches. Rogers came to trial on 8 June, but nine days after his trial the Court was directed to reconvene to consider Rogers' state of mental health, which had been assessed by a consulting neurologist. Although the new medical evidence did not change the Court's original finding and death sentence, a recommendation for mercy was now included. On review the GOC First Army commuted the sentence to penal servitude and suspended it because

> It appears doubtful whether the act of desertion was deliberately committed in order to avoid a dangerous duty.

The third rating, Able Seaman Charles J. Tuffe, LZ/4388, of 'D' Company, was tried by the same Court as Reilly on 8 May and was found not guilty of desertion but guilty of improper absence during the attack on Gavrelle. The GOC First Army remitted eighteen months of his two-year sentence of imprisonment at hard labour and suspended the remaining six months.

In his evidence at the trial of Reilly, Lieutenant Colonel Lewis had stated that

> there is a general slackness throughout the Battalion due to bad training. During the operations of 23rd and 24th April a number of men in one of the Companies took advantage of all the officers becoming casualties in the advance, to straggle back without sufficient reason. Owing to the difficulty of obtaining sufficient evidence against some of these men it has been impossible to bring them to trial by FGCM.

It is possible that these are the words of a new CO trying to stamp his authority by inflating the inevitable small number of stragglers (presumably the rest stood their ground). If true, they are a serious indictment of the state of the battalion handed over to him by Commander Nelson one month earlier, but the lack of evidence for more prosecutions weakens his statement. It has been implied from the trials of these three ratings, the earlier execution of Sub Lieutenant Dyett and Lieutenant Colonel Lewis' comments that Nelson Battalion was considered a weak fighting unit which needed 'shaking up'.[245] However, other battalions had as many or more men found guilty of desertion (there was only one from Nelson) and there is no other evidence to support this opinion. The Nelsons fought bravely at Gavrelle (especially the ORs, given the number of gallantry awards). It was the Nelson Battalion which led the Hoods into Gavrelle and subsequently held the most dangerous north-east corner of the village. As a result they took more casualties than most battalions. If any battalion was acutely aware of the penalties of desertion it must have been the Nelson, whose men had been required to shoot one of their own young officers just over three months earlier. At the trial of Able Seaman Rogers in early June Lieutenant Colonel Lewis, by then two months in command, specifically recorded, in contrast to his earlier comments, 'The discipline of the Battalion is good.'

NELSONS KILLED OR MORTALLY WOUNDED ON THE ARRAS FRONT AND IN THE ATTACK ON GAVRELLE 4 – 25 APRIL 1917,

RANK/RATING NUMBER	NAME DATE	CAUSE	BURIAL / MEMORIAL
AB BZ/3156	ATTWOOD, W 05/04/17	SELF-INF	BETHUNE TOWN CEMETERY
AB R/435	FENN, A 15/04/17	KIA	ARRAS MEMORIAL
AB MZ/465	MARSHALL, W 15/04/17	KIA	ARRAS MEMORIAL
AB R/444	RIVETT, CG 15/04/17	KIA	ARRAS MEMORIAL
AB BZ/3490	SCATTERGOOD, GE 15/04/17	KIA	ARRAS MEMORIAL
LS TZ/2498	MARRIOTT, TW 18/04/17	DOW	ETAPLES MILITARY CEMETERY
AB LZ/1869	HARNETT, A 22/04/17	KIA	ARRAS MEMORIAL
AB TZ/1476	PATRICK, J 22/04/17	KIA	ARRAS MEMORIAL
AB BZ/1367	SEARLE, E 22/04/17	KIA	ARRAS MEMORIAL
AB TZ/3289	SWANSON, C 22/04/17	KIA	ARRAS MEMORIAL
PO TZ/3641	ALDER, J, MM 23/04/17	KIA	ARRAS MEMORIAL
AB TZ/3635	ARMSTRONG, F 23/04/17	KIA	ARRAS MEMORIAL
AB LZ/3162	BARKER, CT 23/04/17	KIA	ARRAS MEMORIAL
AB BZ/3475	BRADBURN, CE 23/04/17	KIA	ARRAS MEMORIAL
AB MZ/638	BROMLEY, H 23/04/17	KIA	ORCHARD DUMP CEMETERY, ARLEUX-EN-GOHELLE
AB TZ/540	BROWN, TB 23/04/17	KIA	ARRAS MEMORIAL
LS TZ/2897	CASS, JG 23/04/17	KIA	ARRAS MEMORIAL
AB TZ/2425	CHARLTON, W 23/04/17	KIA	ARRAS MEMORIAL
AB TZ/945	COWING, M 23/04/17	KIA	ARRAS MEMORIAL
AB CZ/4806	CRAIG, F 23/04/17	KIA	ARRAS MEMORIAL

RANK/RATING	NAME		
NUMBER	DATE	CAUSE	BURIAL / MEMORIAL
AB	CUNNINGHAM, J		
MZ/446	23/04/17	KIA	ARRAS MEMORIAL
AB	DAVIS, PF		
WZ/353	23/04/17	KIA	ARRAS MEMORIAL
CPO	DUNCAN, J		
CZ/3681	23/04/17	KIA	ORCHARD DUMP CEMETERY, ARLEUX-EN-GOHELLE
AB	DUNNETT, CW		
R/381	23/04/17	KIA	ARRAS MEMORIAL
AB	EDWARDS, W		
TZ/4398	23/04/17	KIA	ARRAS MEMORIAL
AB	FLANNIGAN, P		
TZ/5275	23/04/17	KIA	ARRAS MEMORIAL
LS	FOSTER, EW		
LZ/356	23/04/17	KIA	ARRAS MEMORIAL
AB	FULTON, R		
CZ/4603	23/04/17	KIA	ARRAS MEMORIAL
AB	GARNER, W		
TZ/5270	23/04/17	KIA	ARRAS MEMORIAL
LS	GOTTS, JW		
TZ/4306	23/04/17	KIA	ORCHARD DUMP CEMETERY, ARLEUX-EN-GOHELLE
AB	GRIMSDALE, S		
LZ/4365	23/04/17	KIA	ARRAS MEMORIAL
AB	HAMILL, E		
CZ/4286	23/04/17	KIA	ORCHARD DUMP CEMETERY, ARLEUX-EN-GOHELLE
AB	HAMILTON, A		
TZ/4855	23/04/17	KIA	ORCHARD DUMP CEMETERY, ARLEUX-EN-GOHELLE
SUB LT	HEWITT, HC		
	23/04/17	KIA	ARRAS MEMORIAL
AB	HODGE, J		
TZ/7033	23/04/17	KIA	ARRAS MEMORIAL
AB	HUBBALL, J		
R/71	23/04/17	KIA	ARRAS MEMORIAL
PO	HURST, J		
TZ/3150	23/04/17	KIA	ARRAS MEMORIAL
PO	HUSBAND, J		
CZ/3366	23/04/17	KIA	ARRAS MEMORIAL
AB	HUTCHINSON, H		
TZ/5320	23/04/17	KIA	POINT-DU-JOUR MILITARY CEMETERY, ATHIES
AB	IRVINE, H		
CZ/4651	23/04/17	KIA	ARRAS MEMORIAL

RANK/RATING NUMBER	NAME DATE	CAUSE	BURIAL / MEMORIAL
AB CZ/4147	JOHNSON, W 23/04/17	KIA	ARRAS MEMORIAL
AB R/336	LEWINGTON, AW 23/04/17	KIA	ARRAS MEMORIAL
AB TZ/8940	LIGHTOWLER, G 23/04/17	KIA	ARRAS MEMORIAL
AB TZ/8168	LISHMAN, E 23/04/17	KIA	ARRAS MEMORIAL
AB WZ/2485	LOOSEMORE, JW 23/04/17	KIA	ARRAS MEMORIAL
AB CZ/2937	MIDDLETON, W 23/04/17	KIA	ORCHARD DUMP CEMETERY, ARLEUX-EN-GOHELLE
AB TZ/3426	MILLION, G 23/04/17	KIA	ARRAS MEMORIAL
AB CZ/3488	MOIR, RB 23/04/17	KIA	ARRAS MEMORIAL
AB LZ/4453	MORRIS, HJ 23/04/17	KIA	ORCHARD DUMP CEMETERY, ARLEUX-EN-GOHELLE
LS CZ/4283	MORRISON, WT 23/04/17	KIA	ARRAS MEMORIAL
AB TZ/5888	NADIN, H 23/04/17	KIA	ARRAS MEMORIAL
AB TZ/836	NEALE, GW 23/04/17	KIA	ARRAS MEMORIAL
LS WZ/883	O'KEEFFE, A 23/04/17	KIA	ARRAS MEMORIAL
AB TZ/5195	PARKER, H 23/04/17	KIA	ARRAS MEMORIAL
AB BZ/4696	PERKINS, HG 23/04/17	KIA	ARRAS MEMORIAL
PO SZ/59	PUTLAND, HE 23/04/17	KIA	ARRAS MEMORIAL
CPO LZ/128	SALTERN, GF 23/04/17	KIA	ARRAS MEMORIAL
AB CZ/7185	SEATON, A 23/04/17	KIA	ARRAS MEMORIAL
SUB LT	SIDDLE, HA 23/04/17	KIA	ARRAS MEMORIAL
AB LZ/3374	SLINN, R 23/04/17	DOW	ARRAS MEMORIAL
AB LZ/5085	SUGGATE, ED 23/04/17	KIA	ARRAS MEMORIAL
AB TZ/8915	THOMPSON, JE 23/04/17	KIA	ARRAS MEMORIAL

RANK/RATING NUMBER	NAME DATE	CAUSE	BURIAL / MEMORIAL
AB KW/228	THOMPSON, W 23/04/17	KIA	ARRAS MEMORIAL
LT	TRUSCOTT, CA 23/04/17	DOW	STE CATHERINE BRITISH CEMETERY, ARRAS
LT	TURNBULL, GK 23/04/17	KIA	ARRAS MEMORIAL
AB TZ/5201	TYSON, H 23/04/17	KIA	ARRAS MEMORIAL
AB BZ/216	WHITEHEAD, JR 23/04/17	KIA	ARRAS MEMORIAL
AB MZ/613	WILSON, D 23/04/17	KIA	ARRAS MEMORIAL
AB TZ/2995	WILSON, W 23/04/17	KIA	ARRAS MEMORIAL
AB TZ/4317	BINNEY, JA 24/04/17	KIA	ARRAS MEMORIAL
AB CZ/6382	BLAKE, P 24/04/17	KIA	ARRAS MEMORIAL
AB TZ/8515	BOTTERILL, F 24/04/17	KIA	ARRAS MEMORIAL
AB R/183	BROWN, A 24/04/17	KIA	ARRAS MEMORIAL
AB TZ/1883	CARR, GW 24/04/17	KIA	ARRAS MEMORIAL
AB R/285	CHAPMAN, U 24/04/17	KIA	ARRAS MEMORIAL
AB CZ/7443	CLARK, JB 24/04/17	KIA	POINT-DU-JOUR MILITARY CEMETERY, ATHIES
AB LZ/3367	GOODRICH, A 24/04/17	KIA	ARRAS MEMORIAL
AB TZ/5284	GOWLAND, A 24/04/17	KIA	ARRAS MEMORIAL
AB TZ/6365	GUTHRIE, A 24/04/17	KIA	ARRAS MEMORIAL
AB LZ/4395	HAGGAR, JE 23/04/17	KIA	ARRAS MEMORIAL
AB R/320	HOCKIN, LW 24/04/17	KIA	ARRAS MEMORIAL
AB CZ/1900	IMRIE, AG 24/04/17	KIA	ARRAS MEMORIAL
AB TZ/3304	KELLY, J 24/04/17	KIA	ARRAS MEMORIAL
AB TZ/1359	MARCH, GH 24/04/17	KIA	ARRAS MEMORIAL

AB	MURRAY, C		
KP/479	24/04/17	DOW	ARRAS MEMORIAL
AB	MUTCH, AL		
CZ/1792	24/04/17	KIA	ARRAS MEMORIAL
AB	PARKER, H		
TZ/9704	24/04/17	KIA	ARRAS MEMORIAL
AB	PENRY, W		
BZ/205	24/04/17	KIA	ARRAS MEMORIAL
AB	PROUD, H		
TZ/876	24/04/17	DOW	AUBIGNY COMMUNAL CEMETERY EXTENSION
AB	RELF, AS		
LZ/4353	24/04/17	KIA	ORCHARD DUMP CEMETERY, ARLEUX-EN-GOHELLE
AB	SHARP, J		
TZ/1239	24/04/17	KIA	CABARET-ROUGE BRITISH CEMETERY, SOUCHEZ
AB	SMITH, J		
TZ/2453	24/04/17	DOW	AUBIGNY COMMUNAL CEMETERY EXTENSION
AB	SMITH, JW		
TZ/1260	24/04/17	KIA	ARRAS MEMORIAL
AB	STEVENS, JT		
SZ/484	24/04/17	KIA	ARRAS MEMORIAL
AB	TAYLOR, JE		
MZ/814	24/04/17	KIA	ARRAS MEMORIAL
AB	THOMAS, AE		
WZ/1217	24/04/17	KIA	ARRAS MEMORIAL
LS	THOMSON, J		
CZ/3101	24/04/17	KIA	ARRAS MEMORIAL
AB	TURRELL, EG		
R/355	24/04/17	KIA	ARRAS MEMORIAL
AB	WALKER, H		
CZ/6439	24/04/17	KIA	ARRAS MEMORIAL
AB	WEBSTER, JC		
BZ/9076	24/04/17	KIA	ARRAS MEMORIAL
MAJ	WILKIE, D		
	24/04/17	KIA	ARRAS MEMORIAL
AB	WILLOUGHBY, FW		
TZ/5344	24/04/17	KIA	ARRAS MEMORIAL
AB	WINSTONE, HWG		
BZ/1189	24/04/17	KIA	ARRAS MEMORIAL
AB	WYATT, AB		
BZ/1440	24/04/17	KIA	ARRAS MEMORIAL

RANK/RATING	NAME		
NUMBER	DATE	CAUSE	BURIAL / MEMORIAL

AB	BROWN, CB		
LZ/4274	25/04/17	DOW	AUBIGNY COMMUNAL CEMETERY EXTENSION
PO	FRASER, HA		
CZ/3135	25/04/17	DOW	DUISANS BRITISH CEMETERY, ETRUN
AB	SNELL, J		
TZ/1051	25/04/17	DOW	AUBIGNY COMMUNAL CEMETERY EXTENSION
AB	CLASPER, W		
TZ/4336	25/04/17	DOW	DUISANS BRITISH CEMETRY, ETRUN
AB	WESTON, AJ		
LZ/5069	25/04/17	KIA	ARRAS MEMORIAL
AB	LAUCHLAN, W		
CZ/4961	26/04/17	DOW	AUBIGNY COMMUNAL CEMETERY EXTENSION
AB	ROBERTS, A		
TZ/8853	26/04/17	DOW	DUISANS BRITISH CEMETERY, ETRUN
AB	DENMARK, F		
R/438	27/04/17	DOW	ETAPLES MILITARY CEMETERY
SUB LT	PALMER, EJ		
	27/04/17	DOW	AUBIGNY COMMUNAL CEMETERY EXTENSION
AB	WILSON, S		
LZ/5068	27/04/17	DOW	AUBIGNY COMMUNAL CEMETERY EXTENSION
AB	HOPTON, E		
R/357	28/04/17	DOW	ETAPLES MILITARY CEMETERY
AB	GREY, DM		
BZ/486	29/04/17	DOW	DUISANS BRITISH CEMETERY, ETRUN
AB	WILLIAMS, E		
WZ/884	29/04/17	DOW	ETAPLES MILITARY CEMETERY
AB	BREWIS, TF		
TZ/5317	03/05/17	DOW	AUBIGNY COMMUNAL CEMETERY EXTENSION
AB	McDONALD, W		
CZ/556	20/05/17	DOW	ABERDEEN (ALLENVALE) CEMETERY
AB	HALE, W		
WZ/1495	05/06/17	DOW	BAILLEUL ROAD EAST CEMETERY, ST LAURENT-BLANGY
AB	SIDES, A		
TZ/1531	15/09/17	DOW	DEARHAM CHURCHYARD, WESTMORLAND

15

HOLDING THE LINE AT GAVRELLE:

26 APRIL – 2 OCTOBER 1917

Nelson Battalion spent three days at Maroeuil. The men were sent to clean themselves at the baths and their rifles were inspected by the battalion armourer. 27 April saw the men paraded for a 'running and walking parade for half an hour before breakfast', which would become a regular daily routine. Only forty-eight hours after a major battle working parties had to be provided for sanitary work under the Town Major of Maroeuil. On the following day the battalion marched back eight miles to the billets at Villers-Brûlin that they had vacated fifteen days earlier, arriving at dusk. They would stay only one night and the following day the battalion marched the six miles to Beugin. They had last been billeted at Beugin in early June of 1916 when it had been the battalion's base during their first training period with the BEF in the training area of IV Corps of First Army. Here they would have four days of fine weather on the training ground, marching out of camp each day at 9.00 am and returning in late afternoon. During this period the battalion welcomed its new medical officer, Surgeon William P. Starforth RN, as the replacement for Surgeon Cox. Surgeon Starforth had spent the previous month, including the battle for Gavrelle, in 2nd Field Ambulance RND.

On 4 May Nelson Battalion was on the move again after being ordered back to Arras. They started with a ten-mile march to the south-east, passing through the villages of La Comté, Frévillers, Béthonsart and Savy-Berlette to the main road at Haute Avesnes. There buses were waiting to take them on through Arras to near Roclincourt. Their new base was to be in the old German front-line trenches which the enemy had occupied before the Arras offensive. On arrival, after dark, it was found impossible to inspect the area for proper cover and, in consequence, the whole night was spent in the open. It was not until the next morning that a start could be made on putting the new base into proper order and that night the whole battalion was sent forward to provide working parties to dig a series of trenches behind our Oppy-Gavrelle line, the second successive night in the open. This new series of trenches would eventually form the third defensive line, known as the Red Line, and it ran north-south through Bailleul and a mile behind the front-line at Gavrelle. The casualties started immediately, with nine men being wounded, three mortally, on that first night back at the front. One of those killed was Leading Seaman Charles Yates, who had won the Distinguished Service Medal with Hawke Battalion at Gallipoli.[246] The same tasks faced the battalion night working parties for the next two weeks, with respite on only three nights. In the process, steady numbers of Nelson casualties were sustained from German artillery, including bombardments with gas shells. Deaths were mercifully few.

On 20 May Nelson Battalion became part of the Divisional Reserve and moved back to billets and bivouacs in Ste Catherine, close to Arras. Their stay there lasted three days and, although small working parties were called forward to dig communication trenches to the Red Line, it enabled some training to be undertaken. The Nelson War Diary describes a typical day: reveille 5.30, physical drill 6.45 – 7.45, two hours Lewis gun and one hour bombing instruction in the forenoon, an hour each of musketry and bayonet fighting in the afternoon. After a full morning of training on 23 May the battalion moved out later in the day to a hutted camp, known as Wakefield Camp, situated on the Arras to Roclincourt road, where they would continue their training until the end of the month. In preparation for the next tour in the line, training continued apace: live range firing and bombing, lectures and bayonet training were interspersed with the testing of gas respirators, foot inspections, church parades and visits to the baths. Throughout the month of May reinforcements joined the battalion, including six newly commissioned officers.[247] However, it would be June before significant numbers were in post to replace those killed and wounded in April. Sub Lieutenant James Cowan, the battalion Adjutant, had fallen sick in mid May. He was invalided home and his place had been taken by Sub Lieutenant Horace Cooper. At brigade level changes were also taking place, Brigadier General J.F.S.D. Coleridge, DSO, taking over as GOC 189 Brigade from Brigadier General Phillips on 30 May. On 31 May company commanders went forward to look over the trenches and dug-outs in the line north and west of Bailleul where, on the following evening, they would be relieving the Honourable Artillery Company of 190 Brigade.

The Nelson Battalion companies moved off independently on the evening of 1 June to relieve the 1/HAC, 'A' and 'C' Companies establishing themselves around the Battalion HQ in a railway cutting to the west and the other two companies north of the town. The next three days were spent as 189 Brigade support, with the inevitable large working parties being provided at night. Casualties seem to have been mercifully few but one rating was killed on 4 June. On 5 June it was the turn of Nelson Battalion to move back into the front line and the Hawkes were relieved in trenches west and south-west of Oppy. The next five days saw three Nelson companies forward and one in support.

The War Diary records no special events during this period, but two ratings were killed or fatally wounded.

The 11/East Lancashire came into the line and relieved the Nelsons on the night of 10/11 June and the battalion moved back to billets at Roclincourt. Three companies were engaged on night working parties on 12 June, repairing the long communication trench, Ouse Alley, which ran from north of Bailleul towards Oppy. The next day they moved back to the old German front line for a week of hard labour providing large working parties, on occasions the whole battalion, carrying for the Tunnelling Companies. The 189 Brigade Horse Show and Sports Day was held on 21 June but it seems unlikely that many Nelsons had the privilege of attending. On the 22 June their ten days as beasts of burden came to an end and the battalion moved back to Maroeuil, setting off in the morning and taking over a tented camp from Howe Battalion before noon. The twelve days at Maroeuil would be employed in teaching and exercising the full battalion attack procedure in three phases: 1st Phase – attack formations from the trenches; 2nd Phase – attack in the open or over open ground and advancing towards the objective; 3rd (final) Phase – consolidation of position won. On 27 June all of the Nelson officers watched a demonstration of trench-storming by Drake Battalion. On 30 June the phased training came to its conclusion with an exercise of

> The Attack Complete by two Nelson companies on a frontage of 200 yards. Extending from artillery formation and advancing towards objective by sectional rushes, final stages, taking position, pushing forward patrols and consolidating position gained. Remaining two companies watched operations and followed up the advance.

Tactics had come on a long way since the brave but fatal attacks of the Nelson novices at Anzac and Achi Baba Nullah two years earlier.

June and early July saw more reinforcements arriving from England, including a baker's dozen of junior officers. Sub Lieutenant Francis Rees rejoined on 6 June, having been invalided home sick soon after the Battle of the Ancre. As before, he was detached to a trench mortar battery.[248] Lieutenant John C. Watts joined on the same day. He had been first commissioned (ex-LZ/67) in December 1914 and had served with Collingwood and Hood Battalions at Gallipoli. Despite Lieutenant Watts' experience, however, he was sent back to England at the end of August assessed as 'inefficient'. Another long-serving RND officer joined in late June. Lieutenant Herbert L. Reed had first been commissioned in early October 1914, but he had spent all the intervening years at Crystal Palace or Blandford and had seen no action. He joined Hawke Battalion on 16 June, was transferred to Nelson twelve days later and immediately took over as battalion Adjutant from Sub Lieutenant Cooper who had been filling the position for the previous six weeks. The other ten sub lieutenants were all newly commissioned in March 1917 and six of them were former ratings.[249]

As June turned into July Nelson Battalion prepared to move up to the front again. All the company commanders went forward to inspect the support line system that they would soon be taking over. On 4 July the battalion marched out of camp at 7.00 am to take over the support lines south-west of Oppy. They moved forward along the communication trench north of Bailleul, known as Tommy Alley, in the early afternoon and relieved the men of 1/Cheshire Regiment in the support trenches at Sugar Post west of Oppy. The trenches were in a bad condition and subject to German shelling. Casualties were taken as soon as the relief was complete at 3.45 pm. Ahead of the Nelsons, Hood and Hawke Battalions were in the front-line trenches. Work on the support trenches in which they had to live was put in hand and working parties were also provided to the front line over the next days. Reinforcements continued to join from England and were fed forward to the battalion in the trenches. Sub Lieutenant Carlile, who at some stage managed to fall off his horse, had to be invalided and there was a steady toll of wounded. After six days in support, Nelson Battalion moved forward to relieve Hawke Battalion on the left of the 189 Brigade front, completing the handover just after noon on 10 July. The time in the front line would see even more casualties from German snipers, trench mortars and artillery and on 12 July an enemy aircraft dropped a bomb on the right front company, wounding eight men. The Nelson War Diary recorded heavy shelling by the Germans on 14 July and a British bombardment and German retaliation on 16 July, which was the day of their relief. The 1/Devons and 12/Gloucesters came up, the former battalion being so late that the Nelson relief was not completed until 11.00 am on 17 July. After thirteen days in the line the toll of dead stood at four ORs and at least sixteen wounded. Two officers had been wounded: Lieutenant Commander Buckle remained at duty but Sub Lieutenant Scarles was seriously ill with multiple gunshot wounds. He was invalided home and out of the service.

On 17 July the Nelsons marched back to Wakefield Camp near Roclincourt and into Brigade Reserve. The usual mix of inspections and training would fill the rest of July but the routine at Wakefield Camp was broken by a concert by the Royal Marines band and by an opportunity for the whole battalion to go to the cinema. The troops were brought to fifteen minutes' notice to move on the evening of 19 July, probably in readiness to support operations by 188 Brigade, but they were stood down on the following day. 188 Brigade was forward in Gavrelle at this time and Howe Battalion carried out a very successful trench raid in the small hours of 20 July. In this action Sub Lieutenant Arthur B Geden won the Military Cross. A former theological student and able seaman (LZ/321) in Nelson battalion at Gallipoli, he was in No.4 Platoon of 'A' Company at Anzac with the author's father.[250]

On 22 July Hawke Battalion took over Brigade Reserve duties and, accompanied by the Royal Marines band for the first mile, Nelson Battalion marched to new billets in Arras at Anzin- Saint Aubin, arriving there just after 6.00 pm.

On the same day they welcomed back to his old battalion Lieutenant Commander Tom Price, the former Metropolitan Policeman who had last been with the Nelsons on Gallipoli. Wounded (for the second time – he had also been wounded at Anzac) in the Action of Achi Baba Nullah on 13 July 1915, Lieutenant Commander Price had since been 2i/c of several reserve battalions at Blandford. Not one of the officers he met now had been with him at Gallipoli and few of the ratings would have known him from those days. He would, however, only stay with his old battalion for about three weeks before being transferred to Howe Battalion as 2i/c on 13 August.[251] In mid-July, when the battalion was in the trenches, three newly-commissioned junior officers had also joined the battalion. Two of them were former RND ratings and the other was a former soldier commissioned from the Army.[252] At Saint-Aubin, in late July, four more sub lieutenants joined and these were all former soldiers commissioned into the RND.[253] There was great incentive for newly-commissioned soldiers to choose the RND: as RNVR sub lieutenants they were equivalent to Army lieutenants and paid more than an Army subaltern.

The Nelsons would have a week in the Saint Aubin camp, continuing their training, until moving forward to relieve 1/RMLI as Brigade Reserve near Bois de la Maison Blanche on 30 July. The year moved on into August and the routine of training and lectures continued for another week, Lieutenant Commander Price teaching the NCOs while Major Barker lectured to the officers. On 8 August 189 Brigade relieved 190 Brigade in the left sub-sector and, as part of this move, Nelson Battalion moved into the front line, taking over from 7/Royal Fusiliers. The Nelsons were holding the Bradford trenches between Gavrelle and Oppy. It would be a long eight-day spell in the trenches, characterized by generally quiet days, but the nights made dangerous by German artillery bombardments. One of the first casualties was, however, the accidental wounding of Sub Lieutenant Ernest Towler. He had been out on patrol on the first night, 9 August, and was shot in the shoulder near one of the battalion's Lewis gun posts as he was returning. He was invalided home and out of the RND.[254] The shelling and machine-gunning of the Nelson trenches on the following night killed two able seamen and this was repeated two nights later, 12 August, when another two ratings of 'C' Company were killed. Nobody knew it at the time, but, mercifully, these would be the last Nelson deaths in action around Gavrelle. The shelling continued on the next two days, with gas shells in the ordnance mix falling on the ration dump. The support and reserve lines came under a heavy bombardment by German 4·2-inch and 5·9-inch guns. On the last full day in the front line Sub Lieutenant Thomas Baxter was seriously wounded when out on patrol. Shot through the thigh and dangerously ill, he was not fit enough to be sent home until the end of September. He was invalided out of the service. On 16 August the Artists Rifles of 190 Brigade (they had replaced 1/HAC in late June) came forward and the relief of Nelson Battalion was complete by 10.00 pm.

The Nelsons marched back to camp near Arras and were in billets at Aubrey Camp by 1.00 am. The next day was spent on administration and cleaning up after the tour in the front line. More reinforcements arrived from England – about 270 in total would join during August. Kit was inspected and deficiencies made good. The battalion armourer inspected and overhauled all the rifles and Lewis guns. The men marched to the baths at nearby Ste Catherine. On 18 August training began again with some emphasis on night operations in gas helmets, presumably because of the recent experience in the line. The routine was broken by visiting bands from 2/King's Own Scottish Borderers and the Royal Marines, who played in the camp. A brigade sports afternoon was held on 23 August, at which the Nelsons took nine prizes and this was followed in the evening by a battalion concert in the Divisional Theatre.

On 24 August, after only one week out of the line, it was time to go forward again. Company commanders inspected their men in the forenoon and there was a final visit to the baths. At 7.00 pm the battalion paraded and marched off to relieve Anson Battalion in the support line in the right sub-sector. Three companies were in the Naval & Marine Trench system west of Gavrelle, the fourth company further to the rear in the Red Line. In contrast to their previous visit to the front line, this spell to the end of August seems to have been fairly tranquil for the Nelsons. 'Day and night quiet' frequently appears in the War Diary and the working parties could get on with their work relatively un-molested. On 27 August Lieutenant Colonel Lewis temporarily took over as GOC 189 Brigade and Major Barker took his place as acting CO Nelson Battalion.

Two days later two Nelson petty officers[255] were tried by Field General Court Martial (FGCM) on a charge of impeding the Military Police in the execution of their duty. The charge stemmed from the Nelsons' time at Maroeuil in early July. The two POs had been dealing effectively with a noisy crowd of Nelson ratings at estaminet closing time when their efforts were inter-rupted by over-zealous military police (MP) corporals. An argument over jurisdiction ensued and the two POs 'had their names taken'. Both men were acquitted on the charge. On the same day a Nelson junior rating was before a FGCM charged with being in a field of growing potatoes near Maroeuil without lawful authority and carrying an empty sack and an entrenching tool. The local MPs had the field of spuds 'under observation' and arrested Able Seaman Chambers[256] as he left the field. Unfortunately for the MPs his sack was empty and that, together with his excuse that he 'went to get wild stuff', seems to have persuaded the court to find him 'not guilty'.

On the last day of August an eight-hour bombardment by British artillery of German trenches just north of Gavrelle shattered the relative peace. Sub Lieutenant Horace Cooper was hit in the shoulder while repairing shell holes in the Gavrelle Road in the middle of the night. He was invalided home. As the year moved into September, the Nelsons had one more day in the line, Drake Battalion coming forward to relieve them on the evening of 1 September.

The battalion moved back to bivouacs and shelters in the railway cutting near Roclincourt but had only two full days there before going back into the line. There was scarcely time to get two companies through the baths and to assimilate over two hundred reinforcements, who had been held back in the transport lines while the battalion was in the front line. On 4 September the Nelsons went forward again to relieve the 1/Norfolks who were holding the line close to the west of Oppy, the Divisional boundary having moved further to the north. By mid-afternoon the Nelsons were in position with two companies forward, one in support and one in reserve near Bailleul. The relief was achieved without casualties and the men turned-to improving the wiring and the trenches. The next six days in the line seem to have been free of major German bombardments of the front line but hostile machine-gunning and mortaring kept the troops' heads down. The battalion ration dump at a rail-head just behind the front attracted the attention of enemy artillery throughout. On the evening of 8 September this reached a climax with a heavy bombardment by German 5·9-inch guns which succeeded in blowing up the railway line. On the same day a large fighting patrol under Sub Lieutenant John Taylor, with Sub Lieutenant Dolman and 250 ORs, made a raid on the German front line, Fresnoy Trench north of Oppy. Sub Lieutenant Taylor and seventy ORs were wounded but no positive gains were recorded, other than keeping the Germans on their toes. Sub Lieutenant Taylor was, for several days, dangerously ill with severe bomb wounds down his right side and he was eventually invalided home and out of the RND. His leadership in this raid earned him a special mention in the CinC's despatch of 7 November 1917.[257] However, John Taylor owed his life to the bravery of Leading Seaman Arthur Coathup, who was awarded the Military Medal[258] the citation for which stated that it was given

> for gallantry on patrol on the night of 8th/9th September 1917. The O in C of the Patrol having been wounded, this NCO although wounded himself succeeded in carrying him back to the lines.[259]

On the afternoon of 10 September the Nelsons at the front were relieved by 7/Royal Fusiliers with the reserve company handing over to 4/Bedfords. In the evening the battalion marched back to billets at Maroeuil, stopping at Roclincourt for a hot meal. This signalled the end of the Nelson's last turn in the front line around Gavrelle. Another eighteen junior ratings had lost their lives in the trenches or died of wounds since the initial battle for the village in April.

They had less than two days at Maroeuil, enough time for a wash and brush-up, before marching back to Aubrey Camp on the evening of 12 September. This camp was closer to the front and large working parties were sent forward to work in the Red Line each night, those companies not involved continuing their training programme and absorbing newly joined ratings. Co-operation between troops on the ground and aircraft was becoming increasingly important and was the subject of a lecture to all officers and NCOs. After Church Parade on 16 September this lecture was followed by a visit to a local aerodrome where the CO, Sub Lieutenant Arnold and Petty Officer Anson[260] were given introductory flights.

Three new RNVR officers joined in the first half of September[261] and the Battalion Quartermaster, Lieutenant James A Gates RM, who had been with the Nelsons since Gallipoli, was relieved by Lieutenant Richard T Travers RM.

On 17 September the battalion moved camp and went into reserve for the following eight days. The principal task in this period was to undertake a major wiring of Gavrelle village. Almost every night saw three companies going forward to work just behind the front-line trenches. The task was rotated and the company not involved was sent off to the baths in Roclincourt. On 24 September Nelson Battalion was inspected by Rear Admiral Arthur C Leveson, who was flying his flag in the battlecruiser HMS *Australia*. The flag-ship of the Royal Australian Navy, she had joined the Grand Fleet in 1915. The Captain of HMS *Australia* (and Admiral Leveson's Flag Captain) was Captain Oliver Backhouse RN, two years on from his command of the 2nd Naval Brigade at Gallipoli. Backhouse had been the Nelson's Brigade GOC in 1914 and he was doubtless the instigator of this inspection of a naval battalion by a senior naval officer. On the following day 189 Brigade was relieved by 140 Brigade of 47th (London) Division and the Nelson's time at Gavrelle was at an end. Nelson Battalion was relieved by 1/7 London Regiment and moved back out of the line. By train and bus they were moved back to billets near the village of Tincques about fifteen miles to the west of Arras, where they settled in for a period of divisional rest and training.

The rest, however, was short-lived. The Third Battle of Ypres, the fight for the ridge on which the village of Passchendaele sits, had been turning the fields of Flanders into a muddy graveyard since early July 1917, but the gains had been minimal. Within a week of coming out of the line at Gavrelle the RND would be on its way north to provide fresh troops to XVIII Corps in its battle alongside the Canadians north-east of Ypres. The six days at Tincques saw 135 ORs join, mostly new men but some returning from various courses. The battalion also received two officers from England[262] but Lieutenant Herbert Reed, the Adjutant since late June, was detached to 189 Brigade HQ and Sub Lieutenant Bunting, who had only joined in June, was sent home sick. The training programme at Tincques was interspersed with inter-platoon football matches, but it is doubtful that the final was ever held because on the evening of 2 October the battalion, less 'C' Company, marched out of the camp to the railway station at Savy where they boarded their trains and departed for Belgium at around midnight.

In his despatch of 7 November 1917 Field Marshal Sir Douglas Haig included the names of several men of Nelson Battalion for their 'distinguished and gallant services and devotion to duty'. The despatch covered the period from 26 February to midnight 20/21 September 1917. The Nelsons listed in the CinC's despatch were:

Lieutenant [sic] A.W. Buckle	Sub Lieutenant J.H. Taylor
Petty Officer J. Tweddle[263]	Leading Seaman J.W. Todd[264]
Able Seaman S.P. Mascarenhas[265]	

NELSONS KILLED, MORTALLY WOUNDED OR DIED OF DISEASE IN THE GAVRELLE SECTOR, ARRAS, FROM 6 MAY TO 15 SEPTEMBER 1917.

RANK/RATING NUMBER	NAME DATE	CAUSE	BURIAL / MEMORIAL
AB R/571	HICKS, HH 06/05/17	DOW	STE CATHERINE BRITISH CEMETERY, ARRAS
AB CZ/4164	McALEENAN, WJ 06/05/17	DOW	STE CATHERINE BRITISH CEMETERY, ARRAS
LS KP/187	YATES, C DSM 06/05/17	DOW	STE CATHERINE BRITISH CEMETERY, ARRAS
AB R/378	PURKIS, CW 12/05/17	SICK	HAVERHILL CEMETERY, SUFFOLK
AB TZ/5342	PETTY, HP 01/06/17	DOW	LEICESTER (GILROES) CEMETERY
AB LZ/3051	KNIGHT, T 04/06/17	KIA	ARRAS MEMORIAL
AB R/330	ADAMS, GA 07/06/17	KIA	ORCHARD DUMP CEMETERY, ARLEUX-EN-GOHELLE
AB CZ/7372	CHRISTIE, W 18/06/17	DOW	ST HILAIRE CEMETERY, FREVENT
AB TZ/5345	CUMMINGS, W 26/06/17	SICK	CALAIS SOUTHERN CEMETERY
AB R/436	WHITE, SD 10/07/17	DOW	ALBUERA CEMETERY, BAILLEUL-SIRE-BERTHOULT
AB BZ/4735	SHELTON, G 11/07/17	KIA	ARRAS MEMORIAL
AB WZ/1300	PRITCHARD, HJ 12/07/17	DOW	AUBIGNY COMMUNAL CEMETERY EXTENSION
AB TZ/6354	MILLICAN, JG 14/07/17	KIA	ALBUERA CEMETERY, BAILLEUL-SIRE-BERTHOULT
AB LZ/3577	TAYLOR, F 19/07/17	DOW	CREETING ST MARY CHURCHYARD, SUFFOLK
AB R/463	SHEPHERD, H 22/07/17	DOW	NEWMARKET CEMETERY, CAMBS
AB R/360	LYCETT, W 09/08/17	SICK	BIRMINGHAM (WITTON) CEMETERY

RANK/RATING	NAME		
NUMBER	DATE	CAUSE	BURIAL / MEMORIAL
AB	RICHARDSON, F		
WZ/1361	10/08/17	KIA	ALBUERA CEMETERY, BAILLEUL-SIRE-BERTHOULT
AB	RISEBOROUGH, S		
TZ/8309	10/08/17	KIA	ALBUERA CEMETERY, BAILLEUL-SIRE-BERTHOULT
AB	FOLLETT, G		
TZ/8936	12/08/17	KIA	ALBUERA CEMETERY, BAILLEUL-SIRE-BERTHOULT
AB	SMITH, EJ		
WZ/1160	12/08/17	KIA	ALBUERA CEMETERY, BAILLEUL-SIRE-BERTHOULT

16

RETURN TO BELGIUM – FLANDERS AND PASSCHENDAELE:

3 OCTOBER – 9 DECEMBER 1917.

In early October 1917, as the RND moved north to Flanders, the fighting strength of Nelson Battalion's officers had changed yet again:

Commanding Officer	Lieutenant Colonel Frank Lewis DSO *[Leicester Regt]*
2nd in Command	*[Not identified – possibly Lieutenant Commander Buckle.]*
Adjutant	Lieutenant Frank Barrett *[acting]*
Lieutenant Commander RNVR	Archibald W. Buckle
Lieutenant RNVR	Ernest V.G. Gardner MC Leonard Spain Percival Batchelor *[acting]* Herbert L. Reed *[attached 189 Bde HQ]*

Sub Lieutenant RNVR

James E.R. Crawford	Cecil A. Clerk
George W. Bloomfield	William Wellwood
Robert H. Pawson	Norman K. Spoonley
Sidney M. Stringfield	John A. Pennell
William E. Jehring	Perceval Beaumont
Herbert B. Biggs	Robert S. Goodwin
Frank R.G. Richardson	Wilfred H. Appleton
Horace J. Arnold	Joe W. Brearley
Horace S. Page	Walter L. Willison

James W.E. Dolman   Ralph Moore
William Wright   John B.S. Howard
John Connelly   Albert Keep
Harold C. Birch
Francis E. Rees *[attached 'Y' TM Batty]*
Kenneth A. Hucklebridge *[attached 189 Bde LTM Batty]*
William A. Bowler *[detached to RND Signals Company]*

Quartermaster	Lieutenant Richard T. Travers, RMLI
Surgeon	William P. Starforth RN

Although the numbers appear high, the battle experience of the officers was low. Only two officers now had experience which reached back to Nelson Battalion at Gallipoli: Lieutenant Gardner (joined July 1915) and Lieutenant Spain (joined September 1915), although others had served there as ratings. Only Lieutenant Commander Buckle and the three lieutenants had taken part in the Battle of the Ancre. Only six of the sub lieutenants had fought at Gavrelle just five months earlier. For most of them the fighting for Passchendaele would be a baptism of fire in appalling conditions.

The trains carrying the three Nelson Battalion companies reached the Belgian town of Proven on the morning of 3 October and just before noon they were marched off to billets at Nouveau Monde, arriving there at 3.00 pm. 'C' Company, travelling twelve hours behind the main party, arrived in the camp at dawn on the following day. Training resumed immediately, a special class being formed for scouts and observers for each platoon, and another seventy-five reinforcements arrived. On 5 October the Nelsons were on the move again, towards the front. They first moved to Brown Camp, a couple of miles north-east of Poperinghe, and on the following day marched five miles east to Reigersburg Camp, situated north of Ypres near the village of Brielen to the west of the Yser Canal. Arriving at 3.00 pm, they set up bivouacs.

Three successive, set-piece attacks were planned for the RND and these would be executed, in turn, by 188, 190 and 189 Brigades. While the other two brigades were in intensive training, the men of 189 Brigade were sent to work in the forward area. For the Nelsons Reigersburg would be their base for the next week, during which limited training would have to be fitted around a huge demand for working parties. A large team of 600 Nelsons was sent forward on 7 October to work, under the direction of the Canadian Railway Troops Company, extending a light railway beyond St Julien at the rear of the battlefield. Two days later, the Nelson working parties were shifted on to road construction in the battle area between the villages of St Julien and Wieltje, two companies at a time working turn and turn about. At this time the Flanders fighting claimed its first Nelson casualties, Able Seaman Alfred Buckland being killed on 11 October. The next eleven days, during which Nelson Battalion

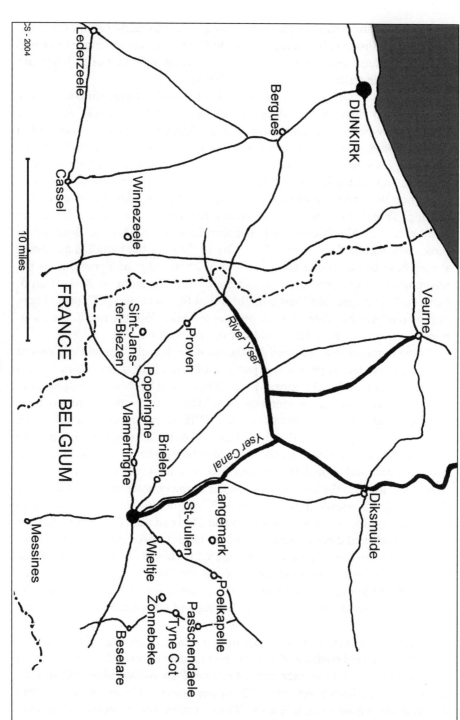

11. Flanders.

provided working parties in the dangerous area immediately behind the front, would see a rising number of casualties. On 13 October came a move to a camp called Kempton Park, a mile north of Ypres and a mile west of St Julien but still well within striking-distance of the Germans.

From 13 to 22 October Nelsons were sent forward in large numbers to work for the Royal Engineers: railways, roads and duckboard tracks across the swamps were being constantly disrupted by German shelling and demanded regular repairs. The toll of those killed and wounded on this task steadily mounted. Nine men were killed and over fifty were wounded, four mortally. Two men were wounded in the Nelsons' camp when it was bombed by German aircraft on the afternoon of 14 October, this raid being followed by a night of shelling. Three officers were wounded and rendered *hors de combat* during the same period.[266] Newly-commissioned Sub Lieutenant Maurice Boys joined three days later as Transport Officer. On 20 October the battalion had again shifted base to La Brique Camp on the northern edge of Ypres but on the morning of 23 October they moved back from the front to Brake Camp, between Poperinghe and Vlamertinghe about five miles west of Ypres. There they would have just three days to prepare for going into the line in the quagmire that was to be their battlefield in front of Passchendaele.

As the battalion readied itself for the front, with both men and equipment subject to detailed inspections, a party of officers, NCOs and runners went forward to reconnoitre the forward area. This would be their first opportunity to see the charnel swamp in which they would fight, although two weeks earlier some had had the opportunity to visit the XVIII Corps 'model ground' of the battlefield. The reality was ghastly and the rest of the battalion did not have to wait long to see it. At 10.00 am on 27 October Nelson Battalion moved forward towards Ypres and at dusk they moved into the line to relieve Hood Battalion, who had come into the line two days earlier as the counter-attack battalion for the initial RND assault carried out by 188 Brigade on 26 October. Such had been the casualties sustained by Anson and Howe of the 188 Brigade that the Hood had relieved them in the front line posts on the evening of that day. Now Nelson Battalion (on the right of the line with Hawke on their left) held the 188 Brigade's few hard-won gains for twenty-four hours until the 190 Brigade came forward to execute the next assault, planned for 30 October. The relief moves were carried out under heavy shelling and completed before midnight 27/28 October.

With 'B' Company in support about half a mile to the rear, 'D' Company moved to a forward position 300 yards east of Varlet Farm and had one platoon of 'A' Company on their right at the Divisional/Corps Boundary. 'A' and 'C' Companies held lines in rear of 'D' Company from the Wallemollen Cemetery and running in front of Inch Houses. The Germans were reported as 'inactive' during the rest of the night but the first Nelsons were already dying in front of

Passchendaele. Able Seaman Gwilym Lloyd died of wounds he received during the move forward. Sub Lieutenant William Jehring[267] was killed when he led out a night patrol.

The Nelsons' first full day in the mud of Passchendaele was marked only by a minor German attack, which was successfully repulsed, and by constant sniping from a pill box seventy-five yards in front of their line. After dark a large fighting patrol of Nelsons was sent forward and successfully captured the position. Not long thereafter the Artists Rifles of 190 Brigade came forward to relieve Nelson Battalion in preparation for the next attack. Nelson Battalion went back over the duckboards to Irish Camp, just north-east of Ypres. They would have less than twenty-four hours' rest there before moving out to act as reserve battalion for the 190 Brigade attack. Those twenty-four hours in the line had resulted in the loss of one officer and seventeen junior ratings and the wounding of at least another thirty. Several of these died later of their wounds. At this time the battalion also lost its Commanding Officer and Surgeon. Lieutenant Colonel Lewis and Surgeon Starforth were both suffering from the effects of gas shells and they were evacuated home. Sub Lieutenant Crawford also took a dose of mustard gas in this attack and was invalided. Lieutenant Commander Robert H. Shelton[268] immediately came over from his position as 2i/c Hawke to take command of the Nelson.

At 5.00 pm on 29 October 'A' and 'D' Companies moved forward in readiness for the assault at dawn the next day. The next morning saw the initial British barrage draw an immediate retaliatory response from the Germans which landed right on top of the massed formations of the Artists Rifles on the right of the line. The problems multiplied in the following hours and it was not long before Nelson Battalion was called forward in immediate support of, and at the disposal of, GOC 190 Brigade. 'A' and 'D' Companies moved to Albatross Farm and 'C' Company moved to Mousetrap Trench.[269] 'B' company were employed as stretcher-bearers for 190 Brigade and, given the scale of casualties and the battlefield conditions, had a hugely daunting task. The gains on the battlefield were minimal for massive loss of life. The first two assaults by RND brigades were now over. Both had been 'traditional' daylight attacks following a barrage, both had failed to achieve their objectives and both had resulted in terrible casualties. For the final assault, by 189 Brigade, the tactics would be changed.

On 31 October Nelson Battalion moved forward into the right of the line with Hawke on their left. The Nelson line, running about 500 yards east and north of Varlet Farm, was held by 'A' Company on the right and 'C' Company on the left. 'D' Company was in immediate support and 'B' Company was held in reserve at Albatross Farm, which was also the Battalion HQ, about a mile to the rear. The new tactics, championed by Commander Asquith of Hood Battalion, rejected the wasteful daylight frontal assault in favour of smaller,

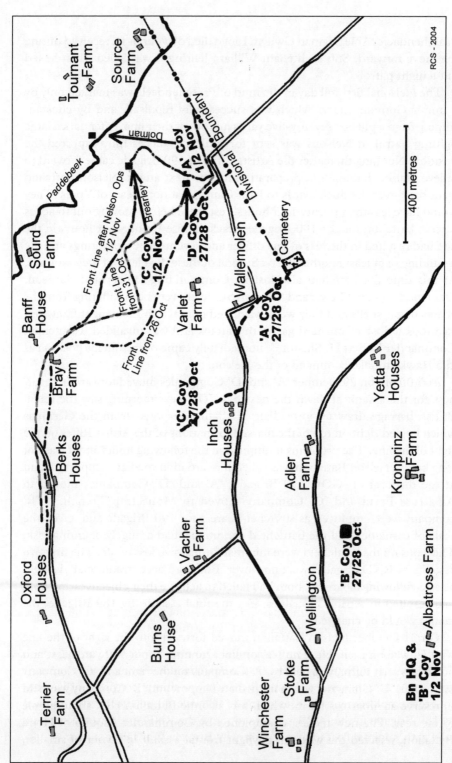

12. Operations at Passchendaele.

commando-style operations against strong points under the cover of darkness, in much the style of the Nelson assault on 28 October but with smaller numbers. These tactics were to prove very successful. Two such fighting raids were carried out by Nelson Battalion on the night of 1/2 November.

The 189 Brigade reports[270] give the fullest description of these raids:

> At 8.10pm one officer (Sub Lt Dolman) and 30 ORs from 'A' Company moved off to capture a concrete building at V.28.a.95.10 but failed to find it. (During these operations confusion was caused by the fact that the concrete structures at V.28.c.5.7. and 4.7. [about 400 yards north-east of Varlet Farm] were believed to exist – in reality they do not: the nearest structures in the neighbourhood being at V.28.a.95.10 and v.28.c.8.8. [about 600 yards north-east of Varlet Farm]. This no doubt caused Sub Lt Dolman's party to lose their way.)
>
> At the same hour one officer (Sub Lt Brearley) and 11 ORs from 'C' Company moved on a concrete structure at V.28.c.8.8. The enterprise was a success. 1 under-officer, 11 ORs and 1 machine gun were captured, 3 ORs killed. The following is the march of events: The officer and his 11 men advanced in extended line about 3 paces apart, the officer in the centre and an NCO on each flank. When the line arrived within 80 to 90 yards of the position, strong wire entanglement and ditches were discovered and a further advance became very difficult. The officer then sent one NCO and three men round to his left and an NCO and two men to his right of the position. He, with the remainder, continued to go straight forward. When about 60 yards from the position the enemy opened fire with a machine gun. The left party were held up by wire and a machine gun. They rejoined the centre party and the whole worked round to the right and eventually rushed the position from the enemy's rear. Lewis guns were placed in position to cover the advance but were only to fire in case of necessity. As events turned out they were not required. Directly the concrete structure had been captured 'A' Company was brought up on the right and the remainder of 'C' Company on the left and the line was consolidated.

The Divisional History clearly recognized the significance of Brearley's raid:

> So fell a post which, through no fault of their own, two battalions had failed to capture in the attack of October 30th.[271]

No men were lost in this exemplary raid. The new tactics were an answer to the particularly difficult conditions in the Passchendaele swamps where a 'front line' was a line in name only and the enemy positions consisted of isolated concrete emplacements in a sea of mud. They would be effectively employed by 189 Brigade in the following days to move the RND line forward successfully with minimal cost in lives. As the 189 Brigade War Diary stated:

Night operations and surprise tactics . . . were a novelty and completely successful. There is no doubt that they are most effective against enemy outpost lines and probably less costly than set-piece attacks under a barrage.

For his part in the action Sub Lieutenant Joe Brearley was awarded the Military Cross:

> For conspicuous gallantry and devotion to duty. With eleven men he attacked a concrete dug-out in the dark. They killed three of the enemy and captured one officer and eleven other ranks and a machine gun. The advance was over boggy ground and the position was strongly wired. The enemy fired on them with a machine gun but he himself shot the No.1 of the gun and rushed the position.[272]

Able Seaman William Stringer was awarded the Distinguished Conduct Medal for his bravery during the attack:

> For conspicuous gallantry and devotion to duty as one of a party of one Officer and 11 other ranks who successfully attacked a concrete dug-out and took an officer and 11 men prisoner. Although wounded, he continued his work of carrying messages for several hours until again wounded so seriously that he was unable to move.[273]

The Nelson War Diary gives slightly different timing for the raid, recording Sub Lieutenant Brearley moving forward at 6.30 pm and completing the operation at 9.00 pm. Although no men were killed during the raid, German retaliation was inevitable and they laid down a significant barrage on the Nelsons at 8.30 pm and again at 2.00 am. 2 November was recorded as a very dull day with low visibility which prevented British contact aircraft coming over the battlefield at first light as planned. The Germans kept up intermittent machine-gun fire and shelling was 'average', but their snipers were very active. As darkness fell, men of 'A' Company went forward and established a line of outposts to fill gaps in the Nelson forward line. No enemy counter-attack was attempted and after dark Hood Battalion came forward and took over the new posts, completing the relief by midnight. Nelson Battalion moved back into Brigade Reserve at Canal Bank.

In the shelling on the night of 1/2 November a number of gas shells landed on the Nelson Battalion HQ at Albatross Farm. Lieutenant Commander Robert Shelton, after barely 48 hours in command, was gassed, together with his Adjutant, Lieutenant Barrett, and other members of the HQ Staff. The Nelson War Diary also records heavy gas shelling during the relief by Hood Battalion on the next night. Those evacuated suffering from the effects of gas also included Major Barker, Lieutenant Reed, Sub Lieutenants Stringfield and Richardson and fifty ORs. Only about six ORs of the Nelson lost their lives as a result of these operations in early November: six too many but a stark and welcome contrast to the slaughter suffered by the Artists Rifles in attempting the same objectives in daylight two days earlier. The dead of 188 and 189 Brigades in the daylight attacks were counted in many hundreds and probably more than 2,000 in total casualties. The casualties of 189 Brigade were not greatly over 100 for better success.

Nelson Battalion spent 3 and 4 November at Canal Bank undertaking the post-battle routine of cleaning kit and reorganizing to take account of those killed or wounded. 188 Brigade relieved 189 Brigade in the line on 5 November, and Nelson and Hawke Battalions, with the Brigade HQ, moved to Dambre Camp. Relieved by 1st Division, the RND's contribution to the Third Battle of Ypres was at and end, although 188 Brigade stayed in the line for another two days. The Canadians, whose left flank the RND had fought to protect down in the swamp, drawing German fire away from their advance on the higher ground, took the village of Passchendaele three days later.

The man who would be the last Commanding Officer of Nelson Battalion joined as the battalion came out of the line. Lieutenant Commander Stuart Gale Jones joined as Acting CO on 3 November from 2i/c Anson. Jones had joined the RNVR before the war as a sub lieutenant in May 1914 and had served with Anson Battalion at Antwerp. He had been promoted rapidly: to lieutenant in November 1914 and to lieutenant commander in June 1915. Appointed 2i/c of Anson in July 1915, he had then been promoted to commander in November when he took command of Anson at the end of the Gallipoli campaign. He remained CO of Anson until May 1916 when he reverted to lieutenant commander and 2i/c. He rejoined Anson Battalion in the BEF as 2i/c in December 1916 after two months sick in UK and attended a Battalion Commander's Course from July to September 1917. His appointment as a commander in command of Nelson Battalion was made permanent in late January 1918. Lieutenant Spoonley took over as Adjutant.

There were several battalion base-changes in early November as Nelson Battalion moved back into the rear area, pulled itself back into shape and took a well-earned and long-overdue, extended rest period. They left Dambre Camp in buses on the afternoon of 6 November and travelled for two hours to Road Camp, near Sint-Jans-ter-Biezen two miles west of Poperinghe and close to the border with France. There the recovery continued with the whole battalion going through the baths to rid themselves of the mud of Passchendaele. On 10 November a three-hour march took the Nelsons further west to Winnezeele, over the border into France. They were now more than twenty miles behind the front at Ypres. Another five hours of marching in pouring rain on the next day, during which twenty-two men fell out, took them to camp at Helsthaege in the Division's rest area in the villages around Lederzeele, a dozen miles south of Dunkirk. Here the battalion stayed for seventeen days.

Reinforcements began to arrive and platoon and company training began again. Five new sub lieutenants[274] joined in the first few days, together with 243 ORs from the Depot. This new intake seemed acceptable as the War Diary noted:

> On inspection, they seemed a very fair draft physically, the majority of them having had 14 weeks training in England.

Drafted to their companies, the new men settled quickly to the routine of company training over the next two weeks. On 18 November Nelson, Hawke and Drake Battalions mustered for church parade at Broxeele. The service was taken by Bishop Gwynne, the Chaplain-General, and, on completion, the battalions marched past the GOC, Major General Lawrie. On the following day Brigadier General Coleridge inspected all the Nelson companies while they were training. Four days later Captain Oliver Backhouse accompanied the GOC II Corps when he inspected the Nelsons training. Two new officers[275] joined during this period with another twenty-nine ORs.

The Military Medal was awarded to thirteen Nelson ratings for their gallantry in the quagmire in front of Passchendaele :[276]

Petty Officer R.A. Gray[277]	Petty Officer E.B .Walsh[278]
Leading Seaman J.G. Cowie[279]	Leading Seaman J.A. Tindall[280]
Able Seaman J. Blackwood[281]	Able Seaman W. Chapman[282]
Able Seaman C.W. Gifford[283]	Able Seaman J. McDonald[284]
Able Seaman A.V. Painter[285]	Able Seaman R. Rodgers[286]
Able Seaman A. Smith[287]	Able Seaman M.P. Stokoe[288]
Able Seaman A. Stuart[289]	

On 28 November it was time to move east again. Six hours of marching took them back to Le Nouveau Monde area and another three hours on the road on the following day brought them back to Road Camp near Sint-Jans-ter-Biezen. With this move back towards Ypres, all the signs were pointing to another spell at the front in Flanders and for the first five days at Road Camp this appeared to be the plan. Training continued in preparation for a cold, wet winter in the trenches and outposts around Ypres . At a church parade on 2 December a number of decorations were announced for service at Passchendaele a month earlier: the Military Cross for Sub Lieutenant Brearley (already described) and for Lieutenant William Wellwood (acting lieutenant since late October); the Distinguished Conduct Medal for Petty Officer Hugh Smith[290] and Able Seaman Frederick Chubb[291]. The citations read:

<u>Lieutenant W Wellwood</u> – For conspicuous gallantry and devotion to duty when in command of his company during minor operations after his company commander had been wounded. He advanced his line 200 yards, but in doing so the two half-companies became separated. He reconnoitred the ground, under heavy machine-gun fire, and had to wade through a swamp, but eventually succeeded in finding the missing half-company.[292]

<u>Petty Officer H Smith</u> – For conspicuous gallantry and devotion to duty. Taking command when the senior petty officers had become casualties and gaining the objective, he personally superintended the selection of the site and consolidated the gained ground.[293]

<u>Able Seaman FG Chubb</u> – For conspicuous gallantry and devotion to duty as one of a party told off to capture a concrete strong point. He had to go up to his waist in water but was the first man to reach the objective, bayoneting one of the crew of a machine gun and helping to capture the gun and twelve prisoners.[294]

Until 4 December the RND was under orders to relieve the 32nd Division on the following night. Late in the night on that day these orders were cancelled and on the next day the battalion was directed to be ready to entrain at short notice. The training programme was cancelled and all ranks prepared to move. The Divisional Order for the move was received on 6 December, but the trains were cancelled the next day and, meanwhile, training resumed pending a decision. This came at midday on 8 December and the Nelsons had one day (a Sunday) to make final preparations and to clean their camp before departure. The move started just after midnight on 9/10 December when 'A' Company left Road Camp, followed four hours later by the remainder of the battalion. The trains took them more than fifty miles south to the sector of the front held by the Third Army to the south-west of Cambrai.

Considering the conditions in the mire in which they fought, the Nelson Battalion casualties at Passchendaele were remarkably few. They were fortunate that a change of tactics saved 189 Brigade from the daylight slaughter suffered by 188 and 190 Brigades. In the months of October and November 1917 in Flanders, Anson Battalion had over 130 killed, Howe Battalion more than 100. In 189 Brigade the Nelson's 47 deaths were exceeded only by Hood Battalion with over 60. The Nelson dead totalled one officer and 46 ORs, 26 of whom have no known grave and are commemorated on the Tyne Cot Memorial. The number of Nelson wounded was probably close to 200.

NELSONS KILLED OR MORTALLY WOUNDED
IN THE THIRD BATTLE OF YPRES (PASSCHENDAELE)
FROM 11 OCTOBER TO 29 NOVEMBER 1917.

RANK/RATING NUMBER	NAME DATE	CAUSE	BURIAL / MEMORIAL
AB R/3273	BUCKLAND, AL 11/10/17	KIA	TYNE COT MEMORIAL
AB R/1534	STOAKES, WH 12/10/17	DOW	MENDINGHEM MILITARY CEMETERY, POPERINGE
AB R/3446	MORGAN, J 13/10/17	DOW	DOZINGHEM MILITARY CEMETERY, POPERINGHE
AB BZ/4698	GAYTON, GW 14/10/17	KIA	MINTY FARM CEMETERY, ST JAN
PO TZ/3996	WATSON, J 14/10/17	KIA	MINTY FARM CEMETERY, ST JAN
AB R/269	DONEY, T 15/10/17	DOW	DOZINGHEM MILITARY CEMETRY, POPERINGHE
AB TZ/2912	KELLY, E 17/10/17	KIA	NEW IRISH FARM CEMETERY, YPRES
AB TZ/2074	REYNOLDSON, JL 17/10/17	KIA	NEW IRISH FARM CEMETERY, YPRES
AB TZ/5504	JONES, AC 18/10/17	DOW	DOZINGHEM MILITARY CEMETERY, POPERINGHE
AB R/374	COLGRAVE, HW 22/10/17	KIA	ST JULIEN DRESSING STATION CEMETERY, LANGEMARCK
AB R/442	EVISON, W 22/10/17	KIA	ST JULIEN DRESSING STATION CEMETERY, LANGEMARCK
AB TZ/188	GOUDY, L 22/10/17	KIA	TYNE COT MEMORIAL
AB WZ/1428	LANDE, E 22/10/17	KIA	TYNE COT CEMETERY, PASSCHENDAELE
AB R/3425	LLOYD, G 27/10/17	DOW	TYNE COT MEMORIAL
AB R/521	BARRATT, C 28/10/17	KIA	TYNE COT MEMORIAL
AB CZ/1063	DUNN, FC 28/10/17	KIA	TYNE COT MEMORIAL
AB R/3423	GARNER, WB 28/10/17	KIA	TYNE COT MEMORIAL
AB R/1489	HARDIMAN, HF 28/10/17	KIA	TYNE COT MEMORIAL

RANK/RATING	NAME		
NUMBER	DATE	CAUSE	BURIAL / MEMORIAL
SUB LT	JEHRING, WE		
	28/10/17	KIA	TYNE COT MEMORIAL
AB	JENVEY, WP		
R/30	28/10/17	KIA	NEW IRISH FARM CEMETERY, YPRES
AB	MACKIE, JD		
CZ/1761	28/10/17	KIA	TYNE COT MEMORIAL
AB	McKENZIE, WJ		
CZ/1442	28/10/17	KIA	TYNE COT MEMORIAL
AB	McLAY, J		
CZ/4024	28/10/17	KIA	TYNE COT MEMORIAL
AB	PARKER, E		
R/3448	28/10/17	KIA	TYNE COT MEMORIAL
AB	POTTER, W		
TZ/5343	28/10/17	KIA	TYNE COT MEMORIAL
AB	RANDALL, FG		
R/3309	28/10/17	KIA	TYNE COT MEMORIAL
AB	RANDLE, WA		
LZ/4293	28/10/17	KIA	TYNE COT MEMORIAL
AB	RINGS, F		
R/3299	28/10/17	KIA	TYNE COT MEMORIAL
AB	ROBERTS, O		
WZ/122	28/10/17	KIA	TYNE COT MEMORIAL
AB	SCHOFIELD, A		
TZ/5365	28/10/17	KIA	TYNE COT MEMORIAL
AB	SMITH, W		
CZ/5608	28/10/17	KIA	TYNE COT MEMORIAL
AB	OWEN, HA		
R/3204	29/10/17	DOW	DOZINGHEM MILITARY CEMETERY, POPERINGHE
AB	PIRIE, JG		
CZ/7269	29/10/17	DOW	DUNHALLOW ADS CEMETERY, YPRES
AB	VICKERS, JT		
LZ/3615	29/10/17	DOW	DOZINGHEM MILITARY CEMETERY, POPERINGHE
LS	DIXON, TW		
TZ/96	30/10/17	KIA	ST JULIEN DRESSING STATION CEMETERY, LANGEMARCK
AB	GREENHALGH, J		
R/3276	30/10/17	KIA	ST JULIEN DRESSING STATION CEMETERY, LANGEMARCK
AB	HATCH, PA		
R/512	30/10/17	DOW	DOZINGHEM MILITARY CEMETERY, POPERINGHE
AB	McFARLANE, A		
CZ/1977	30/10/17	KIA	ST JULIEN DRESSING STATION CEMETERY, LANGEMARCK

RANK/RATING NUMBER	NAME DATE	CAUSE	BURIAL / MEMORIAL
AB LZ/5094	STEWART, SR 30/10/17	KIA	TYNE COT MEMORIAL
AB R/1313	GUNN, JT 01/11/17	KIA	TYNE COT MEMORIAL
AB R/1379	HOWSON, J 01/11/17	KIA	TYNE COT MEMORIAL
AB R/1407	PEARCE, WH 01/11/17	KIA	TYNE COT MEMORIAL
AB R/3313	AWCOCK, E 02/11/17	KIA	TYNE COT MEMORIAL
LS TZ/5303	O'NEIL, JG 02/11/17	DOW	TYNE COT MEMORIAL
LS KW/590	WOOD, J 03/11/17	DOW	TYNE COT MEMORIAL
AB WZ/1700	STOKES, GA 07/11/17	DOW	MENDINGHEM MILITARY CEMETERY, POPERINGHE
AB R/1293	ALFORD 22/11/17	DOW	ST SEVER CEMETERY EXTENSION, ROUEN

17

THE FINAL BATTLE – THE FLESQUIÈRES SALIENT AND WELSH RIDGE:

10 DECEMBER 1917 – 22 JANUARY 1918.

The destination for the men of Nelson Battalion at the end of their train journey south was 'L' Camp near the village of Barastre, four miles south of Bapaume. The front line had moved about twenty miles east since the RND was last on the Ancre. However, the earlier successes of combined infantry and tank attacks by the British Army in driving the Germans back, and taking parts of the Hindenburg Line, had been reversed by the strong German counter-attack in front of Cambrai. The RND had been brought south to take over a sector in the Flesquières salient which now jutted dangerously out into German-held territory. It was defensible only because of the commanding high ground of Welsh Ridge, which trended north-east to south-west and lay about a mile to the east of Villers-Plouich. The British trenches atop this ridge looked towards the German-held village of La Vacquerie a couple of hundred yards to the east. In this context 'high ground' is a relative term because the country was very open and the so-called 'ridges', although of great tactical importance, were little more than undulations in the farming landscape, perhaps only thirty metres higher than the lowest ground between them.

After a day in the trains, the Nelsons were in their billets at Barastre by 9.00 pm on 10 December. Their move to the front was not long delayed, orders for the move being received the next day. On the afternoon of 12 December the battalion moved four miles to Étricourt and an advance party went forward to reconnoitre the line on the following morning. The RND Sector, La Vacquerie – Marcoing, ran to the east and north-east of the village of Villers-Plouich and was on a frontage of nearly seven thousand yards. As the reconnaissance was taking place, most of the battalion moved up to billets in the Bois d'Havrincourt, about three miles behind the front, with the HQ and 'B' Company moving to a position near the village of Beaucamp a mile north-west

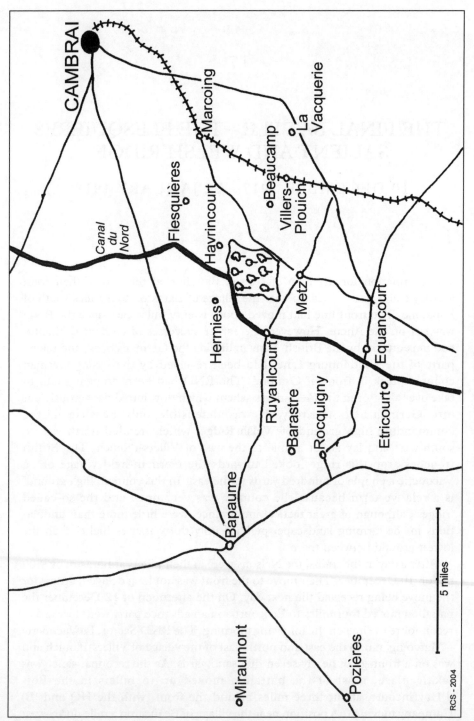

CAMBRAI

Marcoing

La Vacquerie

Beaucamp

Villers-Plouich

Flesquières

Havrincourt

Canal du Nord

Metz

Equancourt

Hermies

Ruyaulcourt

Baraste

Rocquigny

Etricourt

Bapaume

Miraumont

Pozières

5 miles

13. Final Operations – Welsh Ridge.

RCS - 2004

of Villers-Plouich. Beaucamp was on the ridge which ran immediately to the east of Villers-Plouich, Highland Ridge.

On 14 December Nelson Battalion moved into the line as the RND took over a long front that had previously been held by two divisions. Between 5.30 and 8.30 pm the Nelsons relieved 15/Royal Irish Rifles in 189 Brigade's right sub-sector. The exceptionally long four-mile front that the RND took over had to be held by all three brigades at the same time. Each brigade put two of its battalions in the front-line, one in support and one in reserve.

Jerrold described the sector as:

> The apex of the salient, where our line was on the northern slopes of Welsh Ridge, and the whole length of the eastern face of the ridge. On the right of the Division, the southern slopes of Welsh Ridge ran down into a valley, across which our [new] front line, continuing on the line of Welsh Ridge, fell behind our old front line. The Division on the left of the Naval Division, who held the captured sectors of the Hindenburg line forming the northern arm of the salient, was the 19th Division. On the right, holding the re-entrant formed by the German incursion behind our original front, was the 9th Division of the 5th Army. The new front, representing, as it did, a position hurriedly improvised in the stress of battle, was almost lacking in material defences.

Nelson Battalion would have five days in the front line trenches which, yet again, seem to have been left in poor condition by the Army battalion they relieved. The Nelson War Diary notes that all the fire and communication trenches had to be cleaned out and that, when this had been done, the duck-boards which were so important for mobility around the trenches were found to have been covered up in nearly all of them. Getting the defences into order was a high priority and wiring patrols were sent out.

Relieved by Hood Battalion on the evening of 19 December, the Nelsons moved back into support trenches behind Villers-Plouich for two days. Work was started on a new reserve trench about four hundred yards in rear of the front line to be known as Naval Reserve Trench and 'D' Company spent 20 December on that task. Little did they know how important that trench would be in ten days time. Two days earlier Nelson Battalion had said goodbye to Lieutenant Commander Buckle, who was appointed as 2i/c Anson Battalion. Soon to be the Anson's Commanding Officer, it would be with them that he would win the DSO on no less than four occasions in 1918. Lieutenant Commander Gordon Whittaker, DSO, was appointed across as 2i/c Nelson from Drake Battalion as Lieutenant Commander Buckle left, but would not join until 29 December.[295] Whittaker had been awarded the DSO for his part in the Battle of the Ancre a year earlier. When the battalion came out of the line they received another six officers who had joined around 15 December.[296]

The nominal roll of Nelson Battalion's officers as they made ready for their Christmas 1917 tour at the front was close to complement:

Commanding Officer	Commander Stuart G. Jones RNVR *[acting]*
2nd in Command	Lieutenant Commander Gordon W. Whittaker, DSO
Adjutant	Lieutenant Norman K. Spoonley *[acting]*
Lieutenant RNVR	Leonard Spain
	Frank D. Purser
	William Wellwood MC *[acting]*
	Herbert B. Biggs *[acting]*
	Horace J. Arnold *[acting]*
	Wilfred H. Appleton *[acting]*

Sub Lieutenant RNVR	Cecil A. Clerk	John H. Cowan
	George W. Bloomfield	Ralph Taylor
	Robert H. Pawson	Carl P.P. Dieterle
	John A. Pennell	Maurice Boys
	Perceval Beaumont	Frank A. Taylor
	Walter L. Willison	William B. Harrison
	James W.E. Dolman	John G. Coburn
	Ralph Moore	Lewis C.A. Anderson
	William Wright	Francis V.C. Rudnick
	Harold C. Birch	Alexander Brackenridge
	Henry A. Bennett	Thomas White
	Herbert B. Cannin	

Kenneth A. Hucklebridge *[attached 189 Bde LTM Batty]*
William A. Bowler *[detached to RND Signals Company]*

Quartermaster	Lieutenant Richard T. Travers, RMLI
Surgeon	William A. McKerrow RN

The days before Christmas 1917 saw Nelson Battalion moved back to billets in Metz-en-Couture, two companies of the RND's Pioneer Battalion, 14/Worcesters, coming up as relief. The previous six days had seen ten junior ratings killed. The first Nelson officer to fall on Welsh Ridge was Sub Lieutenant Ralph Taylor.[297] He was killed, only five weeks after joining the battalion, while moving back to Metz in charge of an advance party drawn from 'C' Company.

On 23 December, as preparations were being made to go into the line again for Christmas, the proceedings were enlivened by the shooting down of a German aircraft which came down near the Battalion HQ in late afternoon. 'Wreckage soon surrounded by Nelsons,' noted the War Diary, but the fate of the crew went unrecorded. The Nelson advance party went forward after dark on that day, arrived at the Drake Battalion HQ some three hours later and were briefed on the latest battalion dispositions. On Christmas Eve the rest of the Nelsons came into the line for four days over Christmas. The weather was certainly seasonal, with severely cold weather and frequent falls of snow. The Nelson War Diary noted that, despite the cold, there were very few casualties with trench feet, probably because the men were well supplied with hot food. Work on the trenches and barbed wire entanglements continued apace. Patrols were sent out, but it was generally very quiet and there were no signs of an impending enemy attack. Even so, on Christmas Day and Boxing Day five ORs were killed in action. On 27 December Lieutenant Frank Purser was sniped and killed while touring the line among his men and the next day a German shell landed on a dug-out killing Sub Lieutenant Thomas White[298] and seven junior ratings.

After dark on 28 December Drake Battalion came into the front line and the Nelsons moved back a mile and were held in immediate reserve for their brigade, taking over trenches on the eastern slopes of Highland Ridge. They would have just one more day of relative quiet. On 29 December 'C' and 'D' companies went forward to continue work on Naval Reserve Trench and a party of twenty men was sent to the Artillery Brigade HQ just north of Villers-Plouich to spend eight hours making dug-outs. That night the Germans brought down an artillery barrage on Highland Ridge and Sub Lieutenant Maurice Boys was among several wounded. The shells landing on the Nelsons that night were but a foretaste of what was to come at dawn on the following day.

The storm broke at 6.30 am on 30 December with an intense German barrage being laid down on the whole of the RND front using artillery and trench mortars. German 'storm troops' in white overalls were lying on the snow in no-man's-land in the thick, December dawn mist and they assaulted the RND front-line trenches with flame-throwers as soon as the barrage lifted. In the 189 Brigade's centre sector of the divisional line, which was held by Hood Battalion on the left and Drake Battalion on the right, the enemy troops forced a withdrawal which was followed by a counter-attack. However, on the Drake's right Howe Battalion had been forced to withdraw from three successive rows of trenches, Corner Trench, Welsh Trench and Welsh Support. The Drakes had to fall back to Welsh Support to conform. By capturing this trench complex on the very crest of Welsh Ridge the enemy had gained a view down to Villers-Plouich. They could not be allowed to retain it. The Germans then began a bombing battle with the Drakes northwards along Welsh Support Trench. All

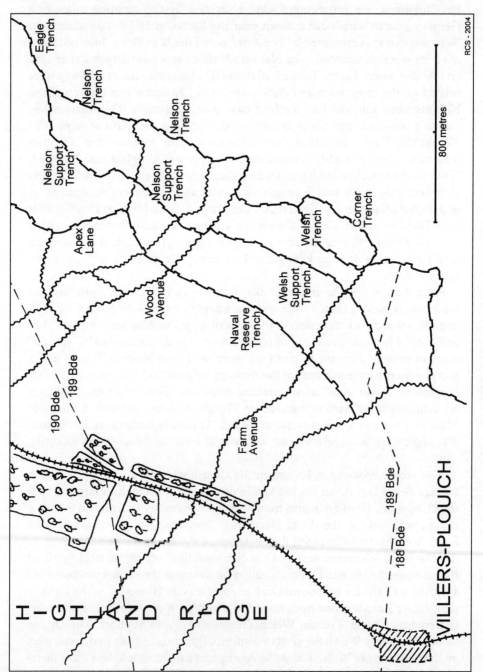

14. Counter-attack Operations on Welsh Ridge.

800 metres

touch with Howe Battalion and with 188 Brigade had been lost. It was in these circumstances that at 7.25 am Nelson Battalion was ordered to send a company to reinforce the Drakes. 'C' Company (Sub Lieutenant Cecil Clerk) moved forward to Naval Reserve Trench, about 300 yards in rear of Welsh Support. The CO of Drake Battalion planned to use them, with one company of Drakes, to counter-attack that southern portion of Welsh Support that the Drakes had been forced to give up. It took time to get the Nelsons forward and to prepare the attack and it was after 2.00 pm when it was executed. Most of 'C' Company went into the assault from Naval Reserve Trench as the Nelson War Diary records:

> Over the top. No artillery barrage. A few men succeeded in gaining the objective, but the right was held up by machine-gun fire. At the same time a bombing party bombed up FARM AVENUE . . . towards the right end of WELSH SUPPORT, meeting considerable opposition. Splendid gallantry was shown by Sub Lieut CLERK oc 'C' Coy, who, although severely wounded, did not relinquish his command until forced to do so through weakness and loss of blood. Petty Officer J.C. WINN, who was in charge of the bombing party also showed splendid gallantry during the attack.

In mid-morning, before this attack, the remainder of Nelson Battalion had been ordered forward to man Naval Reserve Trench. They were in place just as 'C' Company went over the top. Meanwhile, the Divisional Commander and the GOCs of the two naval brigades had met in a conference in the early afternoon. There it was decided that Welsh Support Trench should be re-taken by Nelson Battalion (on the left) with the Ansons (on the right), the latter now temporarily commanded by Lieutenant Commander Buckle. An artillery barrage would be laid down for the attack, which was timed for 4.30 pm. Brigade orders were issued accordingly.

The Nelson War Diary recorded the attack:

> "A' Coy (OC Lieut W.D. WELLWOOD) on the right, supported by 'D' Coy (OC Lieut L. SPAIN) attacked at 4.30pm from NAVAL RESERVE. 'B' Coy (OC Lieut H.B. BIGGS), in co-operation with the Drakes on the left attacked on the immediate left.

The Nelsons went forward, following the barrage, and

> The attack was entirely successful, WELSH SUPPORT re-occupied, and by 5.30pm after a little bombing on our right we were in touch with one of the companies of the Anson Bn (of 188th Bde), who had taken part in the attack. During the operations the enemy put down a very heavy barrage on the area between WOOD AVE and FARM TRENCH along NELSON RESERVE [sic – mistake for Naval Reserve] but fortunately we

suffered very few casualties. Great initiative and courage was shown by Lieut H.B. BIGGS ('B' Coy), Lieut W.D. WELLWOOD ('A' Coy) and Chief Petty Officer J. MARCHANT ('A' Coy). Two platoons from 'A' Coy under Sub Lieut L.C.ANDERSON were sent to reinforce the left company of the Drakes. The coolness and devotion to duty of Sub Lieut ANDERSON were outstanding features.

The entire length of Welsh Support Trench was captured by Nelson and Anson Battalions by 7.00 pm and consolidation of the position started at once and continued through the night. Welsh Support Trench became the new firing line. Corner Trench and Welsh Trench and about 250 yards of ground had been lost but it could have been very much worse had it not been for the spirit of the two counter-attacking battalions. Overnight 30/31 December the Nelsons joined the Drakes in the front line. In Welsh Support Trench Nelson 'C' Company was on the right in touch with Anson Battalion. On 'C' Company's left was Nelson 'A' Company and on their left two platoons of Nelson 'B' Company. The left of Welsh Support Trench was held by Drake 'B' Company and the other two platoons of Nelson 'B' Company. Nelson 'D' Company garrisoned Naval Reserve Trench behind them. The Nelson War Diary noted for that night:

> Food, water and ammunition in ample supplies were carried up to the front line as early as 7.30[pm] by men of 'D' Coy. The remainder of the night of 30th and morning of 31st passed off with intermittent shelling and great activity of enemy TMS [trench mortars], snipers and machine-gun fire. The work of the battalion stretcher bearers during the operations and under cover of darkness enabled us to evacuate all our wounded by 8am of the 31st. The battalion and company runners work was wonderful to the extreme. Every message which had to be carried was at certain points in the open where the ground was being constantly swept by shell fire, machine-gun and rifle bullets.'

The Nelson War Diary concludes its record of the battalion's 'Operations in Counter-Attack' with the following comments:

> When the three companies were ordered to man NAVAL RESERVE Lieut [sic] T.W.WHITTAKER, DSO, second in command NELSONS, and Sub Lieut H.C. BIRCH proceeded to the DRAKE HQ, and thence to NAVAL AVE., to ensure that correct positions were taken up. Their Headquarters were made at Junction of NAVAL and TRENCH AVE. and they acted as liaison between NELSONS and DRAKES. The splendid behaviour of Lieut WHITTAKER in the organising and passing of orders to company commanders and in keeping Bn HQ posted as to the condition of affairs during the operations proved of incalculable value.

The Nelson War Diary was generous in its praise of comrades-in-arms in Drake Battalion:

> Great gallantry was displayed by Lieut HARRIS, MC (Two Bars) officers and other ranks of 'B' Coy Drakes and their splendid work in the re-occupying of WELSH SUPPORT. Their work is spoken of in the highest terms by all who were in the vicinity.'

Lieutenant Harris was awarded the DSO for his part in the action, as was Lieutenant Commander Buckle for his leading of Anson Battalion on the Nelson's right, but, once again, decorations for the Nelsons were few. There was no recognition of Sub Lieutenant Lewis Anderson's efforts while reinforcing the Drakes, or for the courage of Lieutenant William Wellwood. Lieutenant Herbert Biggs received the Military Cross:

> For conspicuous gallantry and devotion to duty. He twice passed through heavy enemy barrage, reconnoitring the ground before a counter-attack. It was entirely due to his coolness and courage that the counter-attack was successful and the position cleared of the enemy.[299]

Drake and Hood Battalions had taken the brunt of the initial German assault, which had been carried out by a large German force equivalent to fifteen battalions. The casualties in Nelson Battalion, in its counter-attack role, were broadly the same as those in the Hood and somewhat less severe than those suffered by Drake. The Nelson War Diary assessed that about 100 ORs had been killed or wounded or were missing. The Divisional Report of Operations breaks this down to twenty killed, seventy-two wounded and four missing. Today's records show the much higher number of forty-four ORs killed or dying of wounds received in the action. Sub Lieutenant Cecil Clerk, who had led the first brave but unsuccessful attack by his men of 'C' Company, died of his wounds on the following day. His 'splendid gallantry' went unrecognized. Two other officers were wounded.[300]

Nelson Battalion spent the first four days of the new year in the line, the time being spent consolidating the new front-line trench system which had been established as a result of the counter-attack and which was in a poor state because of the recent heavy German bombardments. The Nelson War Diary recorded for this period:

> although the men in the line are heavily taxed, physically, the morale and spirits of all are excellent. Hot food is being very well supplied, and the percentage of trench feet very low.

On 1 January 1918 four new officers[301] joined and went straight into the line. Enemy activity had been low since the assault in the last days of December, but snipers were still active. On the day after he joined the battalion Sub Lieutenant Walter Thomas was sniped and hit in the head. He was invalided home and out of the RND. Two days later Sub Lieutenant Albert Robertson was hit and died of his wounds in the 149th Field Ambulance. He was twenty years old and had served just three days in the line. Several ORs also lost their lives during this 'quiet' period in the line in the La Vacquerie sector.

Lieutenant Commander Gordon Whittaker, the Nelson 2i/c, who had only been with the battalion since the end of December, was appointed to a course at the Senior Officers' School, Aldershot, and departed for England on 3 January. His place as 2i/c would be taken on 20 January by Lieutenant Commander Henry G. Andrews, who had been wounded with Nelson Battalion in the Action of Achi Baba Nullah in July 1915.

On the night of 4/5 January most of Nelson Battalion was relieved by Drake Battalion and moved into Brigade Support on Highland Ridge, but Nelson 'C' and 'D' Companies stayed for a little longer in Naval Reserve Trench behind the Drakes. Later on 5 January the whole battalion moved back to Metz as Divisional Reserve, remaining there for the next three days. On the evening of 8 January they went forward to the firing line again to relieve Drake Battalion for a short spell of two days. During this period Sub Lieutenant Herbert Cannin was killed while on patrol. He was the last of nearly fifty officers to be killed in action with the Nelsons, twenty-three officers having been lost at Gallipoli and twenty-five with the BEF.

Late on 10 January Nelson Battalion and 4/Bedfords of 190 Brigade exchanged places, the Nelson moving back to Havrincourt Wood with the last companies arriving there at 3.00 am. They now had a week out of the line in a camp named Nelson Camp. Here they could at last mend and maintain their kit and equipment for the first time since mid-December, but much work also needed to be put in to improve the drainage and duckboards around the camp. The Corps GOC inspected the camp on 13 January and the whole battalion marched off to the baths in Metz on the next day. Advance reconnaissance parties went forward on 17 January and Nelson Battalion went into the line on the following day, relieving 4/Bedfords. The Nelson War Diary notes, yet again, the bad state of the trenches they took over:

> Front line in very bad condition. Men busy building firing positions and cleaning of trenches. Up to the waist in mud and water at parts.

The next four days in the line, making the trenches habitable and installing duckboards, cost the lives of another five ratings killed in action before Nelson and Hawke Battalions exchanged duties on 21 January. Serving under the name of William Higgins, Able Seaman William Doyle was the last Nelson to be killed in action fighting with his battalion on 20 January 1918.[302] The War Diary notes that:

> There was very little sickness and few cases of trench feet during this turn in the line, as was expected because of the bad state of the trenches.

The men of the Nelson marched back to Havrincourt Wood on the evening of 21 January and spent the night there. On the following day they were relieved by 2/Oxford & Bucks and marched five miles to billets at Equancourt, there relieving the 1/KSLI. They did not then know it but Nelson Battalion had completed its last tour in the front-line trenches.

Awards to ratings for gallantry during the operations on Welsh Ridge were announced in routine orders as the battalion left the trenches for the last time. The Military Medal was conferred on[303]:

Chief Petty Officer J Marchant, TZ/2118 (a Bar to the MM he had won at Gavrelle.)

Petty Officer J.C. Winn[304] (dow)   Able Seaman H. Bannister[305]

Able Seaman J. Walsh[306]   Able Seaman F.J. Woodbine[307]

NELSONS KILLED, MORTALLY WOUNDED OR DIED OF DISEASE DURING OPERATIONS AT WELSH RIDGE FROM 14 DECEMBER TO 24 FEBRUARY 1918.

RANK/RATING	NAME NUMBER	DATE	CAUSE	BURIAL / MEMORIAL
AB LZ/4470	BROWN, F	14/12/17	DOW	FIFTEEN RAVINE BRITISH CEMETERY, VILLERS-PLOUICH
AB R/5175	PEAKE, WR	14/12/17	KIA	THIEPVAL MEMORIAL
AB R/4015	MORGAN, EF	15/12/17	DOW	SUNKEN ROAD CEMETERY, VILLERS-PLOUICH
AB R/3921	POULTON, W	15/12/17	KIA	FIFTEEN RAVINE BRITISH CEMETERY, VILLERS-PLOUICH
AB R/5490	DUNSTER, WS	17/12/17	KIA	THIEPVAL MEMORIAL
AB WZ/2258	GRIFFITHS, F	17/12/17	DOW	FIFTEEN RAVINE BRITISH CEMETERY, VILLERS-PLOUICH
AB WZ/1019	LEWIS, JW	17/12/17	KIA	FIFTEEN RAVINE BRITISH CEMETERY, VILLERS-PLOUICH
AB BZ/1380	PHILLIPS, WG	18/12/17	KIA	THIEPVAL MEMORIAL
LS TZ/6357	BATTLE, J	19/12/17	KIA	THIEPVAL MEMORIAL
LS WZ/1425	WARBURTON, C	19/12/17	KIA	THIEPVAL MEMORIAL
AB R/5518	MURKETT, W	20/12/17	SICK	ROCQUIGNY-EQUANCOURT ROAD BRITISH CEMETERY, MANANCOURT
AB TZ/934	SMITH, CB	22/12/17	DOW	RIBECOURT ROAD CEMETERY, TRESCAULT
SUB LT	TAYLOR, R	22/12/17	KIA	METZ-EN-COUTURE COMMUNAL CEMETERY BRITISH EXTENSION
AB R/5179	CONNOP, R	25/12/17	KIA	VILLERS-PLOUICH COMMUNAL CEMETERY
AB R/391	DYE, WH	25/12/17	KIA	VILLERS-PLOUICH COMMUNAL CEMETERY
AB R/3896	JONES, J	25/12/17	KIA	VILLERS-PLOUICH COMMUNAL CEMETERY
AB R/4011	ELLWAY, FRM	26/12/17	KIA	THIEPVAL MEMORIAL
AB R/5181	PALMER, J	26/12/17	KIA	THIEPVAL MEMORIAL

RANK/RATING NUMBER	NAME DATE	CAUSE	BURIAL / MEMORIAL
AB TZ/386	BURRELL, FS 27/12/17	KIA	VILLERS-PLOUICH COMMUNAL CEMETERY
AB R/484	EDWARDS, WG 27/12/17	KIA	THIEPVAL MEMORIAL
AB BZ/3132	GIBBS, E 27/12/17	KIA	THIEPVAL MEMORIAL
AB R/4073	NELSON, JW 27/12/17	KIA	VILLERS-PLOUICH COMMUNAL CEMETERY
LT	PURSER, FD 27/12/17	KIA	VILLERS-PLOUICH COMMUNAL CEMETERY
AB WZ/2584	ANDREWS, TE 28/12/17	KIA	THIEPVAL MEMORIAL
AB TZ/5206	BANKS, J 28/12/17	KIA	THIEPVAL MEMORIAL
AB R/3941	BRERETON, AE 28/12/17	KIA	VILLERS-PLOUICH COMMUNAL CEMETERY
AB CZ/7219	CAMPBELL, W 28/12/17	KIA	THIEPVAL MEMORIAL
AB CZ/3171	GALLOWAY, J 28/12/17	KIA	THIEPVAL MEMORIAL
AB CZ/4013	MAYS, J 28/12/17	KIA	THIEPVAL MEMORIAL
AB CZ/3381	MURPHY, J 28/12/17	KIA	THIEPVAL MEMORIAL
AB R/4038	STATHAM, W 28/12/17	KIA	THIEPVAL MEMORIAL
SUB LT	WHITE, T 28/12/17	KIA	FIFTEEN RAVINE BRITISH CEMETERY, VILLERS-PLOUICH
AB R/5489	RYAN, AH 29/12/17	DOW	ROCQUIGNY-EQUANCOURT ROAD BRITISH CEMETERY, MANANCOURT
AB R/5209	BAILEY, HL 30/12/17	KIA	FLESQUIERES HILL BRITISH CEMETERY
AB R/4846	EVANS, IJ 30/12/17	KIA	THIEPVAL MEMORIAL
AB MZ/389	GRAHAM, TN 30/12/17	KIA	FLESQUIERES HILL BRITISH CEMETERY
AB R/1486	GURNEY, AH 30/12/17	KIA	FLESQUIERES HILL BRITISH CEMETERY
AB R/1473	HALL, JW 30/12/17	KIA	THIEPVAL MEMORIAL
AB R/1380	MARTIN, WJ 30/12/17	DOW	VILLERS-PLOUICH COMMUNAL CEMETERY

RANK/RATING NUMBER	NAME DATE	CAUSE	BURIAL / MEMORIAL
AB CZ/3661	McINTOSH, G 30/12/17	DOW	ROCQUIGNY-EQUANCOURT ROAD BRITISH CEMETERY, MANANCOURT
AB R/3382	PAGE, WF 30/12/17	DOW	THIEPVAL MEMORIAL
AB R/3221	PINNOCK, ECP 30/12/17	KIA	FLESQUIERES HILL BRITISH CEMETERY
AB R/3416	PRITCHARD, J 30/12/17	KIA	FLESQUIERES HILL BRITISH CEMETERY
AB R/5215	RICHARDSON, PW 30/12/17	KIA	FLESQUIERES HILL BRITISH CEMETERY
AB R/1538	SANDERS, WE 30/12/17	KIA	THIEPVAL MEMORIAL
AB R/3222	SELBY, TJ 30/12/17	KIA	THIEPVAL MEMORIAL
AB BZ/3451	ADAMS, H 31/12/17	KIA	CABARET-ROUGE BRITISH CEMETERY, SOUCHEZ
LS R/28	CHUBB, FG, DCM 31/12/17	KIA	MARCOING BRITISH CEMETERY
SUB LT	CLERK, CA 31/12/17	DOW	ROCQUIGNY-EQUANCOURT ROAD BRITISH CEMETERY, MANANCOURT
AB R/3209	DIGHTON, AV 31/12/17	DOW	ROCQUIGNY-EQUANCOURT ROAD BRITISH CEMETERY, MANANCOURT
AB R/3261	DUDLESTON, EM 31/12/17	DOW	ROCQUIGNY-EQUANCOURT ROAD BRITISH CEMETERY, MANANCOURT
AB R/3420	EVANS, WS 31/12/17	KIA	THIEPVAL MEMORIAL
AB R/3176	FOSTER, RG 31/12/17	KIA	FLESQUIERES HILL BRITISH CEMETERY
AB CZ/244	GALLOWAY, W 31/12/17	KIA	THIEPVAL MEMORIAL
PO TZ/5191	GRAY, RA, MM 31/12/17	KIA	THIEPVAL MEMORIAL
AB R/3913	HOLDER, SS 31/12/17	KIA	FLESQUIERES HILL BRITISH CEMETERY
AB R/1533	HYMAN, AL 31/12/17	KIA	THIEPVAL MEMORIAL
AB R/3205	KEELING, SC 31/12/17	KIA	MARCOING BRITISH CEMETERY
AB CZ/7250	LEARMONT, R 31/12/17	KIA	FLESQUIERES HILL BRITISH CEMETERY

RANK/RATING NUMBER	NAME DATE	CAUSE	BURIAL / MEMORIAL
AB TZ/1030	LUTHER, TS 31/12/17	KIA	THIEPVAL MEMORIAL
AB R/5042	MASON, W 31/12/17	KIA	FLESQUIERES HILL BRITISH CEMETERY
AB R/4176	MYCOCK, J 31/12/17	KIA	MARCOING BRITISH CEMETERY
AB R/567	NOAD, H 31/12/17	KIA	FLESQUIERES HILL BRITISH CEMETERY
AB CZ/2293	NOBLE, J 31/12/17	KIA	THIEPVAL MEMORIAL
AB R/4276	ROSEN, H 31/12/17	DOW	RUYAULCOURT MILITARY CEMETERY
AB R/1546	SAVAGE, C 31/12/17	KIA	THIEPVAL MEMORIAL
AB R/3915	SHARP, D 31/12/17	KIA	THIEPVAL MEMORIAL
AB BZ/4014	SMITH, E 31/12/17	KIA	THIEPVAL MEMORIAL
AB BZ/9066	SMITH, OG 31/12/17	DOW	MARCOING BRITISH CEMETERY
AB LZ/4376	SURRIDGE, FC 31/12/17	KIA	FLESQUIERES HILL BRITISH CEMETERY
AB R/4290	TAPP, WJ 31/12/17	DOW	FLESQUIERES HILL BRITISH CEMETERY
LS CZ/7230	THOMSON, W 31/12/17	KIA	THIEPVAL MEMORIAL
AB TZ/7063	TODD, E 31/12/17	KIA	THIEPVAL MEMORIAL
AB WZ/361	WHITE, ST 31/12/17	KIA	METZ-EN-COUTURE COMMUNAL CEMETERY BRITISH EXTENSION
AB R/5164	BOON, F 01/01/18	DOW	ROCQUIGNY-EQUANCOURT ROAD BRITISH CEMETERY, MANANCOURT
AB TZ/8903	BOOTH, A 01/01/18	DOW	ROCQUIGNY-EQUANCOURT ROAD BRITISH CEMETERY, MANANCOURT
AB BZ/9050	PURSALL, HE 01/01/18	DOW	CABARET-ROUGE BRITISH CEMETERY, SOUCHEZ
AB R/3291	WARD, J 01/01/18	KIA	ROCQUIGNY-EQUANCOURT ROAD BRITISH CEMETERY, MANANCOURT
AB R/3303	BISSELL, WF 02/01/18	DOW	ROCQUIGNY-EQUANCOURT ROAD BRITISH CEMETERY, MANANCOURT

RANK/RATING NUMBER	NAME DATE	CAUSE	BURIAL / MEMORIAL
AB R/4006	RENSHAW, TW 02/01/18	KIA	THIEPVAL MEMORIAL
AB TZ/6655	HALL, TC 03/01/18	DOW	THIEPVAL MEMORIAL
AB R/3936	IRONS, GH 03/01/18	KIA	MARCOING BRITISH CEMETERY
AB TZ/2953	LONGSTAFF, JW 03/01/18	KIA	FLESQUIERES HILL BRITISH CEMETERY
AB WZ/835	CLARKE, H 04/01/18	DOW	SUNKEN ROAD CEMETERY, VILLERS-PLOUICH
SUB LT	ROBERTSON, AJ 04/01/18	DOW	THIEPVAL MEMORIAL
AB R/3439	WILLIAMS, LA 04/01/18	KIA	FLESQUIERES HILL BRITISH CEMETERY
AB R/3889	BOULTON, WI 05/01/18	DOW	ROCQUIGNY-EQUANCOURT ROAD BRITISH CEMETERY, MANANCOURT
AB R/518	LEA, H 05/01/18	DOW	ROCQUIGNY-EQUANCOURT ROAD BRITISH CEMETERY, MANANCOURT
AB CZ/4107	BUTCHART, A 08/01/18	KIA	THIEPVAL MEMORIAL
SUB LT	CANNIN, HB 10/01/18	KIA	THIEPVAL MEMORIAL
AB R/6107	KENKNIGHT, JE 10/01/18	DOW	RUYAULCOURT MILITARY CEMETERY
AB R/306	LUGG, RJ 10/01/18	KIA	THIEPVAL MEMORIAL
PO TZ/3841	WINN, JC MM 11/01/18	DOW	ROCQUIGNY-EQUANCOURT ROAD BRITISH CEMETERY, MANANCOURT
AB R/3150	LANE, W 19/01/18	KIA	THIEPVAL MEMORIAL
LS BZ/3493	MILLARD, J 19/01/18	KIA	FIFTEEN RAVINE BRITISH CEMETERY, VILLERS-PLOUICH
AB R/1378	PERRYGROVE, EJ 19/01/18	KIA	THIEPVAL MEMORIAL
AB MZ/800	SMITH, S 19/01/18	KIA	THIEPVAL MEMORIAL
AB R/3979	DOYLE, W 20/01/18	KIA	THIEPVAL MEMORIAL
AB R/3905	BENNETT, A 30/01/18	DOW	ST SEVER CEMETERY EXTENSION, ROUEN

RANK/RATING NUMBER	NAME DATE	CAUSE	BURIAL / MEMORIAL
AB R/3928	JOHNSON, A 16/02/18	SICK	LIVERPOOL (TOXTETH PARK) CEMETERY
AB R/4062	LOWE, W 16/02/18	DOW	BILLINGE (ST AIDAN) CHURCHYARD, LANCS
AB R/67	COWLS, BC 24/02/18	DOW	MONT HUON MILITARY CEMETERY, LE TREPORT

18

THE DISBANDING OF NELSON BATTALION:

23 JANUARY – 23 FEBRUARY 1918.

On 23 January 1918 at 3.00 pm the entire battalion boarded light trains which travelled the five miles to Rocquigny, completing the transfer in about two hours. A short march took them to the battalion billeting area near Barastre where they took over the camp from 23/Royal Fusiliers. The RND was now out of the line, their sector on Welsh Ridge having been taken over by 2nd Division, and they would not go back to the front at Flesquières until mid-February. By then Nelson Battalion had ceased to exist and most of the men had been dispersed to other units.

Jerrold records that the RND now

> put in a month's work on the strengthening and extension of successive defensive positions, all of them unfortunately too close to our front to be of much value when the crisis arose.[308]

The crisis to come was the huge German offensive of March 1918 which would sweep the RND back to its old positions on the River Ancre. Nelson Battalion was not part of that fighting retreat, but many ex-Nelsons, serving in other RND battalions, were to fall or become POWs in its execution.

Through the remainder of January 1918 and into February the Nelsons worked on their camp near Barastre: the rifle and bayonet ranges were improved and, as a protection against German bombing, earthworks were thrown up around all the huts and horse standings. The battalion officers went forward to the village of Hermies, closer to the front, to reconnoitre the defences. The last new officer to join Nelson Battalion arrived on 4 February.[309] On the same date Lieutenant Leonard Spain was struck off the Nelson's strength on leaving the RND to take up an appointment at HMS Excellent for sea service and a gunnery course. He had served almost continuously with the

Nelsons since joining on Gallipoli in September 1915 and in that time he had acted as both 2i/c and CO of the battalion.

Parades, inspections and training continued in parallel to the tasks of the working parties. Such was the routine until Tuesday 5 February 1918. On that day Nelson Battalion were on parade early at 7.15 am for an address by their GOC, Brigadier General Bray. (Brigadier General Coleridge, on moving to GOC 188 Brigade, had been relieved by Brigadier General Asquith. Asquith was severely wounded only two days later and Brigadier General R.N. Bray was brought in as GOC 189 Brigade.) As the Nelson War Diary briefly records:

> GOC 189th Brigade spoke to the battalion, letting them [know] they were to be broken up. News received created profound depression in all ranks.

A decision had been taken a few days earlier to reduce the strength of all British infantry brigades from four to three battalions. In the RND Nelson and Howe Battalions were selected for disbanding, their men to be dispersed to the remaining four naval battalions. The end of Nelson Battalion was now decreed and little time was wasted before its implementation. Working parties were still needed, however, and as soon as the parade, with its depressing news, was completed three hundred men under the 2i/c were marched off to Havrincourt Wood to work on the defence system there. The Divisional Commander, Major General Lawrie, arrived there during the forenoon and inspected their work. One can only speculate on the enthusiasm being put into the job following that morning's announcement.

On 7 February, even as work and training continued and another 150-strong working party went off by bus in the morning to Havrincourt Wood, the first Nelsons were preparing to leave the battalion. The first of these departed at 3.00 pm on that day as two drafts were marched off to their new units: ten officers and 200 ORs were transferred to Drake Battalion[310]; five officers and 100 ORs to Hood Battalion.[311] The only good news on this day was that a Nelson rating, Able Seaman A.W. Boath, had been awarded the Belgian Croix de Guerre.[312]

The next two weeks of February 1918 were taken up with working parties and training as the RND prepared to go back to the front line at Flesquières. The battalion shifted camp on 14 February but remained in the Barastre area. Havrincourt Wood and the various dumps at Ytres and Metz all required manpower and a large party was employed building dug-outs at RND HQ. On 20 February came a Divisional Order to transfer all available officers and 489 ORs to the 7th Entrenching Battalion. The next day saw the scattered working parties return to camp as nominal lists were prepared for this coup de grâce on Nelson Battalion. On 22 February eight officers and 493 ORs were transferred to the 7th Entrenching Battalion[313], leaving Nelson Battalion with just three officers and twenty-three ORs on the strength. Most of the officers sent to the entrenching battalion moved on to Hawke Battalion in mid-March. The ratings were similarly dispersed to other battalions. A significant number were detached on 14 March to 1/RMLI and with that battalion several Nelsons were killed and captured in the RND retreat ten days later. The three officers remaining in the rump of Nelson Battalion were probably the CO, Commander S.G. Jones, the 2i/c, Lieutenant Commander H.G. Andrews, and the Quartermaster, Lieutenant R.T. Travers RMLI. The ratings were probably the senior NCOs (Regimental and Company Sergeant Majors) of the battalion for whom places in other battalions could not be immediately found.

The Royal Naval Division Roll of Honour for Nelson Battalion[314] and the Commonwealth War Graves Commission records for Nelson Battalion contain the names of several ratings who were killed in action, died of their wounds or died as POWs after the February 1918 dispersal of the battalion. The two records are not consistent but the deaths so recorded are included at the end of this chapter for completeness.

The men of Nelson Battalion who were transferred to other RND battalions in February and March 1918 served with great distinction in their new units and many officers and ratings were decorated for their gallantry during the final, victorious months of the war. Among these were:

Commander Stuart G. Jones – the last CO of Nelson Battalion took command of Hawke Battalion in April 1918 and was killed leading them in a bloody action at Thilloy on 25 August 1918 during the Advance to Victory.[315]

Lieutenant Commander Henry G. Andrews – the last 2i/c of Nelson Battalion was invalided home with influenza in March 1918 and later became 2i/c of 2nd Reserve Battalion. He died of influenza and pneumonia just after the Armistice.

Lieutenant Herbert B. Biggs, MC – joined Hawke Battalion in August 1918 and, for his handling of Lewis guns in the same August 1918 action at Thilloy in which Commander Jones was killed, was awarded a Bar to the Military Cross which he had won with Nelson at Welsh Ridge,[316]

Lieutenant Horace J. Arnold – fought with Drake Battalion until being wounded in late September 1918. During that time he was twice awarded the Military Cross for gallant leadership as a company commander.

Lieutenant Alexander Brackenridge – served in Hood Battalion until the end of the war, winning the Military Cross twice in nine days: in late September 1918 on the Escaut Canal and in early October at Niergnies, in the fighting for Cambrai.[317]

Lieutenant Sydney Flowitt – wounded on the Ancre, he was re-appointed to Nelson just as the battalion was disbanding and was cross-posted to

Hawke. In early October 1918 he won the Military Cross for his courage in the battle for the Canal du Nord.[318]

Sub Lieutenant John A. Pennell – served with Drake Battalion until the end of the war. He was awarded the Military Cross on two occasions: for gallantry during the German assault in March 1918 and again in September/October at Graincourt and the Escaut Canal.

Petty Officer James G. Cowie, CZ/2047, MM – transferred to Hood Battalion in the February 1918 draft, he subsequently added a Bar to the Military Medal which he had won with Nelson Battalion at Passchendaele. He also was awarded the Distinguished Conduct Medal on no less than three occasions in the closing months of the war, a truly amazing record of courage.

Chief Petty Officer James Marchant, TZ/2118, MM* – joined Hood Battalion in April 1918 and was awarded the Distinguished Conduct Medal for gallantry at Achiet-le-Petit on 21 August 1918, to add to the two Military Medals he had won with Nelson Battalion.

All of this death and glory for the former officers and men of Nelson Battalion was yet to come. On 23 February 1918, almost exactly three years and six months after the battalion formed up at Deal on the weekend of 21/22 August 1914, the final entry was made in the Nelson Battalion War Diary:

> Battalion Surplus viz. 3 officers and 23 ORs moved to Inf Bde HQ RUYAULCOURT awaiting final disposal. Battalion totally disbanded . . . . WAR DIARY CLOSED.'

On the following day, 24 February 1918, Able Seaman Bertram Cowls[319] died in the 47th General Hospital, Le Tréport, of serious head wounds that he had received in the firing line on 4 January. He was the last man to die from fighting in the line with Nelson Battalion but over the following years many men would have their lives cut short by the wounds they had received in battle.

In early June 1919 many former Nelson men were present in the parade on Horse Guards in London, when the RND was finally disbanded in the presence of the Prince of Wales and watched by its founding father Winston Churchill. They would have been in one of the naval battalions that survived to the end: Hood, Drake, Anson and Hawke. The latter battalion was commanded on the parade by Commander Robert Shelton, DSO, who for a brief period had commanded Nelson Battalion in Flanders. The Anson was led by Commander 'Lofty' Buckle, DSO***, who fought and learned his soldiering with Nelson Battalion in 1916 and 1917.

Six years later, in 1925, other former Nelsons gathered on Horse Guards to witness the unveiling of Sir Edwin Lutyens' graceful memorial to the more than 45,000 casualties of the Royal Naval Division. The memorial was dismantled in 1939 as another world war approached. In 1951 the author, as a young boy, accompanied his father to witness the re-dedication of the RND Memorial on its new site in the grounds of the Royal Naval College at Greenwich. It is to be regretted that no Nelsons survive to see the memorial gloriously reinstated on its original site at Horse Guards in November 2003.

MEN, FORMERLY OF NELSON BATTALION, KILLED, MORTALLY WOUNDED OR DIED OF DISEASE AFTER THE FEBRUARY 1918 DISBANDING.

Recorded as Nelson Battalion by CWGC. The following men had been detached from 7th Entrenching Battalion to 1/RMLI on 14 March 1918 and they were killed or captured in action while serving with that battalion. However, they were still recorded on Nelson Battalion Draft Orders as 7th Entrenching Battalion was only a holding unit for Nelsons pending their permanent posting.

RANK/RATING NUMBER		NAME DATE	CAUSE	BURIAL / MEMORIAL
AB R/5701	‡	COX, B 22/03/18	KIA	ARRAS MEMORIAL
AB R/5045		BROTHERTON, AH 24/03/18	KIA	ARRAS MEMORIAL
AB R/1517	‡	ELLIOTT, C 24/03/18	KIA	ARRAS MEMORIAL
AB TZ/7641	‡	FOX, J 24/03/18	KIA	ARRAS MEMORIAL
AB R/3202	‡	PAGE, AW 24/03/18	KIA	ARRAS MEMORIAL
AB KW/300	‡	SWINDLE, G 24/03/18	KIA	ARRAS MEMORIAL
LS CZ/4167	‡	RAE, T 07/04/18	KIA	POZIERES MEMORIAL
AB LZ/4074		NYE, JB 25/05/18	POW/DD	MONS COMMUNAL CEMETERY
AB R/3406		DESBOROUGH, G 24/07/18	POW/DD	MONS COMMUNAL CEMETERY
AB R/5894	‡	SIMPSON, JJ 27/07/18	POW/DD	NIEDERZWEHREN CEMETERY, CASSEL, GERMANY
LS LZ/2118		WILD, FD 02/08/18	POW/DD	HAMBURG CEMETERY, OHLSDORF
AB R/5695		SMITH, AG 22/11/18	POW/DD	COLOGNE SOUTHERN CEMETERY, GERMANY

‡ = Included in IWM RND Roll of Honour, Nelson Battalion.

POW/DD = Prisoners of war who died of disease in captivity. All were captured on 24 March 1918.

Recorded as Anson Battalion by CWGC. Both of the following men had been posted to Anson in late February 1918 and should not be regarded as Nelson Battalion casualties.

RANK/RATING NUMBER		NAME DATE	CAUSE	BURIAL / MEMORIAL
AB CZ/5225	‡	COWANS, J 14/03/18	DOW	ETAPLES MILITARY CEMETERY
AB R/5562	‡	SPIERS, AH 23/03/18	DOW	GREVILLERS BRITISH CEMETERY

‡ = Included in IWM RND Roll of Honour, Nelson Battalion.

Recorded as Hawke Battalion by CWGC. The following rating had been posted to Hawke in late March 1918 and should not be included in Nelson Battalion.

RANK/RATING NUMBER		NAME DATE	CAUSE	BURIAL / MEMORIAL
AB CZ/7473	‡	BISSET, JK 27/08/18	DOW	BUCQUOY COMMUNAL CMETERY EXTENSION

‡ = Included in IWM RND Roll of Honour, Nelson Battalion.

19

EPILOGUE – EIGHTY-FIVE YEARS ON

On 4 June 2001 the Arras Archaeology Service found human remains while investigating a development site north of Point du Jour on the old Gavrelle battlefield.[320] The remains were identified, by 'RND' and 'NELSON' metal shoulder badges, as belonging to a sailor of Nelson Battalion. No other remains were found in the vicinity and no more detailed identification of the body was possible.

The morning of Friday 25 October 2002 was cool, wet and windy in the Pas-de-Calais. Two miles to the north-east of Arras a small party of about fifteen naval and civilian personnel had gathered in the Commonwealth War Graves Commission (CWGC) cemetery which lies north of the village of Athies, just off the Arras – Gavrelle Road. In Point-du-Jour Cemetery are buried or commemorated more than 760 Commonwealth servicemen who lost their lives in the Great War. Among them are nearly sixty sailors, marines and soldiers of the 63rd (RN) Division who fought and died around the village of Gavrelle, three miles down the road, in 1917. The purpose of the gathering on that wet October morning was to lay to rest the remains of two more sailors of that division whose remains had recently been found, eighty-five years after their death in battle.

One was the unnamed rating of Nelson Battalion. He had probably been killed by a shell on 23 or 24 April 1917. He was one of the fifty Nelsons who died at that time and whose names are inscribed on the Arras Memorial because they have no known grave. The other man was from Hood Battalion: his remains had been found in the village of Gavrelle on 31 August 2001. The burial party was headed by the British Naval Attaché in Paris and the service was, appropriately, conducted by the Chaplain of HMS *Nelson*, HM Naval Base Portsmouth. After the Committal a bugler of the Royal Marines sounded the Last Post and Reveille over the graves. When the service was over, the unknown Nelson sailor had joined two of his comrades-in-arms from the same battalion who lie at rest in the care of the CWGC at Point-du-Jour.[321] His remains are now in Plot 4, Row C, Grave 6. His head-stone is inscribed 'A Sailor of the Great War – Nelson Battn. RND. 23–24 April 1917'.

Nelson Battalion deaths in the Great War totalled 766:
the MEF accounted for 277 deaths;
BEF operations in France and Belgium for 489 deaths.[322]

AS THE STARS THAT SHALL BE BRIGHT WHEN WE ARE DUST

MOVING IN MARCHES UPON THE HEAVENLY PLAIN,

AS THE STARS THAT ARE STARRY IN THE TIME OF OUR DARKNESS,

TO THE END, TO THE END THEY REMAIN.

FROM 'FOR THE FALLEN' BY LAURENCE BINYON (1869–1943)

NOTES

1   NHB: First Lord's Minutes, 5th and 6th Series, July 1914 to May 1915. NA: ADM1/8410/23 – Royal Naval Division – Formation and Development of (1914). These minutes, with a helpful commentary by Captain Christopher Page RN, – the Head of the NHB, have been published in the *RND Journal*, Issues 19 – 21. Editor Leonard Sellers. ISSN.1368–499X. See also Jerrold, Douglas: '*The Royal Naval Division*', Appendix A.

2   Petty Officer Euan Fleming, Clyde 4/1545, was killed in action at Anzac, Gallipoli, on 3 May 1915.

3   Colour Sergeants J. Butterfield, Plymouth/273, Thomas Nowell, Plymouth/2508, Frederick A. Simmonds, Plymouth/4857, and William A.Toates, Plymouth/4414, Sergeants F. Casey, Portsmouth/436, H. Robinson, Portsmouth/3202, of the RMLI, and Sergeant H.W. Lodder, RMA/3216.

4   Jerrold, op cit: p.8.

5   Fevyer, W.H. & Wilson, J.W.: *The 1914 Star to the Royal Navy & Royal Marines.*

6   Sub Lieutenant Clark's full account of his part in Nelson Battalion's time at Antwerp is in the Liddle Collection, Brotherton Library, Leeds University Library (Reference RNMN/NICOL JE) together with notes made by Lieutenant Nicol.

7   Able Seaman Roderick Johnstone, Clyde 3/2251, of Glasgow, joined Nelson battalion at Walmer on 22 August 1914 and was notified as being a POW on 5 December 1914.

8   Jun. R.A. William H. Hall, M/11212, was invited to extend his Non-Continuous Service (NCS) engagement for the duration of hostilities but declined. He was discharged in August 1915 on completing one year of service in the war.

9   The RNASBR was established in 1900 and recruited entirely from members of the St John Ambulance Brigade. At the outbreak of the First World War some 850 members volunteered for service in the Navy. 84 Senior Reserve Attendants (SRA) and Junior Reserve Attendants (JRA) served with the BEF in France and Belgium.

10   Able Seaman Alfred Neesham, KX/81, joined Nelson Battalion at Betteshanger on 9 September 1914. Able Seamen James E. Wilson, Clyde 4/2263, of Glasgow, William Wood, Clyde 3/1755, of Glasgow, John A. Love, Mersey 3/208, of

Liverpool and Arthur Derbyshire, Mersey 6/176, of Birkenhead, all joined Nelson battalion at Walmer on 22 August 1914.

[11] Jerrold, Douglas: *Georgian Adventure*, p.109.

[12] Supplement to *London Gazette*, 1 January 1915, p.5.

[13] Account by Able Seaman Walter Burdon, TZ/90, Nelson Battalion. Department of Sound Records, Imperial War Museum, London, Accession No. SR11041. Recorded 1989.

[14] Able Seaman Charles Leonard Swales, LZ/344, had enlisted on 12 September 1914.

[15] Sub Lieutenant Guy Proudfoot Cooke, a solicitor's clerk before the war, had served at Antwerp with Benbow Battalion as a leading seaman (London 1/2879) and was one of the few members of that battalion not to be interned in Holland. He was subsequently commissioned into the RND in December 1914.

[16] The No.4 Platoon nominal list, by sections (Sections 13–16), was recorded in the diary of Able Seaman Swales and is in the possession of the author.

[17] Captain W.R.C. Murray, 5/Grenadier Guards, died in Portugal in February 1917, aged 30.

[18] See Fevyer, W.H. and Wilson, J.W.: *The 1914 Star to the Royal Navy and Royal Marines*, p.118.

[19] Jerrold, Douglas: *Georgian Adventure*, p.127.

[20] Jerrold, Douglas: *Georgian Adventure*, pp.117–8.

[21] Page, Christopher: *Command in the Royal Naval Division. A Military Biography of Brigadier General A.M. Asquith DSO*.

[22] Sellers, Leonard: *The Hood Battalion, Royal Naval Division: Antwerp, Gallipoli, France 1914–1918*.

[23] Murray, Joseph: *Gallipoli As I Saw It*.

[24] Jerrold, Douglas: *Georgian Adventure*, p.118.

[25] Jerrold, Douglas: *Georgian Adventure*, p.127.

[26] Murray, Joseph, op cit, p.34–5.

[27] Thompson, Julian: *Royal Marines – from Sea Soldiers to a Special Force*, p.74.

[28] Jerrold, Douglas: *The Royal Naval Division*, p.59.

[29] NA, Kew: ADM137/3088A.

[30] NA, Kew: WO95/4290.

[31] NA, Kew: ADM137/3086.

[32] NA, Kew: ADM137/3088A.

[33] Based on The Navy List of April 1915 (effective date 18 March 1915), amended by officers' records.

[34] Both officers served as leading seamen at Antwerp with Benbow and were among the few who escaped internment. Both were from No.1 Company of London Division: Leading Seaman Cooke, L1/2879, and Leading Seaman Lamont-Fisher, L1/3030.

[35] John Edwards did not serve at Antwerp. A former London Division petty officer, L1/3616, and a locomotive engineer, he took over a platoon in 'C' Company when he joined Nelson Battalion as a sub lieutenant on 25 February 1915.

[36] Ordinary Seaman Eric Vivian Rice, LZ/781, a 23-year-old farmer from Kent, had volunteered on 9 November 1914. Initially commissioned from the Public Schools

Battalion into the Hood, he transferred to Nelson Battalion just before embarkation..

37 Account by Private Joseph Clements RMLI, Plymouth/3158(S), Deal Battalion. Department of Sound Records, Imperial War Museum, London. Accession No. SR11268. Reels 3 and 4. Recorded 1990.

38 Jerrold, Douglas: *The Royal Naval Division*, p.67–68.

39 Major F.S. Wilson, RMLI. He was killed in action in late May: 'a particularly grievous loss' (Jerrold) of 'a fine fellow' (Burdon)

40 NA, Kew: WO95/4290

41 Able Seaman Albert E Wilson, KX/127, from Stockton-on-Tees. Diary entry for 15 April. His Gallipoli diary is in the Liddle Collection, Brotherton Library, Leeds University (Reference GALL 113).

42 Built in 1899, Canopus displaced 12,950 tons, carried four 12-inch and twelve 6-inch guns and had a top speed of 18.25 knots.

43 Von Sanders, Liman: *Five Years in Turkey*, pp.63/4.

44 See Sellers and Murray, op cit, for several eye-witness accounts.

45 Rhodes James, Robert: 'Gallipoli', p.174.

46 Account by Private Thomas Henry Baker RMLI, Chatham/263(S), Chatham Battalion. Department of Sound Records, Imperial War Museum, London. Accession No. SR8721. Reels 3 and 4. Recorded 1984.

47 Account by Private Joseph Clements RMLI, Plymouth 3158(S), Deal Battalion. Op cit.

48 Hickey, Michael: *Gallipoli*, p.148.

49 Jerrold, Douglas: *The Royal Naval Division*, p.116.

50 See *RND Journal*, Issue No.21, pp.2043–2070.

51 Rhodes James, Robert: *Gallipoli*, p.170

52 Birdwood, WC: *Khaki and Gown*, p.262

53 Rhodes James, Robert: op cit, p.170.

54 Lance Corporal Walter Richard Parker, Portsmouth/229(S), of Portsmouth Battalion, on 1 May 1915.

55 Able Seaman Wilfred Golden Howes, LZ/299, of 'B' Company and Stoker 1 William James Ferguson, Dev/308717, of 'D' Company were both wounded on 1 May. They died of their wounds in Egypt and are buried in Chatby War Memorial Cemetery. Able Seamen William Humphrey, TZ/1440, from Cumberland, and Charles Lancaster, MZ/50, from Cheshire, both of 'B' Company and killed on 2 May, have no known graves and are commemorated on the Helles Memorial.

56 Rhodes James, Robert: *Gallipoli*, p.179.

57 Aspinall-Oglander, C.F., Brigadier General: *Military Operations, Gallipoli*, Vol.1, pp.309–312.

58 NA, Kew, ADM137/3065.

59 Jerrold, Douglas: *The Royal Naval Division*, p.121.

60 Jerrold, Douglas: *The Royal Naval Division*, p.122.

61 Sub Lieutenant James H. Bookless was wounded and died of his wounds on board HS *Dongola* on 4 or 5 May 1915. His body was buried at sea by Rev P.W. Clarkson en route to Alexandria.

62 Able Seaman John George Scrowther, KX/88, a coal miner from Ashington,

Northumberland, enlisted in the Northumberland Fusiliers on 2 September 1914 and then transferred to the RND. He served at Antwerp.

63 Aspinall-Oglander, C.F., Brigadier General: op cit, Vol.1, p.312.

64 Ibid; p.312.

65 Jerrold, Douglas: *The Royal Naval Division*, p.123

66 Able Seaman Charles Howard Poston, LZ/134, worked as a clerk at Lloyds Bank before enlisting on 7 September 1914.

67 Aspinall-Oglander, C.F., Brigadier General: op cit, Vol.2, p.12.

68 Able Seaman John George Scrowther, KX/88.

69 Able Seaman Robert Glasse Knox, CZ/6, a clerk in civilian life, was one of the first Clyde Division volunteers. He died of a compound fracture of the skull in HMT *Gloucester Castle*. He was just twenty years old.

70 These statistics are based on the complete nominal list of No.4 Platoon, 'A' Company, which was recorded in the diary of Able Seaman Charles Swales.

71 Stoker 1 M. Mulroy, SS103567, had joined the Royal Navy in 1906.

72 Stoker 1st Class, Robert McLaughlin, SS107526 was a married man from Glasgow. He served at Antwerp.

73 Aspinall-Oglander, C.F., Brigadier General: op cit, Vol.2, p.33.

74 Sub Lieutenant Tom Chambers was also wounded on this date. He left Nelson and the RND on his arrival home in September, taking up munitions work.

75 RND Record Card. One of the early Nelson Battalion officers, Harold Thomsett Treves was appointed sub lieutenant on 12 September 1914 and promoted lieutenant on 24 December 1914. He served at Antwerp.

76 Sub Lieutenant Wilfred Valentine Gilbert was commissioned on 7 October 1914. He joined Nelson Battalion on 27 February 1915, the day they left Blandford to embark. He was originally buried by Chaplain B.J. Failes behind the Nelson trenches but is now believed to be buried in Skew Bridge Cemetery, Helles. His younger brother Robert Evelyn Gilbert was also a Nelson sub lieutenant at this time. Robert had received a grave bullet wound to the pelvis on 19 May and was in hospital in Malta when his brother was killed. He was discharged from the RND in February 1916.

77 Chief Petty Officer Mauria Douglas Williams, Dev/165528, a married man from Devonport had served at Antwerp.

78 NA, Kew: ADM137/3084

79 Jerrold, Douglas: *The Royal Naval Division*, p.136

80 Jerrold, Douglas: *Georgian Adventure'*, p.141.

81 Sub Lieutenant Herbert Clyde Evans joined Nelson Battalion after Antwerp on 22 October 1914. He was promoted to temporary lieutenant on 28 February and to acting lieutenant commander on 10 March 1915. He was married and lived in Uckfield, Sussex. His Mention in Despatches was gazetted on 5 November 1915.

82 Jerrold, Douglas: 'The Royal Naval Division', p.137.

83 Burge's diary for the period May to August 1915 is held in the Royal Marines Museum, ARCH 11/13/163.

84 Sub Lieutenant Alan Chadwick Iliff, a 30-year-old manufacturing stationer from London, had volunteered as a rating with London Division, LZ/245. He was advanced rapidly to leading seaman on 21 October and to petty officer on 23

December 1914. Commissioned into Benbow Battalion, he transferred to Nelson when Benbow was disbanded.

85 Able Seamen Samuel Sayes, KW/106, of New Coleford, Gloucs., Wilfred Victor Bailey, LZ/265, of Gillingham, Dorset, and James Wareing, M5/162, of Burton-on-Trent. All died of enteric fever in hospital on Lemnos and are buried in East Mudros Military Cemetery.

86 Among the officers invalided at this time was Lieutenant Warren Barclay. He later won the Military Cross in the BEF with Hood Battalion in Belgium (see Jerrold, Douglas: *The Royal Naval Division*, p.254).

87 Sub Lieutenant William Henry Edwards, joined Nelson Battalion as an acting chief petty officer, Dev/147663, on 22 August 1914. His Pay No. A/1 shows that he was the first rating in 'A' Company. He was be killed in action on 13 July 1915.

88 Sub Lieutenant Arthur Hobbs had been with Nelson Battalion as a CPO, Dev/201206, from first beginnings, serving at Antwerp. Commissioned on 13 May 1915, he would remain with the battalion until it joined the BEF in France, when he was detached to the RND Base Depot at Calais, eventually becoming the Depot Adjutant.

89 Sub Lieutenant Basil Wilson Smyth, joined Drake Battalion as an Ordinary Seaman, L9/2570, from the London Division companies on 22 August 1914. He was a shipbroker's clerk from SE London. He was commissioned in the field on 1 July 1915.

90 Able Seaman John Lymington Price, LZ/236, was shot by Stoker 1 John Simeon, Dev/SS.101676.

91 Able Seaman James Ross, CZ/2686, was shot by Able Seaman Ernest Emery, B2/1191. Able Seaman Edward Armstrong, TZ/2304, was also wounded in the hand by the same bullet.

92 NA, Kew: ADM137/3088B.

93 Able Seaman William Hutchinson's death in Newcastle Infirmary, from a head wound he sustained on 15 June 1915, was reported by his sister in March 1920. His death is not yet commemorated by the CWGC.

94 Aspinall-Oglander, C.F., Brigadier General: op cit, Vol.2, p.109.

95 Ibid, p.110.

96 Jerrold, Douglas: *The Royal Naval Division*, p.146.

97 Lieutenant Commander Price would remain in England for some two years, serving in that time as 2i/c of the 1st, 2nd and 'A' Reserve Battalions. He did not serve with Nelson Battalion again until July 1917.

98 Lieutenant Commander Andrews remained in England until January 1918, when he rejoined Nelson Battalion in France as the battalion's last 2i/c.

99 Lieutenant Commander Nicol was invalided home from Malta in late August 1915 and admitted to the RN Hospital in Plymouth. On 18 October 1915 his appointment to the RND was terminated.

100 Lieutenant Arthur O. Groom, had been a lieutenant in 8/King's Own Scottish Borderers and had transferred to the Royal Marines in March 1915. On 24 April 1915 he was commissioned as a lieutenant RNVR. Invalided off Gallipoli in October, his RND commission was terminated in May 1916.

101 Sub Lieutenants David Galloway (ex-CZ/977), Bernard Dangerfield (ex-LZ/286),

Ernest G. Wood (ex-LZ/537), Bernard W. Kenny and Ernest V.G. Gardner (ex-L7/2982). Sub Lieutenant Gardner was another of the ex-Benbow ratings who had evaded internment or capture at Antwerp.

[102] Pre-Dreadnought sister-ship to HMS *Majestic*, which was torpedoed by *U.21* off Gallipoli – as was HMS *Triumph*.

[103] After two months recovering from enteric fever Able Seaman Wilson was invalided home and was demobilized in June 1916.

[104] Lieutenant Clyde Wickham (invalided November), Sub Lieutenants John Thompson (invalided December), Hedley T. Ely, Cyril A. Truscott and Noel H.E.V. Hale (to hospital September).

[105] Sub Lieutenants William EB Yates (ex-MZ/27), William Lyall, John E Greenwell (ex-TZ/2442), Edmund Langstreth (ex-LZ/1576), Eric W Squires (ex-LZ/815), Leonard Spain, David Francis and Sydney Flowitt (ex-L6/3165). The last-named, as an Ordinary Seaman in Collingwood Battalion, had been interned in Holland after Antwerp. He escaped from internment in April/May 1915. Lyall and Yates were to be invalided sick in October.

[106] Sub Lieutenant Charles Sydney Hosking had served as a Nelson chief petty officer (Dev/147665) since the battalion first formed. Two months after being commissioned he was promoted to acting lieutenant. Sub Lieutenant Charles Henry Reed had joined Nelson Battalion as a petty officer (Dev/193348) and was rated chief petty officer in December 1914. He was evacuated sick only twelve days after being commissioned. Both men served at Antwerp.

[107] Jerrold, Douglas: *The Royal Naval Division*, p.150, records Lieutenant Colonel Burge's new 2i/c as being Lieutenant Commander Edward William Nelson, but Nelson's RND record does not show his taking up this appointment until 29 January 1916.

[108] Lieutenant Commander Wilfred Stewart Miall-Green, from London, was commissioned as a sub lieutenant on 17 September 1914. By March 1915 he was a lieutenant commander and sailed with Benbow Battalion to Gallipoli. He was transferred to Nelson Battalion in the re-organization after the Third Battle of Krithia.

[109] Sub Lieutenants John G. Coburn, Alan L. Ball, George K. Turnbull, James A. Woodgate, Frederick C. Sillar, John Stephens (an ex-RMLI short service volunteer, Deal/930(S)) and James H. Brothers joined in late October. Ball and Sillar were in hospital with fever and dysentery by 11 November. Ball rejoined in April 1916 at Mudros but Sillar was invalided home to be discharged from the RND as medically unfit.

[110] Page, Christopher: op cit, p60.

[111] Muirhead, Thomas: article in *RND Journal*, Issue 18, p.1784, where he notes that Nelson Battalion lost the highest proportion of officers to other ranks (1 to 10.7) and a large number of its sub lieutenants.

[112] Promoted from the ranks, Sub Lieutenant Edward J.B. Lloyd (ex-LZ/1476) was only 19 years old and had been a student at Glasgow University before volunteering in April 1915.

[113] Surgeon Henry Brice Parker MB RN, from Bath, had joined Nelson Battalion on 18 January 1915. He would remain with the battalion until late September 1916

when he broke his femur in an accident in France. His work as a surgeon would not be recognized until mid-1918, when he was awarded the Distinguished Service Cross 'in recognition of exceptionally good work done by him as Medical Officer of the Nelson Battalion, Royal Naval Division, in Gallipoli.' (Supplement to London Gazette 21 June 1918, p.7304)

114 Sub Lieutenant Bernard William Kenny was commissioned in February 1915 and joined the Nelson from 2nd Reserve Battalion in July 1915. He was struck down with dysentery in early September and spent two months in hospitals in Egypt and Cyprus. He was killed in action on 19 December 1915, five weeks after rejoining the battalion.

115 Chief Petty Officer Edward Jones, C5/1744, from Glasgow, had joined Nelson battalion on 22 August 1914 and served at Antwerp.

116 Chief Petty Officer Thomas McLaughlin, CZ/245, had volunteered in mid-September 1914 and had advanced rapidly to that rating by September 1915. In Collingwood Battalion he was wounded in the Third Battle of Krithia and joined Nelson Battalion when he returned from hospital in Egypt in August 1915.

117 Able Seaman Joseph Bowles, CZ/4395, a labourer from Paisley, volunteered on 11 May 1915, joining Nelson Battalion on the peninsula with the 22 November draft.

118 Lieutenant Colonel Burge's full description of the evacuation is contained in his letters home in the collection of the Department of Documents in the Imperial War Museum (P.216).

119 Petty Officer Arthur Victor Hunt, M3/214, had been with Nelson battalion since its first formation, serving at Antwerp. He had been a civil servant, surveyor of taxes, before the war. Buried at Yozgat by the Turks, his body was moved after the war to the Baghdad (North Gate) War Cemetery in Iraq, where the bodies of many Commonwealth POWs were concentrated.

120 Jerrold, Douglas: *The Royal Naval Division*, Appendix C, quotes total casualties as 332 Officers and 7,198 Other Ranks, of which 133 Officers and 2,491 Other Ranks were killed or died.

121 Muirhead, Thomas: op cit, pp.1781–1784.

122 Supplement to *London Gazette*, 13 September 1915, pp.9065/6

123 Supplement to *London Gazette*: 5 November 1915, pp.10999 – 11000; 28 January 1916, p.1206; 1 November 1916, p.10617.

124 Petty Officer Barker was later commissioned and was killed in action with Anson Battalion on 24 December 1917.

125 Supplement to *London Gazette*, 13 July 1916, p.6952–3.

126 Chief Petty Officer John Caldwell Thompson was Battalion Sergeant Major. He was Mentioned in Despatches on a second occasion when serving in Hawke Battalion in 1918.

127 Petty Officer Barrett was also awarded the Medaille Militaire by the President of the French Republic. Supplement to *London Gazette*, 5 October 1920, p.9694.

128 Able Seaman William Charles Short, SZ/21, was one of only two Sussex Division volunteers in the platoon. He survived the fighting at Anzac and at Helles, was invalided to Egypt with pyrexia and returned to Gallipoli in mid-August. He was killed in action on 6 September 1915, one day after his 20th birthday.

129 Sub Lieutenants P. Batchelor, ex-LZ/686; J.H. Emerson, ex-LZ/1426; A.K.

Smithells, ex-LZ/700. Sub Lieutenants A.P. Mecklenburg, ex-L7/3545 and A.P. Taylor, ex-L7/3339, were both former Benbow able seamen who had escaped together from internment in Holland in May 1915.

[130] Lieutenant Robert E.L. Davies, who had been invalided home in September 1915, also transferred to the RNAS. These were the first of several Nelson officers who would make this move. Davies joined the RNAS as a pilot in late 1916 and was awarded the Distinguished Flying Cross in January 1919.

[131] Jerrold, Douglas: *The Royal Naval Division*, p.169.

[132] For a detailed insight into the garrison routine on Lemnos, see *RND* Issues Nos.19 and 20: the diaries of James Curzon Hilton of Hood Battalion.

[133] Sub Lieutenants Edwin L.A. Dyett, Harold R. Pearson (ex-ZP/1206), William D. Redmond (ex-LZ/46), Francis E. Rees, James D. Black, Reginald A. Carder and William D. Walker. Sub Lieutenant Carder would move across to Hood Battalion soon after the move to France.

[134] Able Seamen James A. Bell, T3/213, and Edward Goss, T4/204, were taken into the 3rd Reserve Battalion at Blandford and then discharged to sea service at Chatham on 3 May 1916. Both had come through the Gallipoli experience relatively unscathed: Bell had been slightly wounded on 13 July and evacuated to Egypt; Goss had been in hospital in Malta with debility from fly-borne disease. They both survived the war.

[135] Sub Lieutenants Leonard S. Gardner and Herbert S. Strickland. Sub Lieutenant Leonard Gardner was the elder brother of Sub Lieutenant Ernest Gardner, who had joined the battalion in July 1915 and been invalided home in October.

[136] Both of these officers were killed in action before Beaucourt in the Battle of the Ancre, 13 November 1916. Their deaths are commemorated on the Thiepval Memorial.

[137] Able Seaman Thomas Thomas, WZ/1510, was 36 years old and came from Morriston, Swansea.

[138] NA, Kew: WO32/5075.

[139] Able Seaman Joseph Pigott, TZ/5517, from Sheffield, was twenty years old.

[140] Sub Lieutenant Greenwell would be severely wounded in the battle for Beaucourt and he joined the RNAS as a pilot in November 1917. Absorbed into the RAF as a Lieutenant, he was killed in July 1918 flying a Short 184 seaplane of 408 Flight at Newhaven. His aircraft collided with a house on the seashore.

[141] Nelson Battalion War Diary. NA, Kew, ADM137/3065

[142] The notes of this Court of Enquiry, handwritten on sheets from a field notebook, are in the papers of Leading Seaman Procter at the Fleet Air Arm Museum. The correct service number of Able Seaman Little is TZ/7536.

[143] Jerrold, Douglas: *Georgian Adventure*, p.169.

[144] Also joining at this time, and new to the battalion, were: Lieutenant Frank D. Purser; Sub Lieutenants Douglas R.G.P. Alldridge (ex-L5/2898), Ernest W. Cashmore, James R. Savary (ex-LZ/252), Frederic W. Chardin (ex-LZ/432), George A. Reddick and Reginald C. Whiteside. Sub Lieutenant Savary had been wounded in the defence of Anzac on 1 May 1915 when an able seaman in 'B' Company of Nelson Battalion. Sub Lieutenants John Thompson and Reginald Whiteside would remain with Nelson Battalion for only three months. In October

they were struck off the strength of Nelson Battalion and transferred to the Royal Flying Corps as Observers on probation. Lieutenant Thompson RFC was killed in action with 45 Sqn on 11 March 1917 and is buried in Lijssenthoek Military Cemetery, Poperinghe, Belgium. Whiteside was killed in action with 18 Squadron RFC, where he was still serving as an RNVR sub lieutenant, on 20 December 1916. His death is commemorated on the Arras Flying Services Memorial. His name is also included in the IWM Nelson Battalion Roll of Honour.

145 Jerrold, Douglas: *Georgian Adventure*, p.168.

146 Ibid, p.170.

147 Ibid, p.171.

148 Petty Officer Albert P Wedel, WZ/140, came from Cardiff and was a very young petty officer aged 20.

149 Jerrold, Douglas: *Georgian Adventure*, p.175.

150 Able Seaman Thomas Hendrie, CZ/4306, was killed in action while serving in Hawke Battalion in September 1918.

151 The first Nelson killed on the Ancre was Able Seaman George Scott, TZ/1436, who was aged 23 and came from Workington, Cumberland,

152 Jerrold, Douglas: *Georgian Adventure*, p.188.

153 Able Seaman Fred Robson, TZ/46, had been a fireman with the NE railway Co. before enlisting on 8 September 1914. He was shot in the back during the defence of Anzac but was back with the battalion by mid-June and had been a Nelson ever since. He was 23 years old.

154 Lieutenant H.T. Ely, the Adjutant since December 1915, was sick in hospital at this time. He was invalided home and would not rejoin the Nelsons. Appointed to Hood Battalion in April 1918, he was killed in action in the following August during the 'advance to victory'.

155 NA, Kew, ADM137/3065, pp. 121–126.

156 Jerrold, Douglas: *The Royal Naval Division*, p.188.

157 Jerrold, Douglas: *Georgian Adventure*, pp190–191.

158 See inter alia Jerrold, Douglas: *The Royal Naval Division*, Chap. IX; Sellers, Leonard: *The Hood Battalion*, Chapters 17 & 18; Page, Christopher, Captain RN *The Royal Naval Division on the Ancre, 1916* in RND Journal, Issue No.2, pp108–126; Thompson, Julian; *The Royal Marines*, pp148–157.

159 Jerrold, Douglas: *Georgian Adventure*, p.192.

160 Ibid: pp194–195.

161 NA, Kew: WO95/3093.

162 NA, Kew: WO95/3112.

163 See Sellers, Leonard: *For God's Sake Shoot Straight!*, pp.41–42, for Sub Lieutenant Gardner's testimony on the course of the action, given in the trial of Sub Lieutenant Dyett.

164 Also killed on 13 November were Sub Lieutenants J.H. Brothers and J.D. Black, who had transferred from Nelson Battalion to 189 Brigade Machine Gun Company earlier in the year

165 Lieutenant Commander Galloway did not return to Nelson Battalion. He was awarded the French Croix de Guerre in early 1917. He served as 2i/c Drake

Battalion April-August 1918 and then, briefly, as CO of Hood Battalion until seriously wounded on 2 September 1918.

166 Lieutenant Flowitt was re-appointed to Nelson Battalion in February 1918 just as the battalion was being disbanded.

167 Sub Lieutenant Lloyd did not return to Nelson Battalion. Specializing as a Signals Instructor in 1917, he served in Hawke Battalion in 1918.

168 Sub Lieutenant Smithells transferred to the RNAS as a pilot in November 1917, subsequently being absorbed in the RAF in 1918.

169 Sub Lieutenant Chardin, permanently unfit for general service, left the RND in March 1918 and was appointed Assistant to the Naval Vice Consul, Santander.

170 Sub Lieutenant Savary joined Hawke Battalion in March 1917 and was transferred from the RND to the Army in November 1917.

171 Sub Lieutenant Mecklenburg MC (later Mexborough) served in reserve battalions until February 1918 when he was transferred from the RND to the Ministry of Shipping as an Admiralty Liaison Officer.

172 Jerrold, Douglas: *The Royal Naval Division*, p.204.

173 Supplement to *London Gazette*, 10 January 1917, p.458.

174 Supplement to *London Gazette*, 26 January 1917, p.1017.

175 Supplement to *London Gazette*, 26 January 1917, p.1019.

176 Supplement to *London Gazette*, 19 February 1917, pp.1749 – 1755.

177 A/Petty Officer George Price, MM, WZ/1564, a Welsh miner, was confirmed petty officer with Nelson and served with the battalion until its disbanding in February 1918. Thereafter he fought with Anson Battalion, being severely wounded in October 1918. He was invalided a year later with 50 per cent disability.

178 A/Petty Officer Thomas Matthew, MM, TZ/368, a Northumberland miner, transferred to Hood Battalion in February 1918. He was captured by the Germans in late March 1918 and repatriated after the Armistice.

179 Petty Officer James Alder, MM, TZ/3641, died in action at Gavrelle on 23 April 1917.

180 Able Seaman Robert Foster, MM, KX/69, was an Antwerp and Gallipoli veteran from the original 'A' Company, No.4 Platoon in which the author's father served. Foster's right arm was amputated as a result of his wounds on the Ancre and he was eventually discharged medically unfit in March 1918.

181 Able Seaman John Fox, MM, CZ/4669, formerly a hairdresser, had joined the battalion on Gallipoli in October 1915. Shot through the elbow on the Ancre and sent home, he was invalided from the RND in August 1917.

182 Able Seaman James McLeod, MM, CZ/257, was wounded in the battle for Beaucourt and invalided home, rejoining in June 1917. Transferred to Drake Battalion in February 1918, he fought with them as a petty officer until the Armistice.

183 Able Seaman David Nixon, MM, TZ/5213, joined Nelson Battalion on Gallipoli in October 1915. In December 1916 he was transferred to 189 Brigade Machine Gun Coy and in August 1917 to 223rd MG Coy. He was killed in action in the first RND (188 Brigade) attack at Passchendaele on 26 October 1917.

184 Corporal Joseph Vernon, MM, Deal/3025(S), enlisted in the Royal Marines in December 1914. A bricklayer by trade, he was posted to the RND Medical Unit

and attached to Nelson Battalion, sailing with them in the MEF in March 1915. He stayed with the Nelsons until invalided home with hepatitis in September 1917, returning to serve in the Medical Unit from January to October 1918. Born in 1876 he won his Military Medal at the age of 40.

185 Supplement to London Gazette 4 January 1917, p.192

186 *The Globe and Laurel*, Volume XXIV, No.255, 7 January 1917.

187 The very first of these men was drafted to Nelson Battalion. A carpenter from Chudleigh, Devon, Able Seaman Horace Caunter, R/1, enlisted on 17 August 1916 at the Exeter Depot of the Devon Regiment and was attached to 'A' Reserve Battalion RND for training. In February 1918, with the demise of Nelson Battalion, he was cross-posted to Hawke and remained with them until he was demobilized in 1919.

188 Sub Lieutenant James Crawford had joined on arrival at Le Champ Neuf but was posted to 6th Entrenching Battalion a week later. He did not rejoin the Nelson until the following May. Joining in mid-December were: Lieutenant Archibald W Buckle (ex-L10/1523) and Sub Lieutenants George W. Bloomfield (ex-LZ/2722), William A. Bowler, Ernest P.G. Bridge, Denis S. Brown, Cecil A. Clerk, Horace E. Fair, Winthrop J. Crosland-Taylor, Holt C. Hewitt, John B.S. Howard, Kenneth A. Hucklebridge, Louis F. Hunt (ex-L2/3118), Henry E. Nowell, Herbert A. Siddle, William Wellwood, Ernest E. Wicks, Arthur F. Wolfe (ex-LZ/1515).

189 See *RND Journal*, Issue No.18, pp.1733 – 1747: 'RND Personality – Commander 'Lofty' Archibald Walter Buckle, DSO★★★' for a full description of his career.

190 Sellers, Leonard: *For God's Sake Shoot Straight! The Story of the Court Martial and Execution of Sub Lieutenant Edwin Dyett*. See also his follow-up article in *RND Journal*, Issue No.16, pp.1550–1554.

191 See *RND Journal*, Issue No.6, pp. 496–508: Tasker, Trevor: *RND Graves in the Abbeville area of France*.

192 Jerrold, Douglas: *The Royal Naval Division*, p.211.

193 Sub Lieutenants Hewitt, Siddle, Crosland-Taylor, Howard and Nowell. All but Sub Lieutenant Nowell would rejoin the battalion at a later date.

194 Sub Lieutenant Ernest P.G. Bridge, who hailed from Co. Tipperary, was transferred to the 6th (Service) Battalion, Royal Irish Regiment on 21 January 1917.

195 Griffiths, R.J.H. (grandson): *RND Journal*, Issue No.21, pp. 2098 – 2101.

196 One such was 8767, CSM J. Toogood of 2/Royal Scots Fusiliers.

197 Able Seaman Albert Needham, TZ/6680, is also recorded as having died on 1 February as a POW in German hands but he was originally reported missing on 3 February. His death on the earlier date was reported by the German Red Cross but the circumstances of his death are not clear.

198 NA, Kew: WO95/3112.

199 Jerrold, Douglas: *The Hawke Battalion*, pp.147–8.

200 Leading Seaman Colin Bain Wheeler DCM MM, CZ/2224, a motor mechanic from Speyside, enlisted in November 1914 and was transferred to Nelson from Benbow Battalion on Gallipoli. Shot in the feet in the Action of Achi Baba Nullah, he rejoined from hospital in Egypt in January 1916. Transferred to the 2nd Brigade LTM Battery in June 1916, he was promoted to petty officer immediately after the attack on Puisieux Trench. Commissioned in April 1918, he joined Anson

Battalion in September and was detached to the 188 Brigade LTM Battery, where he won the Military Cross a week later near Cambrai. (Supplement to *London Gazette*, 30 July 1919, p.9785.)

201 Supplement to *London Gazette*, 26 March 1917, p.2993.

202 Supplement to *London Gazette*, 17 April 1917, p.2694

203 Sub Lieutenant Arthur F. Wolfe, from Wolverhampton, had enlisted in London Division (LZ/1515) in April 1915, just after his eighteenth birthday. He served with Hawke Battalion at Gallipoli and was invalided home sick. Commissioned in October 1916, he was killed on the Ancre two months before his twentieth birthday.

204 Able Seaman N. Richardson, LZ/526, volunteered in October 1918, the day after his eighteenth birthday. He had come through the whole of the Gallipoli campaign totally unscathed and considered it the healthiest time of his life.

205 Lieutenant Wilfred F. Webb and Sub Lieutenants Edward H. Smith (ex-London5/3393), Horace A. Cole, Robert M. Macaulay, Charles V. Davis, James H. Anderson, Arthur D.H. Simpson, William A. Nicoll, Robert H. Pawson, Edmund J. Palmer and James M. Jamieson. Lieutenant Webb was a Gallipoli veteran of Benbow and Hood Battalions. All the sub lieutenants except Smith, Cole and Palmer had been commissioned into the RND from Officer Cadet Battalions in late November 1916. Edward Smith had served at Antwerp as an able seaman with Benbow Battalion and was one of the few to avoid internment. Sub Lieutenant Pawson was formerly a corporal in the Yorkshire Regiment. Sub Lieutenant Jamieson would be in hospital from the end of March, not rejoining until January 1918.

206 See *RND Journal*, Issue No.21, pp. 2098 – 2101.

207 Supplement to *London Gazette*, 26 March 1917, pp.2990 – 2993 and 26 April 1917, p.3947

208 Petty Officer Robert L Barrie, MM, CZ/70, had been among the first RNVR recruits to join Nelson Battalion in late October 1914. He had served with them continuously with only short spells away for illness. He was advanced to chief petty officer later in 1917, serving with Hawke Battalion after Nelson disbanded.

209 Leading Seaman Albert J. Jupp, MM, S6/56, had fought with Howe Battalion at Gallipoli until he was struck down with enteric fever in early July 1915. He joined Nelson Battalion at Le Champ Neuf in December 1916. Promoted to petty officer at Welsh Ridge, he transferred to Anson in February 1918 and finished the war with that battalion.

210 Able Seaman John R Campbell, MM, CZ/1562, had fought with Benbow and Nelson Battalions at Gallipoli, where he was shot through the neck on 13 July 1915, only rejoining at Mudros. At Puisieux Trench he was badly frost-bitten and all his toes had to be amputated. He was invalided in August 1918.

211 Able Seaman William Duthie, MM, CZ/2274, had been with Nelson Battalion since February 1915. Wounded at Gallipoli, he also received serious wounds in June 1917 while in the firing line near Gavrelle.

212 Able Seaman Anthony Steele, MM, LZ/5079, had only been in Nelson battalion since December 1916. At Gavrelle he received a serious wound to his arm. Its

protracted treatment resulted in his not being invalided from the Service until April 1920.

213 Supplement to *London Gazette,* 15 May 1917, p.4744. Petty Officer Ernest Rennie, LZ/147, enlisted in early September 1914 and was among the first draft of 'Z' ratings to join Nelson Battalion in October 1914. He had been with the Nelson ever since. He was commissioned in October 1917 and was killed in action in May 1918, three weeks after joining Drake Battalion.

214 Supplement to *London Gazette,* 15 May 1917, p.4744. Able Seaman James W Inns, TZ/4936 had joined the battalion on Mudros. He also won a Military Medal at Gavrelle.

215 The papers of the FGCM and the Court of Enquiry are in Attwood's papers at the Fleet Air Arm Museum.

216 Lieutenant William C. Mathew had been commissioned as an RMLI subaltern, Motor Owner-Driver, in which capacity he had gone to Belgium in October 1914, earning the 1914 Star. He subsequently transferred to the RNVR and served at the 2nd Brigade HQ at Gallipoli from where he was invalided sick in October 1915. He would only stay with Nelson Battalion for two months before going to England to take a commission in the Indian Army.

217 Page, Christopher: op cit, pp. 109–110.

218 Macmillan, Thomas: *The War To End War. 1914 – 1918.* Department of Documents, Imperial War Museum.

219 Jerrold, Douglas: *The Royal Naval Division,* p.228.

220 Page, Christopher: op cit, pp.116 and 133 Note 2.

221 While this narrative has concentrated on the actions of Nelson Battalion, the mixing of Nelsons and Hoods, on the left, and of Hoods and Drakes, on the right, complicates the battle for Gavrelle. For a fuller picture of the battle see Jerrold, Douglas: *The Royal Naval Division* and Tallet, Kyle & Tasker, Trevor: *Gavrelle – Arras* in the Battleground Europe series published by Leo Cooper.

222 On 7 July 1918, Lieutenant Bernard Dangerfield MC (by then RAF) was flying as Observer in a Short Admiralty 184 Type seaplane operating from Newhaven. During the sortie they dropped a 230-lb bomb on a German U-boat. Oil was seen after the attack.

223 Major David Wilkie, (5/Black Watch (Royal Highlanders)) aged 36 and from Kirriemuir, was another of the Army imports to the RND's naval battalions.

224 Sub Lieutenant Arthur Taylor's colourful career as an escaper, which had begun as a Benbow leading seaman escaping from internment in Holland in May 1915, continued after his transfer to the RNAS as a flight sub lieutenant. As Flight Lieutenant AP Taylor RAF he was awarded the Military Cross for escaping from German captivity as a POW (*London Gazette,* 16 December 1919).

225 Petty Officer Horace E Putland, SZ/59, from Eastbourne, volunteered on 16 September 1914 and had served with Nelson Battalion since completing training. He was killed on the first day of the attack on Gavrelle, aged 22.

226 Supplement to *London Gazette,* 18 July 1917, p.7225. Sub Lieutenant Crosland-Taylor had been in hospital for most of February 1917, latterly with shell shock. Two months after winning his MC at Gavrelle he went on leave to England and

was assessed unfit for general service because of neurasthenia. In March 1918 he was transferred to the Royal Marines Submarine Miners at Chatham.

227 Supplement to *London Gazette*, 9 July 1917, pp.6827 – 6837 and 18 July 1917, p.7277 – 7278.

228 Chief Petty Officer Albert J Collins, MM, CZ/797, had been with Nelson Battalion since joining as a leading seaman at Mudros in January 1916. He rose rapidly to chief petty officer by July 1916 and served with Hawke Battalion in 1918.

229 Petty Officer James Marchant, MM, TZ/2118, had enlisted in November 1914 but did not join a fighting battalion (Nelson) until February 1917. He won a Bar to the MM at Welsh Ridge and the DCM in August 1918.

230 Petty Officer John Tait, MM, TZ/1713, had been wounded with Collingwood Battalion at Gallipoli on 4 June 1915 and was wounded again at Gavrelle. When Nelson Battalion was disbanded he was detached to 1/RMLI and was captured by the Germans on 24 March 1918 as the RND was retreating. He was demobilized in February 1919.

231 A/Petty Officer James Duncan, MM, CZ/2895, had been made an acting petty officer on the day of the attack on Gavrelle but was later deprived of this rating as a result of an offence of absence. A few days after this he requested to revert to able seaman. He transferred to Hawke when Nelson Battalion disbanded and shortly thereafter he was gassed in action and became a prisoner-of-war. He was demobilized in February 1919.

232 Leading Seaman Walter Dudley, MM, TZ/2023, joined Nelson Battalion on Gallipoli in July 1915. Advanced to petty officer after Gavrelle, he finished his time with the RND in Hawke Battalion where he won a Bar to his Military Medal in September 1918. He was demobilized in January 1919. He had managed to survive more than three years of continuous front-line service without being wounded.

233 Leading Seaman Charles Dockrill, MM, TZ/3903, had served at Gallipoli in Hawke Battalion and joined the Nelson in early 1917. He lost a leg in fighting on Welsh Ridge in January 1918 and was invalided just after the Armistice.

234 Leading Seaman Alexander R Hamill, MM, CZ/4607, had served in Nelson Battalion since October 1915. A wound to his arm at Passchendaele led to his being invalided out of the RND in July 1918.

235 Able Seaman William Barnfather, MM, TZ/4281, joined Nelson Battalion at Gallipoli in September 1915. In February 1918 he was transferred to Drake Battalion and detached to 189 Brigade Trench Mortar Battery. Petty Officer Barnfather was killed in action in October 1918.

236 Able Seaman John W. Candlish, MM, TZ/7445, joined Nelson Battalion at Mudros in February 1916. At Gavrelle he sustained a serious bullet wound in the foot and was invalided home. He was wounded again in September 1918 while serving in Hawke Battalion. He was discharged in February 1919.

237 Able Seaman Frederick L. Chettle, MM, BZ/4448, joined Nelson Battalion as a signaller in August 1916. He was cross-posted to Hawke when Nelson Battalion was disbanded in 1918. His Military Medal was presented to him by the King at Aldershot in June 1918. He was later discharged to sea service.

238 Able Seaman Harry Hollis, MM, TZ/5744, had been with the Nelsons since

Mudros. He transferred to Hawke Battalion when Nelson disbanded and served with them until demobilized in April 1919.

239 Able Seaman James W. Inns, TZ4936, was serving with 189 Brigade LTM Battery and had already been Mentioned in Despatches. He transferred from Nelson to Drake in February 1918 and to Anson a month later, continuing to serve in the 189 Brigade LTM Battery. He was demobilized in January 1918.

240 Able Seaman Charles Johnston, MM, CZ/6435, had been in Nelson Battalion since February 1916. He was wounded at Gavrelle and invalided home. When fit again he joined Hawke Battalion and there won a Bar to his MM in 1918.

241 Able Seaman John Martin, MM, CZ/4949, fought on Gallipoli with the Nelsons for the last six weeks of that campaign. In February 1918 he was cross-posted to Anson Battalion, serving with them to the end of the war.

242 Able Seaman John H. Spicer, MM, LZ/5101, had been with Nelson Battalion since December 1916. He transferred to Hawke in March 1918 was demobilized in March 1919.

243 Able Seaman Henry J. Webb, MM, LZ/3340, joined Nelson Battalion on Mudros in March 1916. He was cross-posted to Hood Battalion in March 1918, was wounded shortly thereafter, but returned to the Hood for the final two months before the Armistice. He was demobilized in March 1919.

244 The FGCM papers for all three ratings are held at the Fleet Air Arm Museum.

245 See article by Tallet, Kyle: 'Death sentences passed on men of the RND, which were never carried out'. *RND Journal*, Issue No.12, pp.1099 – 1113.

246 Leading Seaman Charles Yates, KP/187, DSM, from Upper Norwood, London, had joined at Crystal Palace on 10 September 1914. He was 22 years old when he died.

247 In early May Sub Lieutenants John H. Taylor, Horace Cooper and Douglas A. Stuart (ex-C1/2473) joined. Later in May they were joined by Sub Lieutenants Charles D. Carlile, Thomas D. Baxter and Norman K. Spoonley. Sub Lieutenant Stuart had been with the RND since its establishment, serving with Hood at Antwerp as an able seaman and winning the Distinguished Service Medal at Gallipoli. He was badly wounded on 9 May, the day after he joined Nelson Battalion, and was invalided home.

248 Sub Lieutenant F.E. Rees subsequently transferred to the RNAS as a pilot in October 1917. Later transferring to the RAF, he was killed when the Handley Page O/400 bomber he was flying failed to return from a raid on Folpesweiler aerodrome on 22/23 August 1918.

249 Sub Lieutenants Percy Scarles, Frank Barrett (ex-LZ/367), Sidney M Stringfield (ex-L9/3529) and William E Jehring (ex-LZ/73) also joined on 6 June. Barrett and Stringfield had served at Gallipoli as ratings. Lieutenant Watts and Sub Lieutenant Jehring had both enlisted on the same day in September 1914 and both joined Benbow Battalion. Jehring was not commissioned until after he had served at Gallipoli with Benbow and Drake Battalions. Joining in mid-June were Sub Lieutenants John A. Pennell (ex-BZ/9042), Harry Bunting (ex-LZ/3253), Perceval Beaumont, Herbert B. Biggs, Robert S. Goodwin and Ernest W.J. Towler (ex-BZ/1477), none of whom had previous fighting experience.

250 See Tallett & Tasker: *Gavrelle – Arras*, pp.91 – 93.

251 Lieutenant Commander Price was only 2i/c Howe for two months before being invalided home sick. Fit only for Home service, he later commanded the Regimental Depot at Aldershot as an Acting Commander.

252 Sub Lieutenant Horace J. Arnold (ex-L9/3294) had been with Drake Battalion at Antwerp and Gallipoli, Sub Lieutenant Wilfred H Appleton (ex-LZ/107) had served with Benbow and then Drake Battalions at Gallipoli. Both were invalided home sick. Sub Lieutenant Joe W. Brearley had been a Private in 1st Rhodesian Regiment and King Edward's Horse of the South Africa Union Defence Force.

253 Sub Lieutenant Robert G. Richardson was former A/Corporal of 11th TR Battalion, Sub Lieutenant Horace S. Page was a Company Sergeant Major in the Essex Regiment, Sub Lieutenant James W.E. Dolman had served in the Royal Fusiliers and Sub Lieutenant Ralph Moore was formerly a Lance Corporal in the King's Shropshire Light Infantry

254 Sub Lieutenant Towler, 24 years old, was a former schoolmaster, who had volunteered in January 1916. He had only served two months with Nelson Battalion.

255 Petty Officers William Allchorn, SZ/152, and William Blogg, TZ/3434. The FGCM papers are included with the service papers of Petty Officer Allchorn in the FAA Museum.

256 Able Seaman Arthur B. Chambers, LZ/4404. His FGCM papers are in the FAA Museum.

257 Supplement to *London Gazette,* 11 December 1917, p.12908.

258 Supplement to *London Gazette,*12 December 1917, p.13009.

259 Leading Seaman Arthur Coathup MM, MZ/428, first saw service with Hawke Battalion at Gallipoli. He joined Nelson Battalion in May 1917. Invalided for the wounds received in this action, he rejoined Hawke Battalion in September 1918 and was killed in action twenty days later at the crossing of the Canal d'Escaut.

260 Petty Officer Russell W. Anson, TZ/8880, joined the battalion in late 1916 and was commissioned in September 1918.

261 Sub Lieutenants Walter L. Willison, John Connelly and Albert Keep. Connelly had been a private in King Edward's Horse before being commissioned.

262 Sub Lieutenant John B.S. Howard rejoined Nelson Battalion on 29 September. He had first joined in mid-December 1916 but was invalided home sick a month later. Sub Lieutenant Harold C. Birch had served in the King's Rifle Regiment as a Sergeant before being commissioned.

263 Petty Officer John Tweddle, TZ/1978, enlisted in November 1914 and served in Anson and Nelson Battalions at Gallipoli. Wounded in the hand on the Ancre, he was rated Acting Pioneer Sergeant in May 1917. After Nelson Battalion disbanded he was posted to Hawke in mid-March 1918 and died on 22 March of wounds received in action. He has no known grave and his name is on the Arras Memorial. See *RND Journal,* Issue No.11, pp.1028 – 1034.

264 Leading Seaman John W. Todd, TZ/5332, a clerk in civilian life, enlisted in June 1915 and joined Nelson Battalion at Gallipoli in October. In July 1917 he joined the 253rd Divisional Employment Company and in October was posted to duty with the Field Cashier as a Writer 2nd Class. He was demobilized in May 1919.

265 Able Seaman Sydney P. Mascarenhas, LZ/525, enlisted in October 1914. His father lived in Lisbon. He went to Gallipoli with Benbow Battalion and there was

transferred to Nelson, later being invalided home with dysentery. In December 1916 he was posted back to Nelson and made an acting petty officer while serving as an interpreter with the British Mission attached to the Portuguese Expeditionary Force in France. In this posting he was Mentioned in Despatches and was awarded the Meritorious Service Medal and the Portuguese Military Medal for Good Services (Copper).

[266] Sub Lieutenant John B.S. Howard, after only two weeks back with the battalion, was wounded on 14 October, evacuated home and subsequently transferred to the Royal Marines Submarine Miners. On 17 October the Nelson's longest serving officer, Lieutenant Ernest V.G. Gardner, MC, was wounded by a shell, evacuated home and declared permanently unfit. A/Lieutenant Percival Batchelor, a company commander, was wounded on 22 October and invalided home, subsequently being discharged with traumatic neurasthenia.

[267] Sub Lieutenant Jehring had survived a bullet wound to the neck while serving at Gallipoli as a rating in Drake Battalion.

[268] Lieutenant Commander Robert Howard Shelton, DSO, had been a Leading Seaman (L4/3301) with Hawke Battalion at Antwerp, where he had evaded internment and captivity. Commissioned immediately after Antwerp, he rejoined Hawke at Gallipoli as a lieutenant in May 1915 and was a lieutenant commander by November 1915 when he was invalided home sick. Rejoining Hawke with the BEF in early 1917, he was awarded the DSO at Puisieux Trench and became 2i/c in July 1917. He later commanded both Hawke and Anson Battalions either side of the Armistice.

[269] Sub Lieutenant Albert Keep, only six weeks with the Nelsons, was gassed at this time, invalided home and transferred to the Royal Marine Submarine Miners.

[270] NA, Kew: WO95/3112.

[271] Jerrold, Douglas: *The Royal Naval Division*, p.260. For a starkly contrasting account of the conditions of the frontal assault on 30 October see *RND Journal*, Issue No.22, pp.2187 – 2205. Extracted from *War is War* by ex-Private X (Victor Gollanz Ltd, 1930), this is an account by a soldier of The Artists Rifles.

[272] Supplement to *London Gazette*, 25 April 1918, p.4996.

[273] Supplement to *London Gazette*, 28 March 1918, p.3876. Able Seaman William J. Stringer, DCM, BZ/9067, from Birmingham, was 36 years old. He enlisted in October 1915, but was not called up until June 1916, and had been with Nelson Battalion since November 1916. He received bullet wounds to his right arm, chin and chest. Invalided home, he was discharged invalided in October 1918.

[274] Sub Lieutenants Ralph Taylor, Frank A. Taylor, William B. Harrison, Carl P.P. Dieterle and Henry A. Bennett. The two Taylors were not related: Ralph was from Sydney, Australia, Frank from Sheffield. Sub Lieutenant Harrison was formerly a Sergeant in 21/Manchester Regiment. Sub Lieutenant Bennett, ex-M6/56, an RNVR rating since 1906, had been at Antwerp as an able seaman in Anson Battalion. He came through the whole Gallipoli campaign unscathed, was rated chief petty officer on 1 January 1916, and seems to have led a similarly charmed live with Anson in the BEF. He left Anson at Christmas 1916, when he went to UK for a commission.

275 Sub Lieutenant John H. Cowan was new to the battalion. Lieutenant Frank Purser rejoined, having been invalided sick at Christmas 1916.

276 Supplement to *London Gazette* 28 January 1918, p.1386 – 1398 and 23 February 1918, p.2417 – 2431.

277 Petty Officer Robert A. Gray, MM, TZ/5191, was be killed in action on 31 December 1917 at Welsh Ridge.

278 Petty Officer Edward B. Walsh, MM, TZ/5282, had been with Nelson Battalion since Gallipoli, where he joined in October 1915 and had been rated petty officer on the day of the attack on Gavrelle. Cross-posted to Hawke Battalion when Nelson disbanded, he was killed in action on 27 March 1918 when the RND had retreated to the River Ancre.

279 After the disbanding of Nelson Battalion, Leading Seaman James G. Cowie, MM, CZ/2047, gave exceptionally gallant service as a petty officer in Hood Battalion, being decorated on four occasions in 1918.

280 Leading Seaman James A. Tindall, MM, KW/240, had served in the RND since September 1914 and in Nelson Battalion since November 1914. He served as a petty officer with Drake Battalion from February 1918 until being gassed a month later. His medals are now held in HMS *Nelson*, Portsmouth.

281 Able Seaman John Blackwood, MM, CZ/3071, had served with Drake Battalion at Gallipoli, joining Nelson in May 1917. Wounded at Welsh Ridge, he later joined Hawke Battalion and was killed in action with them in August 1918.

282 Able Seaman William Chapman, MM, TZ/124, was one of the earliest Nelsons. He enlisted in September 1914 and joined Nelson Battalion two months later. He was missing, later found wounded, at Achi Baba Nullah and was wounded again on the Ancre. Transferred to Hood Battalion in February 1918, he died on 6 September 1918 of wounds received in action.

283 Able Seaman Charles W. Gifford, MM, TZ/4236, had been with the Nelson since September 1915. He received a severe neck wound in Belgium and was invalided home. He joined Hawke Battalion in June 1918.

284 Able Seaman John McDonald, MM, CZ/6391, joined Nelson Battalion at Mudros. He later fought with Hawke Battalion and was captured in the German advance in late March 1918.

285 Able Seaman Albert V. Painter, MM, R/66, was one of the first 'R' ratings to join. He fought with Drake Battalion from February to October 1918, being twice wounded.

286 Able Seaman Robert Rodgers, MM, CZ/3527, first joined Nelson battalion at Mudros. He served with Drake Battalion for a month from February 1918 until being gassed. He was demobilized in February 1919.

287 Able Seaman Albert Smith, MM, CZ/1260, served at Gallipoli with Hawke Battalion and was wounded right at the end of that campaign. In August 1918, while serving in Drake Battalion, he was captured by the Germans.

288 Able Seaman Michael P. Stokoe, MM, KP/809, was a Gallipoli veteran of Anson Battalion. He moved to Drake Battalion in February 1918 but was gassed a month later. He returned to employment as a Durham miner in January 1919.

289 Able Seaman Andrew Stuart, MM, CZ/3081, would be cross-posted to Hawke

Battalion when Nelson disbanded in early 1918 and served there until the end of the war.

290 Petty Officer Hugh Smith DCM, MM, CZ/5603, a valet in civilian life, transferred to Drake Battalion in March 1918. With them he won the Military Medal. Transferred for a commission, he failed the course and was demobilized in February 1919.

291 Able Seaman Frederick G Chubb, DCM, R/28, was one of the early 'R' conscripts (a watchmaker and jeweller by trade) to join Nelson Battalion in December 1916. He died in action on Welsh Ridge during the Nelsons' counter-attack on the last day of 1917.

292 Supplement to *London Gazette* 25 April 1918, p.5018.

293 Supplement to *London Gazette* 28 March 1918, p.3874.

294 Supplement to *London Gazette* 28 March 1918, p.3849.

295 Lieutenant Commander Gordon William Whittaker, DSO, had been commissioned as a sub lieutenant in May 1915 but did not join Drake Battalion until February 1916 at Imbros. Wounded in the attack on Beaucourt, he did not rejoin the Drakes until June 1917. He was promoted quickly, making lieutenant commander five months later.

296 Sub Lieutenant John G. Coburn had served with Nelson Battalion in the MEF from October 1915 until March 1916 when he was invalided with appendicitis. Sub Lieutenants Thomas White (ex-MZ/30), Francis VC Rudnick, Lewis C.A. Anderson, Alexander Brackenridge and Herbert B Cannin were all newly-commissioned in May and June 1917. Sub Lieutenant Anderson was formerly a Corporal in the Worcester Regiment. Sub Lieutenant Cannin had enlisted in the RNVR (LZ/444) in September 1914 but had been transferred to the Divisional Train as a Royal Marine Corporal (Deal/2259(S)) in March 1915.

297 Sub Lieutenant Ralph Taylor, from Sydney, Australia, celebrated his twenty-fourth birthday just after joining.

298 Killed after only six weeks in the battalion, Sub Lieutenant White was a former seaman who had served with first Benbow and then Anson Battalions in the MEF and BEF. Rated chief petty officer in January 1916, he was discharged to UK for a commission in December 1916.

299 Supplement to *London Gazette,* 16 August 1918, p.9563.

300 Sub Lieutenant Henry A. Bennett was invalided home and was transferred to sea service in March 1918. Sub Lieutenant John G. Coburn was invalided with a head wound but would rejoin Hawke Battalion one month before the Armistice.

301 Sub Lieutenants Walter W. Thomas, Arthur B. Dutton, John R .Bluett and Albert J. Robertson. Walter Thomas (ex-LZ/247) had enlisted in September 1914. He joined Nelson Battalion in November 1914 and sailed with them to Gallipoli as an ordinary seaman. He had been advanced to chief petty officer by October 1915. He left the Battalion on Christmas Eve 1916 for Cadet School. John Bluett (ex-Deal/3611(S)) was a 34-year-old Sunderland coal miner when he enlisted in the RM in March 1915. He served with the RND Medical Unit in the 2nd Field Ambulance before he was commissioned.

302 Able Seaman William Doyle, R/3979, from County Wexford, Ireland, had joined Nelson Battalion in November 1917.

303 Supplement to *London Gazette*, 19 March 1918, pp.3458–3472.

304 Petty Officer John C Winn, MM, TZ/3841, had served briefly with Hawke Battalion at Gallipoli and joined Nelson in February 1917. He was mortally wounded on 10 January 1918, dying before learning of his award.

305 Able Seaman Harry Bannister, MM, CZ/4435, had been with Nelson Battalion since November 1915 and was wounded at Beaucourt and on Welsh Ridge. He transferred to Hood Battalion in February 1918.

306 Able Seaman John Walsh, MM, R/4063, transferred in February 1918 to Drake Battalion, where he was severely gassed a month later. He was demobilized in February 1919.

307 Able Seaman Frederick J. Woodbine, MM, R/3090, had served six years in the Army before transferring to the RND. He later served in Anson Battalion until demobilized in February 1919.

308 Jerrold, Douglas: *The Royal Naval Division*, p.273.

309 Sub Lieutenant John L Were. A few more officers were later appointed to Nelson Battalion, but they were cross-posted to other RND battalions before they could join.

310 Officers transferred to Drake Battalion on 7 February 1918: Lieutenants H.J. Arnold (on leave) and W.H. Appleton; Sub Lieutenants R.H. Pawson, J.M. Jamieson, J.A. Pennell, R. Moore (in hospital), H.C. Birch (on leave), W.B. Harrison, J.R. Bluett, J.L. Were. Lieutenant Appleton was Mentioned in Despatches later in the year.

311 Officers transferred to Hood Battalion on 7 February 1918: Lieutenant W. Wellwood, MC; Sub Lieutenants J.W.E. Dolman (on leave), F.A. Taylor, J.H. Cowan, A. Brackenridge

312 Able Seaman Alexander Wood Boath, CZ/4860, of Forfar. *London Gazette*, 14 September 1918. He had fought with the Nelsons since the last month on Gallipoli. Wounded at Welsh Ridge in early 1918 he transferred to sea service in May of that year.

313 Officers transferred to 7th Entrenching Battalion on 22 February 1918 included: Lieutenants N.K. Spoonley (Adjutant) and H.B. Biggs, MC; Sub Lieutenants W.A. Bowler, P. Beaumont, W.L. Willison and A.B. Dutton. Other officers were transferred before they could join Nelson Battalion.

314 Department of Printed Books, Imperial War Museum, May 1996.

315 Jerrold, Douglas: *The Royal Naval Division*, pp.307/8.

316 Ibid

317 Ibid, pp.323/4.

318 Ibid, pp.313 – 315.

319 Able Seaman Bertram C Cowls, R/67, had been among the first 'R' conscripts to join the battalion in December 1916.

320 The remains were discovered at trench map reference 51b.H.4.a.9.5.

321 Also buried in Point-du-Jour cemetery are Able Seaman James Burnett Clark, CZ/7443, from Torphichen, Bathgate, West Lothian, and Able Seaman Henry Hutchinson, TZ/5320, from Chester-le-Street, Co. Durham. They were killed in action on 23 and 24 April 1917, respectively.

322 Only Howe Battalion, the other battalion disbanded early, also had more than 700

men lost over the comparable period (about 740). Deaths in the other naval battalions were between 540 and 690, approximately, to the end of February 1918. In the battalions disbanded on Gallipoli, Collingwood had some 230 deaths, Benbow less than twenty.

INDEX

Sanders, Liman von, Gen, 29
Savary, James R., Sub Lt RNVR, 96 (n.144), 106, 114 (n.170)
Sayes, Samuel, AB, KW/106, 57 (n.85), 60
Scarles, Percy, Sub Lt RNVR, 162 (n.249), 163
Scott, George, AB, TZ/1436, 103 (n.151), 121
Scrowther, John G., AB, KX/88, 38 (n.62), 42 (n.68), 44, 86
Sharer, Edmund M., Lt RNVR, 5, 23, 58, 80
Shelton, Robert H., Lt Cdr RNVR, DSO, 175 (n.268), 178
Short, William C., AB, SZ/21, 87 (n.128)
Shute, Cameron D., Maj Gen, DSO, 103, 105, 111, 115, 119, 131, 136
Siddle, Herbert A., Sub Lt RNVR, 118 (n.188), 131 (n.193), 141, 150, 151, 156
Sillar, Frederick C., Sub Lt RNVR, 76 (n.109)
Simeon, John, Stoker 1, SS101676, 59 (n.90)
Simmonds, Frederick A., Col Sgt RMLI, Ply/4857, 6 (n.3)
Simpson, Arthur D.H., Sub Lt RNVR, 136 (n.205), 150, 151
Smith, Albert, AB, CZ/1260, MM, 180 (n.287)
Smith, Edward H., Sub Lt RNVR, 136 (n.205), 150, 151
Smith, Hugh, PO, CZ/5603, DCM, MM, 181
Smithells, Arthur K., Sub Lt RNVR, 87 (n.129), 91, 106, 114 (n.168)
Smyth, Basil W., Sub Lt RNVR, 58, 59 (n.89), 69
Sowerby, Frederick W., Lt RNVR, 24, 38, 58, 81
Spain, Leonard, Lt RNVR, 74 (n.105), 85, 88, 91, 93, 106, 117, 119, 131, 150, 171, 188, 191, 202
Spicer, John H., AB, LZ/5101, MM, 152 (n.242)
Spoonley, Norman K., Lt RNVR, 161 (n.247), 171, 179, 188, 203 (n.313)
Squires, Eric W., Sub Lt RNVR, 74 (n.105), 85, 90, 106, 113, 125
Standring, Robert C., Lt Cdr RNVR, 5, 16; *Plate 5*
Starforth, William P., Surgeon RN, 160, 172, 175
Starkey, Herbert J., Lt RNVR, 23, 58, 65
Startin, Francis H.J., Sub Lt RNVR, 24, 58, 65, 70
Steele, Anthony, AB, LZ/5079, MM, 137 (n.212)
Stephens, John, Sub Lt RNVR, 76 (n.109), 85, 91, 93
Stokoe, Michael P., AB, KP/809, MM, 180 (n.288)
Strickland, Herbert S., Sub Lt RNVR, 88 (n.135), 91, 106, 118, 131, 150
Stringer, William J., AB, BZ/9067, DCM, 178 (n.273)
Stringfield, Sidney M., Sub Lt RNVR, 162 (n.249), 171, 178
Stuart, Andrew, AB, CZ/3081, MM, 180 (n.289)
Stuart, Douglas A., Sub Lt RNVR, DSM, 161 (n.247)
Swales, Charles L., AB, LZ/344, xiii, 16 (n.14, n.16), 22, 25, 28, 29, 31, 35–36, 37; *Plate 16*

Tait, John, PO, TZ/1713, MM, 152 (n.230)
Taylor, Arthur P., Sub Lt RNVR, MC, 87 (n.129), 90, 106, 131, 150, 151 (n.224)
Taylor, Charles H.S., Surgeon RN, 5, 24; *Plate 7*
Taylor, Frank A., Sub Lt RNVR, 180 (n.274), 188, 203 (n.311)
Taylor, John H., Sub Lt RNVR, 161 (n.247), 166, 168
Taylor, Ralph, Sub Lt RNVR, 180 (n.274), 188 (n.297), 196
Tepper, Roland H., Lt RNVR, 24, 80; *Plates 11, 13*

Thomas, E., AB, MZ/172, 81
Thomas, Thomas, AB, WZ/1510, 89 (n.137)
Thomas, Walter W., Sub Lt RNVR, 193 (n.301)
Thompson, John C., CPO, C2/1801, 81 (n.126)
Thompson, John, Sub Lt RNVR, 74 (n.104), 96 (n.144)
Tindall, James A., PO, KW/240, MM, 180 (n.280)
Toates, William A., Col Sgt RMLI, Ply/4414, 6 (n.3)
Todd, John W., LS, TZ/5332, 168 (n.264)
Toogood, J., CSM, 8767, 131 (n.196)
Towler, Ernest W.J., Sub Lt RNVR, 162 (n.249), 164 (n.254)
Town, J., Hon Lt RM, Quartermaster, 5, 24, 59, 74; *Plate 14*
Travers, Richard T., Capt RMLI, 167, 172, 188, 204
Trevanion, Cecil V., Sub Lt RNVR, 118
Treves, Harold, Sub Lt RNVR, 4 Lt, 5, 23, 47 (n.75), 53; *Plates 8, 15*
Trotman, Charles N., Brig Gen RMLI, CB, 41, 62, 92
Truscott, Cyril A., Lt RNVR, 74 (n.104), 85, 90, 106, 112, 118, 131, 150, 151, 157
Tuffe, Charles J., LZ/4388, 153
Turnbull, George K., Lt RNVR, 76 (n.109), 85, 90, 141, 150, 151, 157
Tweddle, John, PO, TZ/1978, 168 (n.263); *Plates 19, 20, 21*

Vernon, Joseph, Corpl RMLI, Deal/3025(S), MM, 114 (n.184)

Walker, William D., Sub Lt RNVR, 88 (n.133), 90, 106, 131, 150
Wallace, William, PO RN, DSM, 14
Walsh, Edward B., PO, TZ/5282, MM, 180 (n.278)
Walsh, John, AB, R/4063, MM, 195 (n.306)
Wareing, James, AB, M5/162, 57 (n.85), 61
Watts, John C., Lt RNVR, 162 (n.249)
Webb, Henry J., AB, LZ/3340, MM, 152 (n.243)
Webb, Wilfred F., Lt RNVR, 136 (n.205), 151
Wedel, Albert P., PO, WZ/140, 98 (n.148), 101
Wellwood, William, Lt RNVR, MC, 118 (n.188), 131, 150, 171, 180, 181, 188, 191,
      193, 203 (n.311)
Were, John L., Sub Lt RNVR, 202 (n.309), 203 (n.310)
Wettern, Eric F., Captain RMLI, 34, 35 (n.50)
Wheeler, Colin B., LS, CZ/2224, DCM, MM (later Sub Lt RNVR,MC, DCM,
      MM), 134 (n.200)
Whitaker, Hubert J.I., Sub Lt RNVR, 24, 44
White, Thomas, Sub Lt RNVR, 187 (n.296), 188, 189 (n.298), 197
Whiteside, Reginald C., Sub Lt RNVR, 96 (n.144)
Whittaker, Gordon W., Lt Cdr RNVR, DSO, 187 (n.295), 188, 192, 194
Wickham, Clyde, Lt RNVR, 74 (n.104)
Wicks, Ernest E., Sub Lt RNVR, 118 (n.188), 131
Wilkie, David, Maj (Black Watch), 150, 151 (n.223), 158
Williams, Mauria D., CPO RN, Dev165528, 47 (n.77), 53
Willison, Walter L., Sub Lt RNVR, 167 (n.261), 171, 188, 203 (n.313)
Wilson, Albert E., AB, KX/127, 28 (n.41), 36, 40, 57, 63, 72 (n.103)
Wilson, James E., AB, C4/2263, 13 (n.10)